Cognac

Cognac

Nicholas Faith

MITCHELL BEAZLEY

Cognac
by Nicholas Faith

First published in Great Britain in 2004 by Mitchell Beazley, an
imprint of Octopus Publishing Group Limited, 2–4 Heron Quays, London E14 4JP.

A CIP catalogue record for this book is available from the British Library.

ISBN: 1 84000 903 9

Commissioning Editor: Hilary Lumsden
Executive Art Editor: Yasia Williams
General Editor: Margaret Rand
Production: Gary Hayes

Phototypeset in Berkeley Book by Intype Libra Ltd

Printed and bound by Mackays of Chatham

Contents

Acknowledgments

For this new, totally rewritten edition of a book first published nearly twenty years ago, I have been able to rely on many friends, old and new, including, but not only, Alain Braastad – who has forgotten more about the history of cognac than I will ever know – Claire Coates and Laurence Nolay at the BNIC, Bernard Hine, Colin Campbell, Alfred Tesseron, Georges Clot, Gerard Allemandou, whose restaurant La Cagouille, in Paris offers an incomparable selection of cognacs, and, finally but not least, my colleagues at the International Spirits Challenge. Anyone involved in producing a book of mine inevitably has problems and Hilary Lumsden, Margaret Rand, and Julie Sheppard, all of Mitchell Beazley, rose nobly to this particular challenge.

Introduction

In winter you can tell you are in cognac country as soon as you turn off towards Cognac on the road from Paris to Bordeaux at Barbezieux. The landscape does not change at all dramatically; it is more rounded, perhaps a little more hilly, than between Bordeaux and Barbezieux, and there are an increasing number of vines. But the major impact has nothing to do with the sense of sight. It has to do with the sense of smell. At night during the distillation season from December to March, the whole atmosphere is suffused with an unmistakable aroma, a warmth that is almost palpable: brown, rich, grapey. It emanates from dozens of otherwise unremarkable groups of farm buildings, distinguished by the lights burning as the new brandy is distilled.

Cognac emerges from the gleaming copper vats in thin, transparent trickles, tasting harsh and oily, raw yet recognisably the product of the vine. If anything, it resembles grappa; but what to the Italians is a saleable spirit is merely an intermediate product to the Cognaçais. Before they consider the product ready for market it has to be matured in oak casks. Most of the spirits, described by the more poetically minded locals as "sleeping beauties", are destined to be awakened within a few years and sold off as relatively ordinary cognacs, but a small percentage is left to sleep for much longer. Every year expert palates sample them and eliminate – or, rather, set aside for immediate sale – those deemed incapable of further improvement. As the survivors from this rigorous selection process mature, so their alcoholic strength diminishes and within forty or fifty years is down to forty degrees of alcohol – the strength at which cognacs, old and new, are put on the market. These aristocratic brandies are then transferred to the glass jars – demi-johns, known to the Cognaçais as *bonbonnes* – each holding twenty-five litres of the precious fluid, and stored, even more reverently, in the innermost recesses of their owners' cellars – the aptly named *paradis* familiar to every visitor.

Hennessy has the most famous *paradis* in Cognac itself, but an even more impressive collection is hidden away in the crypts of the medieval church of the small town of Châteauneuf, a few kilometres, to the east used to store their brandies by the Tesseron family. For nearly a century three generations of the family have supplied even the most fastidious of the cognac houses with at least a proportion of the brandies they require for their finest, oldest blends. The Tesserons' two *paradis* contain over 1000 *bonbonnes* dating back to the early nineteenth century. I was privileged to taste a sample of the 1853 vintage.

The world of cognac is governed by certain immutable rituals. Even when pouring the 1853, the firm's general manager swilled out the empty glass with a little of the cognac and dashed it to the floor to ensure that the glass was free from impurities. Astonishingly, my first impression of the cognac was of its youth, its freshness. Anyone whose idea of the life span of an alcoholic beverage is derived from wines is instinctively prepared for the tell-tale signs of old age, for old wines are inevitably faded, brown, their bouquet and taste an evanescent experience. By contrast even some of the oldest cognacs can retain their youthful virility, their attack. It seems absurd: the brandy was distilled when Queen Victoria was still young, and some of the grapes had grown on vines planted before the French Revolution. Yet it was no mere historical relic, but vibrantly alive. But then the perfect balance of such a venerable brandy is compounded of a series of paradoxes: the spirit is old in age but youthful in every other respect; it is rich but not sweet; deep in taste though relatively light, a translucent chestnut in colour. Its taste is quite simply the essence of grapiness, without any hint of the overripeness that mars lesser beverages.

But the secret of a great cognac lies in its "nose", its bouquet. In the words of Robert Delamain, scholar and cognac merchant, what one looks for in a cognac is: "above all a scent, a precious scent that exists nowhere else in nature, not in any flower, not in any herb; a soft aroma that engulfs you in successive waves; a scent that you examine, you explore, in order to uncover other agreeable, if indefinable, aromas".[1]

[1] Robert Delamain, *Histoire du Cognac*, Paris, Stock, 1935.

The warmth and delicacy Delamain is describing linger long after the glass has been emptied. In the wine tasters' vocabulary the crucial attribute is that the brandy is "long". At the end of the nineteenth century – when the 1853 was probably being transferred from oak to its appointed *bonbonnes* – Professor Ravaz claimed: "The bouquet of a good *eau-de-vie* from the Grande Champagne lasts for a week or more."[2] He was not exaggerating. In the distilleries themselves the aroma lingers on throughout the eight or nine months in every year when the stills themselves are empty. Cognac's essential difference from most other spirits is that its aromatic components derive directly and exclusively from the grapes, their quality itself dictated by the nature of the terroir where they are grown. Not surprisingly no other spirit is as clean, and leaves no sense of thickness on the palate.

Only after tasting a cognac of that age and quality can you appreciate the truly miraculous nature of the whole enterprise and begin to understand how it is that the name of a small town in western France has become synonymous with the finest distilled liquor in the world. As a result, Cognac is by far the best-known town in France, Paris only excepted; yet even today Cognac has only 30,000 inhabitants, and when it first rose to fame in the eighteenth century a mere 2,000 people sheltered behind its walls. Whatever the town's size, the reputation of its brandy would have been a prodigious achievement, for anyone with access to grapes and the simplest of distillation apparatus can make brandy of a sort. But only the Cognaçais can make cognac, a drink with qualities that are enhanced by age until it becomes the very essence of the grapes from which it was distilled.

The success of the Cognaçais is due to a multitude of factors – a combination of geography, geology, and history. They had the perfect soil, the right climate, and the ability to market their products to appreciative customers the world over. Yet at first sight nothing about Cognac, a small town in the middle of an agreeable, albeit unremarkable landscape, is special. On more detailed investigation almost everything about the region is out of the ordinary. The most obvious distinction is geological, as it is for most of the *terroirs* producing France's finest wines and spirits. But whereas the soils and sub-soils of Bordeaux and Burgundy, if

[2] Louis Ravaz and Albert Vivier, *Le Pays du Cognac*, Angoulême, 1900.

unusual, are not unique, the Cognac region includes formations found nowhere else. In Delamain's words:

> So far as the super-Cretaceous period is concerned, it appears in the Charentais in so specially characteristic a form that in the international language of geology these terrains are referred to by their Charentais names: Angoumois (from Angoulême), Coniacien (from Cognac) and Campanien (referring to the Champagne country of the Charente).

These last three formations are especially rich in chalk, and they produce the best cognacs. But geology by itself provides an inadequate explanation. As Delamain says:

> To confine yourself to the chemical make-up of the soil narrows and falsifies the problem. The physical nature of the earth appears to have a much greater importance: the most appreciated qualities derive from chalky soils composed of especially delicate and porous chalk lying on a similar type of chalk subsoil. Because it is so porous the subsoil accumulates rainwater, which it releases gradually as it is required, like a humidifier.

Cognac's geography and its weather are both special, though they are less easy to pinpoint than its geological peculiarities. Cognac is at the frontier of the geographical divide separating the northern "Langue d'Oïl" from the southern "Langue d'Oc". In the later Middle Ages the linguistic boundary passed through Saintes, due west of Cognac, and Matha, a few miles north of the town. The change between the two cultures is not as dramatic as in the Rhône Valley, where you are suddenly aware of the influence of the Mediterranean, but it is nevertheless abrupt enough to emphasize that you are in a different world.

Travellers have long been aware of the change. Delamain again:

> For sailors from the whole of northern Europe, the coast of France below the Loire estuary was the region where, for the first time, they felt they were in the blessed South, where the heat of the sun makes life easier, where fruits ripen and wine flows. The Bay of Bourgneuf, and the Coast of Saintonge sheltering behind its islands, were for them the first sunny shores they came across. Cognac itself still retains some of the elements of a sleepy southern town, closing at midday, drowsing in the hot summer sun. Its inhabitants, however businesslike, lack any northern brusqueness.

Cognac is at the heart of a very special border region, a rough oblong bounded on the north by the Loire, between the Bay of Biscay and the mountains of the Massif Central. The French themselves would call it Aquitaine, but the region I am trying to define is rather more restricted, since it peters out to the south of Bordeaux, its special softness lost in the heat of the Basque country. The whole area is remarkable for its gentleness. There are no abrupt slopes, no cliffs, no obvious drama in the landscape at all. Often it appears dull to the uninstructed eye until one begins to appreciate its subtleties. Its most obvious characteristic is its weather, like the landscape gentle, temperate, but more emollient than further north. Everything is softer, lighter, gentler, and Cognac epitomizes those qualities.

Naturally the river Charente, which bisects the area, is a gentle river: "the most beautiful stream in all my kingdom," said King Henry IV four hundred years ago. The French would call it *molle*, the soft sweet Charente, which twists and turns on its leisurely way to the sea. Bordered by willows and poplars, troubled only by fishermen (and the town's ever-energetic oarsmen), the Charente is an almost absurdly picturesque river. Echoing its breadth, its alluvial basin is broad, and the slopes above, like the river, are spacious and gentle. It is on these slopes that the grapes for the best cognac are grown.

As you can see from the map on p. 2 the heart of the region – where today most of the grapes are grown – is an irregular rectangle, which naturally distils the climatic advantages enjoyed by the region as a whole. It is near enough to the coast for the winters to be mild. To the east it is bounded by the first foothills of the Massif Central, and as the country gets increasingly rounded the weather becomes a little harsher, the brandies less mellow. Cognac itself enjoys the best of both worlds. The climate reinforces the initial advantages provided by the geological make-up of the soil and sub-soil. Because Cognac is so northerly a vineyard, the long summer days allow the grapes to ripen slowly and regularly, giving them the right balance of fruit and acidity required for distillation purposes. But the sunlight is never harsh, for the microclimate is unique. Even the most transient visitor notices the filtered light, its unique luminosity – more intense sunlight would result in overripe grapes with too much sugar. In his book on cognac, Cyril Ray quotes a variety of authors, including the novelist Jacques Chardonne, the mapmaker Louis Larmat, and Louis Ravaz. They all use the word soft, "doux" or "douce", to describe the region, its weather, and above all the light – which Jacques de Lacretelle describes as "tamisée" ("filtered"). As Jacques Chardonne,[3] the region's most famous novelist, put it, "The quality of the light in the Charente is without any parallel in France, even in Provence".

The weather has another contribution to make after the grapes have been fermented into wine and then distilled, but only those who live in Cognac fully appreciate how this quality of diffused intensity extends even to the rain. The Charente region is wetter than many other regions of France, but, in the words of Professor Ravaz, the rain falls "often, but in small amounts . . . sometimes it is only a persistent mist which provides the earth with only a little moisture, but which keeps the atmosphere saturated with humidity and prevents any evaporation". Ravaz's description sounds remarkably like that of a Scotch mist. This is no coincidence, for both cognac and malt whisky require long periods of maturation in oak casks and their special qualities emerge only if the casks are kept in a damp, cool atmosphere.

The individual components of the cognac formula could, in theory, have been reproduced elsewhere, but the result is unique. According to Professor Ravaz, who did a great deal to help replant the Cognac vineyard after the phylloxera disaster:

The same variety of grape can be grown anywhere and in the same way as in the Charente: distillation can be carried out anywhere else as at Cognac and in the same stills; the brandy can be stored in identical casks as those we employ in our region; it can be cared for as well, or maybe even better. But the same combination of weather and terrain cannot be found anywhere else. As far as the soil is concerned, it is not enough that it should belong to the same geological formations; it must have the same physical and chemical composition. And no one has ever found such a duplicate. In addition, the climate of the region must be identical to that of the Charente, and that is almost inconceivable. There is therefore very little chance that all the elements which influence the nature of the product should be found together in any region apart from the Charente; and

---

[3] *Le bonheur de Barbezieux*, Stock, Paris, 1938. Chardonne was the son a of a Cognac merchant called Boutelleau and took his pseudonym from the town of Chardonne, near Vevey in Switzerland, where he lived for five years.

thus no other region can produce cognac. The slightest difference in the climate, the soil, and so on is enough to change completely the nature of the brandy; and that is as it should be because there are, even in the Charente, a few spots (small ones, it is true) which produce mediocre brandy. All the trials which have been made all over the place to produce cognac with the same varieties and the Charentais methods have resulted only in failure. And this lack of success could have been foreseen if people had only remembered this one principle: that the nature of products is dependent on a combination of conditions which occurs only rarely.[4]

Even Professor Ravaz omits one crucial element in the creation of cognac – the unique qualities of the people themselves. The combination of conditions that he outlines provides only the potential for making cognac and ignores the very different qualities needed to spread its fame throughout the world. For the potential could be realized only through a very special type of man, combining two superficially incompatible qualities. The making and storage of the spirit demands painstaking patience, a quality usually associated with peasantry in general and especially marked in a country with such a troubled past as that of the Charente. As Maurice Burès says: "Scarred for a long time by incessant wars, the Charentais became reserved, introverted, discreet."[5] But this combination was precisely the opposite of the open outlook required if cognac were to be marketed successfully the world over. Indeed most of it has always been destined for sale abroad, for, unlike Northerners, the Charentais did not need spirits to keep themselves warm in winter and have always drunk sparingly of their own product.

Their instinctive unwillingness to allow anyone to intrude on the intensely private life of the family is symbolized by the classic face of the Cognac farm with its dour stone walls interrupted only by stout, permanently shut wooden doors that enclose spacious cobbled farmyards surrounded by fermentation vats, still rooms, storehouses. Outsiders find the blank stone walls sad and menacing; the inhabitants find them deeply reassuring. *Cagouillards* ("snails"), they are nicknamed, shut in their fortresses. This collective introversion, this native defensiveness, is not confined to the countryside but extends to the small country towns –

---

[4] Ibid.

[5] Maurice Burès, "Le type saintongeais", *La Science Sociale*, vol. 23, Paris, 1908.

including Cognac itself. Even the Charente – a complicated stream, with its traps, its numerous weirs, its treacherous sandbanks – shares this regional desire for shelter, for along much of its course it is so narrow that the trees close in, forming a roof, their green reflected in the water.

Yet, miraculously, the inhabitants have managed to combine the two qualities. The fusion was best expressed by the region's most distinguished native, the late Jean Monnet, the "founder of Europe". He was the son of one of Cognac's leading merchants, and he remembers how every evening "at dusk, when we lit the lamps, we had to shut every shutter. 'They can see us,' my mother would say, so greatly did she share the anxiety, the fear of being seen, of exposure which is so marked a trait of the Charentais character."[6]

The paradox was that in the household of the Monnets, as in those of many other merchants, guests were not exclusively aged aunts or squabbling cousins but also included buyers from all over the world. As a result, the little world of Cognac provided the young Jean Monnet with "an enormously wide field of observation and a very lively exchange of ideas. I learned there, or springing from there, more than I could have done from a specialized education." Moreover, he found that abroad the name of Cognac was deeply respected, a sign of refinement among the "rude" inhabitants even in far-off Winnipeg. This combination of a patient peasant obsession with detail and an international outlook is as unusual, and as important, as Cognac's geology and geography.

Cognac is the fusion of so many factors, that there is no simple or obvious way to arrange a book on the subject. But it is obviously essential to start with an analysis of the reasons for its superiority and the skills required in its production.

[6] Jean Monnet, *Memoires*, Paris, Fayard, 1976.

part I

Cognac

Todays vineyard

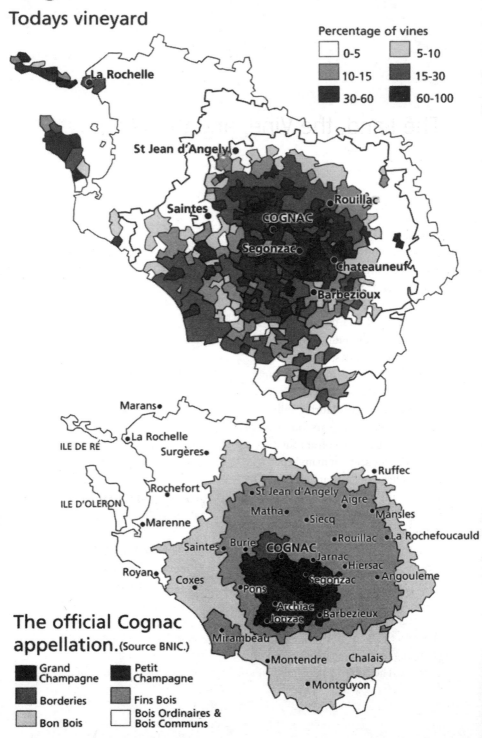

Percentage of vines

- 0-5
- 5-10
- 10-15
- 15-30
- 30-60
- 60-100

La Rochelle

St Jean d'Angely

Saintes

COGNAC

Rouillac

Segonzac

Chateauneuf

Barbezioux

Marans

La Rochelle

ILE DE RÉ

Surgères

Rochefort

Ruffec

ILE D'OLERON

St Jean d'Angely

Aigre

Matha

Siecq

Mansles

Marenne

Rouillac

La Rochefoucauld

Saintes

Burie

COGNAC

Jarnac

Hiersac

Royan

Coxes

Segonzac

Angouleme

Pons

Archiac

Jonzac

Barbezieux

Mirambeau

Montendre

Chalais

Montguyon

The official Cognac appellation. (Source BNIC.)

- Grand Champagne
- Petit Champagne
- Borderies
- Fins Bois
- Bon Bois
- Bois Ordinaires & Bois Communs

1

The Land, the Vine, and the Wine

Over the past few years the French have been battling to defend the idea of terroir, the physical conditions governing the making of wine, against cheeky persons from the New World who assert that the skills of the winemaker are more important. The French are naturally touchy, for the idea of terroir forms the basis for their system of *appellations contrôlées*. They could do worse than call the Cognaçais to testify on their behalf. For geological and climatic factors are the only variables in the cognac equation. All the brandies entitled to the appellation are made from the same grape varieties, harvested in the same way at the same moment of the year, fermented in the self-same vats, distilled in the same stills, and matured in the same oak. Nevertheless, his colleagues in other firms would agree with Maurice Fillioux of Hennessy that "after cognac has been in cask for ten years, out of all the hundreds we taste, ninety-five per cent of the best come from the Grande Champagne". The phrase *premier cru de Cognac* seen on many a placard throughout the Grande Champagne is not official; merely an indication that, in the opinion of the inhabitants anyway, the Grande Champagne really is the finest cru. Nevertheless, man still matters, and as one local puts it: "the Grande Champagne is in the inhabitants' minds and not in the landscape".

In theory, and in legal status and administrative practice, Cognac's *crus* form a series of concentric circles, with the Grande Champagne as a rough semi-circle at its heart, surrounded by a series of rings of steadily decreasing quality. This is rather misleading, for in geographical fact there are three separate areas (four including the Borderies), not the seven indicated on the map. To the west there is the coastal plain, with its vast, ever-changing skies, its marshes, sandy beaches, oyster beds – and thin, poor cognacs. The heterogenous mass of the Bois is mostly anonymous, rolling countryside which could lie anywhere between the Loire and the Gironde, the vines mingling with the arable and pasture. The Borderies[1] are by far the smallest of all the *crus* at a mere 13,440 hectares (33,210.93 acres). The Fins Bois are nearly thirty times the size, 354,200 hectares (875,246.49 acres); the Bon Bois are even bigger, 386,600 hectares (about 953,825.93 acres); and the Bois Ordinaires are smaller, 274,176 hectares (677,503.05 acres).

The divergence between history, as expressed in the official definition and the contemporary reality has vastly widened recently, as the maps on p. 2 show vividly. The result is that the official map is now increasingly misleading. In 1966 the two outer regions included over two-fifths of the vines, a figure which was down to a fifth by 1981 and a mere seventh by 2001 – and the vast bulk of the reductions in acreage had been in the Bons Bois. Not surprisingly the proportion of the land occupied by vines had also gone down. By 2001 the three smallest regions, the Champagnes and Borderies, with only an eighth of the cultivable land in the region, accounted for over two-fifths of the vines. By contrast the outer ring, the Bois Ordinaires, have been totally irrelevant for a generation – they now include a mere 2,000 hectares (4,942 acres) of vines, a token 1.3 per cent of all the cultivable land in the region. The Bons Bois are only slightly more relevant, with 12,000 hectares (29,652 acres) of vines, 5.4 per cent of the total agricultural land, virtually all concentrated to the east and southeast of Jarnac.

Even in the Fins Bois, there are few vines west or northwest of Cognac and the 33,000 hectares (81,544 acres) of vines in the appellation cover only one-seventh of the cultivated land in the region, leaving the outer ring virtually free of vines. These figures contrast with the Grande Champagne and the Borderies, where half the land is covered in vines, and the Petite Champagne, where the figure is thirty per cent. In other words Cognac, by and large, has retreated to the region which first made its brandies famous in the eighteenth century and to a mere third of the total to which it had expanded in the pre-phylloxera glory years of the middle of the nineteenth century.

The result is that the vines have become concentrated, not in

[1] The name derives from the *bordes*, the *metairies* or smallholdings cultivated by sharecroppers who were tenants of the outside investors who had settled in the area in the late sixteenth century.

concentric circles, but in a much more compact, if irregular, rectangle. Its western limits extend south from Saint Jean d'Angely through Saintes to the Gironde estuary between Royan and Mortagne. To the east it runs from Saint Jean again down to the estuary via Barbezieux. The only exceptions are the vines on the islands of Ré and Oléron, which produce Pineau de Charentes and cognacs almost entirely for the tourist trade. The heart of the region remains the Champagnes, Grande and Petite – a landscape unlike that of the Bois and resembling rather the Sussex Downs, albeit covered in vines and not pasture, with the same mixture of gentle, rolling hills and snug, wooded valleys – together with the Borderies and the northern and eastern parts of the Fins Bois.

The comparison with the Sussex chalk is no accident: "Cognac is a brandy from chalky soil" is the repeated theme of the standard work on distillation.[2] For the finest cognac there is no substitute for the pure chalk found only on the south bank of the river. In an irregular quadrilateral, bounded on the north by the Charente, to the west and south by the river Nie, and petering out towards Châteauneuf to the east, are found the famous "cretaceous" soils which make up the Grande Champagne. This comprizes twenty-seven parishes and 35,700 hectares (88,216 acres) in the canton of Cognac, devoted almost exclusively to the vine for over 300 years.

The various formations were first defined by H. Coquand, the mid-nineteenth-century geologist who did the first scientific study ever undertaken of any wine-growing area[3] (before his time all of them had been lumped together more generally as *Maestrichtien*). The heart of the Grande Champagne is composed of a special sort of chalk, the Campanian, a name which echoes the Latin origin of the word "champagnes". But the Campanian emerges only on the crests of the gentle, rolling slopes of the Grande Champagne, for it is one of three layers of variously chalky soils which come to the surface in the area. The other two are also rather special: the Santonian – named after the old name for the province, Saintonge – covers much of the Petite Champagne, the belt

[2] René Lafon, Jean Lafon and Pierre Coquillaud, *Le Cognac sa distillation*, Paris, J.B. Baillière et Fils, 1964.

[3] H. Coquand, *Description Physique*, Paris, 1858.

round the Grande Champagne; while the town of Cognac itself is built on the appropriately named Coniacian chalk.

The Grande Champagne, like all other chalky soils, was formed by the accumulation of small fossils, including one particular species found nowhere else, *Ostrea vesicularis*. In the words of the French Geological Survey, it is "a monotonous alternation of greyish-white chalk, more or less marly and siliceous, soft and incorporating, especially in the middle of the area, faults made up of black pockets of silica and lumps of debased marcasite". Marcasite is composed of crystallized iron pyrites, and this iron (also found across the Gironde in Pauillac) is important, but it is the sheer intensity of the chalkiness in the soil which is crucial – that and its physical qualities, its crumbliness, its friability.

The second best soil, the Santonian, is described as "more solid, less chalky, but incorporating some of the crumbliness of the Campanian slopes, into which it merges by imperceptible degrees". (One good test is the density of the presence of the fossil of *Ostrea vesicularis*.) The heart of the Grande Champagne, its backbone, is formed by the ridge between Ambleville and Lignières above Segonzac. But the colouring of the modern geological map is specifically designed to underline how blurred is the boundary between the Santonian and the Campanian. As a geologist told me recently: "The boundaries established by H. Coquand and H. Arnaud have been adhered to, although they are vague round Cognac itself where the visible features are much the same."

The only *cru* whose boundary is completely clear-cut is the Borderies, with their very special clay soils known as *groies* dating geologically from the Jurassic era. Ever since the Tertiary period some ten million years ago, when the Charente was carving out its riverbed, the soil has become steadily more decalcified, but the process is still incomplete and the result is a mixture of chalk which is breaking down and intermingling with the clay. The mixture produces a unique, and often underrated, cognac.

Inevitably, in an area the size of the Bois, the geology is much less well defined than it is in the Champagnes or the Borderies. Even Professor Ravaz is rather vague, saying that the brandies of the Bois are "produced on slopes formed by compacted chalk or by arable soils covered with sands and tertiary clays",[4] the first being better because of the chalk. The

---

[4] Louis Ravaz and Albert Vivier, *Le pays du Cognac*, Angoulême, 1900.

finest pockets in the Fins Bois are the so-called Fins Bois de Jarnac to the north and east of the town, which are much sought after. Moreover, there is one curious little pocket of virtually pure chalk on the east bank of the Gironde extending inland to Mirambeau, whose growers have long wanted re-classification from Fins Bois to Grande or at least Petite Champagne. By the river at St-Thomas-de-Conac (one of the many spellings of the name) the "estuarial" Fins Bois can produce excellent long-lived brandies – as witness the quality of those from the Château de Beaulon. These prove the unfairness of the canard that they are iodiny because of the proximity of salt water – anyway, the water in this stretch of the estuary is fresh, not salty.

I have come to believe, however, that the distinction between different terroirs – and this applies to other wine regions as well – is due far more to the physical characteristics of the soil than to its precise chemical composition. Hence the general suitability of chalk soils, not only in Cognac but also, for instance, in Champagne and Jerez. For chalky subsoils provide excellent drainage, but can also store substantial quantities of water to which the roots of the vine can gain access. Crucially, too, chalky soils provide very few nutrients, which helps the quality of the grapes.

Professor Ravaz himself turned his back on a purely geological explanation of cognac's qualities. As he said: "The clayey, siliceous soils of the Borderies produce brandies of a higher quality than those of the dry *groies* or even some of the chalkier districts in the southwest of the Charente-Inférieure [the former name for the Charente-Maritime]. For the geological make-up of the earth is not as important as Coquand makes out." Ravaz emphasized the combination of the chemical and physical constituents of the soil, with the physical predominant: "the highest qualities are produced from chalky soil, where the chalk is soft and highly porous and where the subsoil is composed of thick banks of similar chalk". The topsoil is invariably merely a few centimetres thick. In these soils, said Ravaz, "the subsoil hoards rainwater, thanks to its sponginess and its considerable depth, and releases it slowly to the surface soil and to the vegetation. It is thus to a certain extent a regulator of the soil's moisture content, and so, in chalky soils, the vine is neither parched nor flooded." This description explains why the Borderies, relatively poor in chalk, produce such good brandies: the soil is friable and is thus physically, if not geologically, perfect.

The same factors apply in the Médoc on the other bank of the Gironde, where the thicker the gravel banks, the better the drainage and the steadier and more reliable the growth as the water seeps through to the roots in a sort of drip irrigation. The parallel extends to the importance of the lie of the land. A well-drained slope is obviously preferable to a flat stretch of river valley, liable to clogging. Obviously, too, north-facing slopes are less highly prized. The sunlight is less strong, and in grey years, when the best southern slopes produce wines of a mere seven degrees of alcohol, the northern slopes cannot even manage that.

The politicians and the administrators responsible for defining Cognac's crus could not afford Ravaz' fine distinctions and naturally followed Coquand's clearer definitions. Broadly speaking, the classification accords with that established by market forces before the geologists moved in, a pattern found in other regions, like Bordeaux. Inevitably, those responsible for guarding cognac's reputation adhere to it, for no one can face the problems which any attempt at re-classification would present.

There is no dispute about the validity of the distinction between the various categories; only the boundaries are in question. The first, and most obvious, is that the river Charente marks the frontier – with one exception, the pocket around Bourg-sur-Charente, the only land north of the Charente entitled to call itself even Petite Champagne. Nevertheless, the Grande Champagne includes the alluvia of the riverbed and the strip of Santonian chalk that separates the alluvium from the Campanian, which starts several miles south of the river at Segonzac. This sleepy little town is the heart of the Grande Champagne (not surprisingly, the only merchant located in the town is Frapin, which sells only cognacs from its estate in the Grande Champagne). At the other boundary, the farther bank of the River Né towards Archiac, officially in the Petite Champagne, produces cognac arguably superior to some from the Grande Champagne. But most of the blenders agree with Maurice Fillioux that the Grande Champagne should never produce bad brandy and that its boundaries are broadly correct. Francis Gay-Bellile, late of the Bureau Viticole, does not sound ridiculous when he affirms that they are ninety-five per cent accurate.

No one disputes the borders of the Borderies, nor the quality of the brandies they produce, two-thirds of which are bought by Martell and Hennessy. As we saw, even the vast region of the Fins Bois is now more clearly defined so far as the market is concerned. None of them buys even Fins Bois from the west, brandies they find too "foxy", with too much *goût de terroir* – an unappetizing earthiness. Few reputable firms buy much brandy from the Bons Bois and serious firms concentrate their purchases in a narrow strip to the south around Chevanceaux and Brossac.

If the terroirs of the Cognac region vary wildly, the grape varieties used have only changed a couple of times in the past four centuries. When cognac first made its name the region was largely planted with the Balzac grape, which had several characteristics found in today's favourites. It was highly productive; it was a Mediterranean variety and thus did not fully ripen as far north as the Charente, and it was relatively late-budding and thus not susceptible to the region's late spring frosts. Its major rival at the time was the Colombat or Colombard widely planted in Armagnac, now mostly used for making table wine. This reminded Ravaz of the Chenin Blanc grape used in Anjou, but Munier[5] found that "its wine is the most powerful and is indeed needed to provide backbone for those which lack this quality". These were "the fattest, that is to say, the most oily" grapes. Indeed, when Rémy Martin used the Colombard to make "alembic brandy" in California it found that it produced brandies which were rich and fruity but relatively short on the palate.

In the nineteenth century the Balzac, and to a great extent the Colombard, were almost entirely replaced by the Folle or Folle Blanche. As a 1774 almanac put it, the wines should be thin, should have *peu de corps*; the Cognaçais already understood the importance of acidity in the wines they distilled. Folle Blanche, which had arrived from Italy as early as the fourteenth century, had already been planted before the Revolution and was also a great favourite of the Armagnaçais. In the words of Professor Ravaz, its wine was "so acid, so green, that it is something of a struggle to drink it". Nevertheless it is still planted round Nantes – by no coincidence a former brandy-producing region – under the name of Gros Plant, and not surprisingly most of the wines are as acid as they come.

---

[5] Etienne Munier, *Sur la manière de bruler ou disteller les vins*, Bruno Sepulchre, Paris, 1981.

But it was the ideal grape for producing fine, aromatic, fragrant cognacs, and brandies made from it are still cherished – not least by me. Ravaz described how "an old bottle of wine made from the Folle gives off a bouquet which can be detected from far off and which provides an adequate explanation for the perfume of brandies made from this variety. For it produces the softest brandies and the ones with the strongest and most lasting scent."

But its fate was sealed by the devastation wrought by the phylloxera louse in the 1870s. When the variety was grafted on to American rootstock it flourished so vigorously, its bunches were so tightly packed, that the grapes in the middle were liable to the dreaded grey rot (they are still beyond the reach of modern anti-rot sprays). A good many overproductive hybrids were planted after the phylloxera, but the brandies they produced smelled foul. As a result, since 1900 a single variety has been triumphant, and although other vines are permitted, they now account for only a tiny percentage of Cognac's production – although over the past few years some intrepid souls have planted some Folle Blanche.

The triumphant variety is known in Cognac as the Ugni Blanc or the St-Emilion. It's an Italian variety which originated as the Trebbiano from the hills of the Emilia Romagna around Piacenza. It's a relatively neutral variety and much in demand in Italy for use as a base wine when blended with more aromatic varieties. The Italians also use it for brandy-making, but even in Italy it matures late, and in Cognac, at the very northern limit of its cultivation, it remains relatively green and acid, and produces a different type of juice than when grown in Italy. Its other major advantage is that it starts budding late and is, therefore, like the Balzac, less susceptible to the area's late spring frosts. Cognac's long, light but not hot summers ensure that there is a certain intensity in the juice. Since the grapes are not fully ripe when they are picked, they lack even the little aroma and bouquet they develop when fully mature.

Until phylloxera, cultivation was higgledy-piggledy. Replanting was carried out either in rows or in blocks. In the past twenty years the vineyard has been adapted for harvesting by machine. The vines have been trained far higher than previously. It is easy to see the result, with the older, thicker trunks pruned right back, the newer trained up to 1.2–1.5 metres (4–5 feet) high on trellises (the Cognaçais replace their vines roughly every thirty-five years). For the same reasons the space between the rows has been doubled to just over 2.8 metres (nine feet), and although the vines are planted more closely, there are still only 3,000 to each hectare, 1,000 fewer than under the old system. The major disadvantage of the change is that the grapes ripen a week later because they are farther away from the ground and therefore benefit less from the sun's rays reflected from the chalky-white soil.

Vines are pruned less severely than in Bordeaux, say, allowing for higher production of inevitably more acid wines (unless the owner is looking for the richness required for grapes destined for table wine or Pineau de Charentes). Nevertheless, the viticultural assembly lines of the Charente share one important characteristic with their nobler brethren elsewhere in France. Growth must not be encouraged, either by pruning too lightly to leave room for more bunches of grapes, or by lavishing too much manure on them: otherwise the balance will be disturbed, and the acid level will inevitably be reduced.

The St-Emilion matures so late that even the relatively unripe grapes used for making Cognac are ready for picking only in October. But the only limit to the date of the harvest is the frost generally expected in late October, which, in a bad year like 1980, can ruin the quality of the wine. Harvesting machines would seem a natural choice for the region because the Cognaçais are not particularly interested in quality, but they were hesitant before taking to them. With early models of the machines the wines were rather "green" for the very obvious reason that the machine sucked in everything, twigs and leaves as well as grapes. Opponents even alleged – incorrectly – that the machines' hydraulic machinery was badly insulated and tended to leak tiny quantities of oil on to the grapes, resulting in an oiliness which was inevitably exaggerated by distillation. The machines have steadily improved over the past thirty years and now feature flayers which make the vines vibrate and which don't maul the bunches.

Until the late 1980s there was a long tradition of treating wine as a mere raw material, the more productive the better – indeed in that sense cognac had never been a traditional wine-making region. Nevertheless, as Roger Cantagrel of the Station Viticole puts it, "the wines have always been clean and came from well-tended vines" – you see far fewer of the straggly patches found in other French wine-making regions. Moreover the nine-fold concentration of the inherent qualities of the wine in the distillation process reinforces the Cognaçais' obsession with its purity and reliability.

Even so, in the past fifteen years there has been a real revolution. "We didn't worry about vinification," says Yann Fillioux of Hennessy, but "now we realize every day that the quality of the wine is important." As so often with such changes there were several factors involved: first the problems involved in the change from coal and wood to gas heating had to be sorted out so that the technicians could turn to other factors in improving cognac – itself a reflection of the general tendency throughout France to return to the vineyard.

But it was 1989, a year in which the summer heat extended into October, which was the turning point. Hot years are not necessarily a bad thing – 1947 was a case in point – but in 1989 the wines were too strong, well over eleven degrees, and the fermentation was too quick. So the wines contained too much ethanol, with its appley overtones, aromas which are intensified when it is bound to sulphur dioxide (SO_2). Some of the distillers managed to cope. For instance Jean Marc Olivier escaped any serious problems by severe selection of the wines he allowed to be distilled. But then he had been a director of a Chambre d'Agriculture before he arrived as maître de chai at Courvoisier in 1985, and immediately initiated a policy of direct contact with the growers. Since then he has gone in for micro-vinification of everything he buys to ensure that there are no faults.

Nevertheless, even its rivals admit that it was Hennessy that led the revolution in wine-making when it hired Jean Pineau to take charge of the firm's vinification. Pineau had previously worked for a cooperative in Languedoc and found that the Cognac region lacked both what he calls any network of advice about wine-making, or the type of technical high school that had proved invaluable in educating the children of growers in regions like Champagne and Burgundy. He immediately started a systematic analysis of thousands of samples of the wines made by the firm's suppliers. More generally he persuaded his suppliers – and thus a major cross-section of the region's growers – to install more modern pneumatic presses to ensure that the grapes were not squeezed too hard, which would give too much tannic material from the pips and skins – though it has to be said that the Cognaçais have always been conscious of the need not to press the grapes too fiercely. Indeed one of the many regulations issued in the 1930s banned the continuous presses in use since the late eighteenth century, which pressed and squeezed the grapes at the same time. The additional pressure crushed the pips and released a stream of undesirable tannic and oily substances into the must.

But Pineau was original in that, as he puts it, he "started to treat Cognac like any other wine-making region". Unfortunately the notorious refusal of the major firms to cooperate with each other has prevented a more widespread research programme so there is no general pressure on growers, many of whom, as Pineau says, "are still hoping that they can muddle through". Nevertheless, by the millennium viticulturalists were roaming the vineyards so that they could recognize immediately after harvest if the grapes were rotten, even though some of the problems were not immediately visible to the naked eye.

At the same time yields were reduced, helped by changing pruning methods because of oversupply, and global warming increased the average strength of the wines and ensured that they could be harvested up to a couple of weeks earlier. Indeed the combination of global warming and the technical advances in grape-growing and wine-making should mean that no longer are unripe or rotting grapes used. For there has been a general tightening up of wine-making since 1995 with, for instance, the temperature of fermentation being controlled, and as a result of his efforts Olivier finds that the wine is now much more complex, with more taste.

With a greater concentration on the wine has come a much closer look at the nature of each vintage – particularly as single-vintage cognacs are now becoming increasingly fashionable (see chapter eleven). The characteristics of each vintage depend on the weather in the month before the harvest. Distillers are looking for the right alcoholic content and above all for balance – in 2002 for instance the lack of rain meant that the alcohol emerged through concentration and the wine was not well balanced. In theory there should be a negative correlation between vintages in Cognac and Bordeaux, since the Bordelais are looking for grapes that are not overly acid, a quality greatly prized by the Cognaçais, but there isn't any such correlation, not all the time anyway. As Eric Forget of Hine points out, the two regions are actually looking for the same things, "balance, acidity and quality", and because harvests in Cognac start on average three weeks later than in the Médoc, Cognac has a second chance. It also helps that the weather in Cognac is sunnier through the summer and less rainy during the crucial weeks in September. For instance 1972 was a lousy year in Bordeaux because the weather had been cold and rainy, but there was a warm "after-season" which led to some very good cognacs.

Of course there are still problem years. In 1980 the season was late, and the grapes were picked very cold, so their juice had almost been neutralized, rectified by the cold. This in turn made it difficult to get fermentation started. As a result the wines were thin and flat, and their faults were duly multiplied in the distillation process. In 1962 the problem had been exactly the opposite. The grapes were picked in very hot weather, up to 35°C (95°F), and because the winemakers could not control the temperature the precious yeasts were killed before they had time to complete their work. (Today the Charentais use natural yeasts developed from local strains by the Station Viticole.) Better cooling techniques prevented a repetition of these worries in the unprecedentedly hot summer of 1982. In 1976, another hot year, the grapes could not be picked until they contained a full twelve degrees of alcohol and thus produced cognacs that were flat and uninteresting.

The wines used for distillation are obviously undrinkably acid. They are also very weak, between seven and ten degrees of alcohol, for one very basic reason: the weaker the wine, the greater the degree of concentration involved in producing a freshly distilled cognac of around seventy degrees. When the St-Emilion is fully ripe its wine will reach ten to eleven degrees. But even a wine of ten degrees would be concentrated only seven times; one of seven degrees (the lower limit of practical distillation) will be concentrated ten times, so it will be infinitely more aromatic. The ideal strength is between 8.5 and 9.5 degrees of alcohol, resulting in wines which provide the right balance of qualities – Olivier tries not to buy grapes with over 9.5 degrees of potential alcohol. In theory wine as weak as three or four degrees could be turned into acceptable brandy. But the lower the strength, the less likely the grapes are to be wholly sound or even half-ripe.

Even today the wine-making itself is naturally pretty basic. The object is a quick alcoholic fermentation lasting around seven days followed immediately by "the malo" – malolactic fermentation – when the malic acid in the wine is transformed into lactic acid. As Francis Gay-Bellile, the former director of the Station Viticole, points out, it relies on nature: "We adapt our wine-making techniques to the needs of the still." For all they are doing, as he says, is to "preserve the interesting elements in the juice".

The must is fermented in vats holding 100–200 hectolitres. Until recently these were made from concrete, but modern winemakers now prefer vats made from soft iron lined with epoxy resins or resins reinforced with glass fibre. In the past few years the fermentation of the first few vats has been triggered off by the use of cultured yeasts, but otherwise there has been total reliance on nature as the juice ferments for an average of five days at a temperature of 20–25°C (68–77°F).

Modern scientific knowledge has led to remarkably few changes in the tried and tested historical methods, the major difference being a fuller understanding of the wine-making process and its problems. For a long time, for instance, it was thought that the taint of bitterness, of greenness, found in some cognacs could be traced back to tannin from the skins of the grapes. But there is virtually no tannin in a wine made, as in Cognac, by lightly pressing the St-Emilion grape, and any residual tannins are eliminated by the distillation process. The disagreeable bitterness did indeed come from tannins – not from the skins but from volatile substances like hexanol and haxanal contained in the pips, leaves, and twigs swept up in the harvesting process. As one distiller put it, "if you put perfect wines into the still the distiller can concentrate his efforts on capturing its aromatic components". The longer a wine remains undistilled the more of its valuable aromatic esters it loses. So distillers have to conserve more of the *têtes* (the first flow of spirit from the still, usually put back to be redistilled) if they distil too late, which in effect means after the end of February following the harvest, a month before the legal limit of March 31.

Nevertheless, the wines used for distillation by the Charentais have several advantages. They are so acid – the level of residual sugar is a mere one gram per litre, lower than that of many wines made for drinking (technically they have a pH of 3–3.4) – that they keep well, do not suffer from bacterial problems, and lack the pectins which can make wine rather cloudy. But the need for purity creates one major problem. White wines being prepared for drinking are invariably dosed with a little sulphur to prevent oxidation and deter bacteria. It is simply impossible to use sulphur dioxide (SO_2) when making wine for distillation. Even without SO_2 the yeasts produce a certain quantity of aldehydes. Encouraged by SO_2 they produce up to twenty times as much. The compound formed by the SO_2 and the aldehydes decomposes when heated in the still, and the resulting mixture of aldehyde and alcohol produces acetal, giving off a smell reminiscent of hospital corridors.

Before the wine can be distilled it should undergo *le malo*. Fortunately the wines are precocious: when wines are sufficiently acidic, are free from sulphur, and have not been racked, the lactic acids develop very quickly. In most wines this sort of viticultural puberty does not take place until the spring following the fermentation, too late for the Cognaçais, who have to finish distillation before warm weather stimulates fresh fermentation. You can distil pre-malo wines, but you must not distil them in mid-malo, as the resulting brandies give off a rather foetid smell. But by early December, a mere six weeks after the grapes have been picked, most of the wines are ready for distillation.

2

Distillation: the Heart of the Matter

Wine is the raw material of cognac, its major influence potentially negative if it is not correct, healthy, and free from any impurities that would
inevitably be multiplied, concentrated, in the distillation process. The
newly distilled brandy may be merely an intermediate product, yet the
still has transformed the wine not into any ordinary spirit but into
cognac. "It is one thing to manufacture alcohol," wrote Professor Méjane;
"it is quite another to create a high-grade brandy with the same raw materials, brandies produced in batches are greatly superior to those produced
in continuous stills."[1] This vital improvement in quality justifies all the
inconveniences of double distillation: increased energy consumption, the
need for the distiller's skills, its reduced, limited, discontinuous flow. For
even the fiery liquids trickling from Cognac's stills have real, and different, characteristics: some are fuller than others, some obviously have
more depth, more potential. By contrast some are showing a hint of
mustiness, or rawness, or of smokiness, due to faults in the wine or the
distillation process. There is no doubt that the average quality, especially
at the basic VS level, has improved over the past thirty years, which is not
to say that cognacs are as characterful as they were – the distinctive "qualities" found in earlier years were often due to faults in the brandy.

Distillation is a simple enough process, based on the fact that alcohol
vaporizes at a lower temperature than water. So when a fermented liquor
(wine, or the sort of "mashes" used to produce malt whisky) is heated, the
alcohol vaporizes and the qualities – or faults – of the wine or other raw
materials are concentrated. It is then trapped in a pipe leading from the
top of the still and cooled. Of course, there are an infinite number of

[1] *Annales de technologie agricole,* 1975.

practical problems involved: the shape and size of the vessel, the metal from which it should be constructed, the type and quality of the liquor to be distilled, the shape of the pipe conducting the spirit to the cooler, the moment at which the liquor is acceptable – and the cut-off point after which it is either too weak or too full of impurities (or both). But all these problems are matters of trial and error, and most had been solved by the end of the seventeenth century. Then, as now, the wines were made into a *brouillis*, a half-strength spirit, in a first distillation before the second (*la bonne chauffe*) produces the real stuff. It has always been a matter of pride to the Cognaçais that their brandies are produced by a double distillation process. The only other spirits traditionally made in this way are the cal-vados of the Pays d'Auge in Normandy and Scotland's malt whiskies. Other, lesser spirits (like most calvados or armagnac) are made from a single *chauffe*.

Even the distillation process in Cognac is unlike that used elsewhere. Ordinary distillation involves the separation of the volatile elements in the original liquid according to their boiling points, whereas in distilla-tion *à la charentaise* the alcoholic vapours simply sweep through the dis-tillation apparatus. A local author writing at the end of the nineteenth century, in an attempt to ban more efficient but less satisfactory stills, compared "the cooking of brandy to that of pot-au-feu. Who does not prefer a nourishing home-made broth to that made in a restaurant, even though it has been made by steam?"[2] Michel Caumeil, the now-retired research director of Hennessy, put it even more simply: "The production of cognac is simply controlled evaporation."[3] The process is not com-pletely scientific but is an art, a balancing act between the desire to pre-serve the character provided by the grapes with the need to eliminate undesirable elements by "rectification", or distilling the spirit to a higher strength. It is at this point that the crucial element of personal judgment, the "distiller's skills" referred to by Professor Méjane, enter into the equa-tion. For distillation is a complex process involving a number of chemi-cal reactions such as esterification and hydrolysis.

The still has to heat the wines, trap the alcoholic vapours, and then cool them. In theory this is simple enough. But, as with the wine-making,

[2] Quoted in: A. Baudoin, *Les eaux-de-vie et la fabrication du Cognac*, 1983.
[3] Michel Caumeil, *Pour la science*, December 1983.

everything has to be perfect: the heat has to be about 1600°C – a higher temperature is favourable only for less volatile components. The heat must be applied uniformly to all the liquid in the container; only the desirable vapours must be extracted; they must flow smoothly; and the cooling process, like the heating, must be gradual and regular. Yet by the mid-seventeenth century the locals, with a certain amount of help from the Dutch – the biggest customers for the brandy – had found solutions to all these problems most still valid today.

As a result the first detailed picture we have of an "alembic Charentais", dating from 1710, would be instantly recognizable to a distiller today. So indeed would that written by Etienne Munier, a well-known engineer whose description, written half a century later, remains our basic source of information about cognac in the later eighteenth century. The still itself, the alembic or *chaudière à eau-de-vie* (literally a "spirit boiler"), is surmounted by a smaller *chapiteau* – literally, a circus tent, the "big top" – to trap the vapours, which are then led down a *bec* ("beak") to a cooling coil. The alembic is still housed in a massive square, brick-built oven containing an open fire, for cognac is heated from outside whereas most malt whisky is now heated internally through a system of steam-heated pipes in the vat. Only the dimensions of the alembic – and the fuel employed – have changed.

Then, as now, the whole apparatus was constructed of "several pieces of red beaten copper, fitted together with copper nails and without solder". Copper is an ideal material for the purpose. Physically it is malleable, easy to work, resists any corrosion resulting from the fire, is impervious to most acids, and a good conductor of heat. But copper also has a chemical role to play. It fixes the fatty acids in the wine, as well as any of the sulphurous products in the vapours that would harm the quality of the cognac. Copper also reacts with components such as sulphur and fatty acids which enrich the brandy and serves as a general catalyst for fixing different components of the wine without changing the taste of the spirit. Experiments using alternative materials, like steel and glass, were conducted at the beginning of the twentieth century. They merely confirmed how ideal copper was for the purpose. The copper used today is special, very pure (electrolyzed) and polished to smooth out the pores in the metal.

The shape of the apparatus has not changed either. The *cucurbite*, the vat in which the wine is heated, has always been onion-shaped, "*un cone tronqué*" (a truncated cone). This provides an expansion chamber in which the fumes released by heating can swirl like those in a tornado. They sweep upwards into the *chapiteau*. This is also rounded, the combination resembling an old-fashioned cottage loaf sculpted in gleaming copper. In Munier's day it varied in shape, although it always broadened above the neck, to help it capture the alcoholic vapour rising from the *cucurbite*. Munier's own text was illustrated with a *chapiteau* which strongly resembled an old-fashioned stove-pipe hat, but he also provided a sketch of a much more modern-looking, more rounded shape he had devised himself. The *chapiteau* prevents the froth from spilling over to the condenser, allows the less volatile elements in the vapour to fall back into the *chaudière*, and thus guarantees the quality of the spirit. The *chapiteau* should be about one-tenth the size of the *cucurbite*. If it is any bigger, the vapour gets too strong, too rectified.

The vapours then trickle down the *bec* or, as it was called locally in Munier's time, the *queue* ("tail"), which is effectively an extension of the *chapiteau*. Then as now the individual components were not merely nailed together but "strongly soldered with a compound of tin and zinc", which "helped to ensure that [the *bec*] was not blown off by the expansion of the vapours during distillation". This insistence on the construction of the apparatus was not accidental, for every element had to be gas-tight. Munier was a "physiocrat", one of the small band of inquiring spirits who believed that it was their mission to improve anything they came across. In his case the obvious problem was the *col* ("neck"). As he put it: "I have heard a number of progressive distillers say that the neck of the still was usually too flat; that there was not enough distance between the surface of the liquor and the roof of the *chapiteau*, so that the vapours do not travel far enough to rid themselves of 'phlegms' [undesirable congeners], and the liquid spills over too easily." Until his time the *bec* had been a straight pipe.

Observers of Munier's day thought that the combination resembled a Moor's head (*tête de Maure*). To modern eyes it resembles, rather, a bullet-headed cartoon animal with a long sharp nose. Earlier in the century Claude Masse had suggested bending the pipe, and Munier went farther towards the modern idea, the elegantly shaped *col de cygne* ("swan's neck") which provides an infinitely smoother flow path than the earlier, more angular designs. It is not surprising that the distillers of Munier's time found the flow problem delicate, as some unwanted *mousse* ("froth") seeped into the *serpentin*. With the older shape, as Bruno Sepulchre notes[4]: "You got very personalized brandies. The evolution of the present olive or onion shape of the *chapiteau* also reflects the evolution towards brandies that taste more neutral and standardized because they are rectified by the increased height of the *col de cygne*."

To correct this problem the biggest *chapiteaux* were only about one-tenth the size of the still itself, and care was taken that the "swan's neck" did not arch upwards too much. Nevertheless the *chapiteaux* used in peripheral regions still capitalize on this point: they are larger in order to block off some of their undesirable *goûts de terroir*. Cognac is a conservative place: it was not until well into the twentieth century that the *col de cygne* triumphed over the much more angular *tête de Maure*. The distillation apparatus was completed by the cooling coil, described by Munier as "the *serpentin*, which forms five circles in a slope of three and a half feet, submerged into a barrel called the pipe, the spirit flows from the *serpentin* into a circular double-bottomed (*foncé de deux bouts*) tub; it is called a *bassiot*. The *serpentin* . . . condenses the vapours and cools the vapours before filtration."

In terms of size the apparatus used in Munier's day was a mere pilot plant for the much bigger stills employed today which provide much more standardized, less erratic brandies. Then – and indeed, right through the eighteenth and nineteenth centuries – when most cognac was distilled by thousands of growers, the *cucurbite* was relatively tiny, with an internal diameter of a mere 53 cm/20.9 inches and only 75 cm/29.5 inches high. The size varied, but overall it held only between three and four *veltes* (216–288 litres; a *velte* was a Dutch measure). Everything else was in proportion: the furnace was 0.9 metres/35.4 inches in diameter; the bec was only 0.5 metre/19.68 inches long; the *serpentin* a mere 1 metre/39 inches tall and, according to Munier, the whole apparatus could be contained in a "small one-storey building, consisting of single room about three by four metres (9.84 feet)".

Modern technology has changed all that. Some of the stills used for the *première chauffe* hold up to 130 hl, although those used for the second

---

[4] *Le Livre de Cognac*, Hubschmid & Bouret, Paris, 1983.

chauffe are legally limited to a maximum of thirty hectolitres and can be filled only with twenty-five hectolitres of liquid. If they are any bigger, the brandy they produce cannot be called by any of the *sous-appellations* ("sub-appellations"), and can only be plain "cognac". For the balance has to be preserved: the bigger the still, the more neutral the spirit. But in any case there is an absolute limit to size: above a certain point too little of the wine or *brouillis* is in actual contact with the alembic.

The stove heating the wine has always been crucial. Now, as in Munier's day, it is made of thick masonry, with a large door occupying a third of the front, strong enough to resist the heat of the furnace. Behind it the chimney was in brick, as was the lining of the furnace. Considerable skill was required to ensure that the heat was absolutely steady. In Munier's words: "Too high a flame upsets everything; with the strong spirit water it carries off acids and oils, which do not have time to mix and which alter the taste of the brandy; too low a fire provides a light, pleasant brandy but one that is too strong, with too burning a taste; it removes neither enough water nor all the bitterness." Even today if the flame is too high, it overheats the copper, and the resulting brandy can be *rimé* ("burnt").

For a *bouilleur de cru* distilling his own wine the fuel was by far the biggest cash cost he incurred – two-thirds of a cubic metre (over twenty cubic feet) of wood or 100 kilos (220.5 lbs) of coal were required to produce a hectolitre of cognac. Until the nineteenth century wood from the Bois or from the forests to the east provided the normal fuel. But wood burns quickly, so the furnace had to be refilled every two or three hours during a distillation season that lasted, day and night, for up to three months. This imposed a colossal strain: James Long[5] recounts how when the distiller wanted a nap he would "hang a tin on the swan's neck suspended on the end of a piece of string stuck there with wax; so that when the wax melted the tin would fall and wake him up!". Munier insisted that the vat house (*brûlerie*) had to be separate from any other building to reduce the danger of fire, for he had seen "distillers grown sleepy and careless who had, through sheer clumsiness, lit with their candles the spirit that came out of the serpent"; the fire spread up the "stream of spirit" and could be stopped only by blocking the outlet at the bottom of

[5] *The Century Companion to Cognac and Other Brandies*, London, Century, 1983.

the *serpentin* with a wet rag. A nineteenth-century visitor, Henry Vizetelly, was only half-joking when he wrote: "Various little precautions have to be observed; among others, not to set the premises on fire."[6]

During the nineteenth century wood was gradually replaced by coal, which required less frequent attention, although this meant rebuilding the furnaces to provide more draught. Fuel oil was tried but proved difficult to insulate from the still. Fortunately, the natural gas discovered at Lacq in the southwest of France in the early 1950s has proved an ideal fuel – reliable, regular, and requiring no attention. Even so, it took over twenty years for the infrastructure of pipes and tanks of propane or butane to be fitted to the region's thousands of scattered stills. The gas is adjusted to heat the liquid at the same speed as wood and has many advantages, notably that it provides more regularity – with wood even the strength and direction of the wind mattered because of the change in draught involved. An even more modern heating method, electricity, is strictly forbidden, indeed the alembic has, legally, to be heated by a naked flame.

Distillation needs less heat, and thus less fuel, if some of the heat dissipated in the cooling process is transferred to the wine through a heat exchanger. So during the nineteenth century the idea of heating the wine by using a *chauffe-vin* gradually caught on. The pipe containing the wine was simply diverted through the barrel-shaped cooling chamber. But conservatives like Martell still do not employ a *chauffe-vin*; they are afraid that the more complicated refrigeration chamber could not be properly cleaned, that the pipes would be blocked and the incoming wines overheated. Supporters of the *chauffe-vin* say that it is simply a mechanical process, designed to save heat, but even they admit that it can be dangerous if the wine is heated above 40–45°C. The *chauffe-vin* can then cause oxidation, so it is often used only for a few hours during a *chauffe*, and usually the last few.

The wine can, of course, be distilled with or without its lees. To outsiders it is surprising that many producers do not utilize at least part of the lees, for they are now forming an increasingly important weapon with which winemakers can increase the complexity of their products as part of their effort to extract the qualities directly linked to each specific ter-

[6] Viztelly, *Household Words*, 1855.

roir, especially for brandies destined to spend a relatively long time in cask. This reluctance is often due to the Cognaçais' continuing lack of interest in the qualities of the wine. Nevertheless, using the lees is a complex business, for only now are researchers gradually separating the two different types of lees: those from the grapes, their skins and twigs, and the relics of the yeasts. Moreover the lees need protecting from the air before the wines are distilled and cannot safely be used late in the distilling season, once the external temperature has risen much above 10°C. They can also stick to the wall of the alembic. And, as one distiller pointed out, "lees means that you need time for the brandies to mature and provide their additional complexity".

Not surprisingly the major firms differ in their approach. In the early 1950s Rémy separated itself from the other producers by using the lees to produce eaux de vie which were rich and could cope more easily with the wood, giving them greater fullness and richness after a few years in wood. "The 6000°C heat of the fire cooks the lees and infuses the cognac with their aroma," says Robert Leauté. The yeast lees contain a number of esters, including three fatty acids, which turn out to be absolutely critical in giving the cognac its much prized *rancio* (a particular rich, cheesy flavour) quality when it is in cask. For its part Courvoisier "keeps the lees only when the grapes are clean and free from rot" and uses them only when producing brandies that are strongly structured. Hennessy is pragmatic, insisting on the need for pure wines – an attitude inherited from a production director in the 1960s who disliked the idea. At the other extreme from Rémy, Martell has always set its face against the practice in its efforts to produce purer cognacs. But it is noticeable that virtually all the producers in the Grande Champagne I have come across distil on at least some of the lees, if only because they are producing brandies destined to mature long enough to absorb the resulting richness in the brandy.

Distillers start work in late November or early December, as soon as the wine has completed its fermentation, but have only three months to complete their work before an early warm spell might awaken the dormant wines, although they are legally permitted to continue distilling until March 31. They work day and night, for distillation is a long process, with the first *chauffe* taking eight or nine hours and the second up to fourteen hours for distillers anxious to extract the maximum grapiness from the wines. The first distillation produces a *brouilli* of between twenty-six and thirty-two degrees of alcohol, over three times the strength of the wine. The first vapours to emerge are much stronger, about fifty-five degrees, and are removed because they are bound to contain impurities already in the system. At the other end of the cycle the flow is cut off when the hydrometer below the *serpentin* shows that the spirit contains less than five degrees – the instrument serves as a checkpoint not only for the strength but also for the temperature of the cognac. Because the *première chauffe* produces what is purely an intermediate product and, moreover one which is difficult even for an experienced distiller to taste, outsiders assume that it is less important than the second *chauffe*. Precisely the opposite is true: virtually all the chemical reactions that provide the cognac with its final quality take place during the first, not the second, *chauffe*. The professionals all agree that it does sixty per cent of the work and that the *bonne chauffe* merely concentrates the cognac still further.

The stills used for the *première chauffe* are usually bigger, but there is inevitably a short time during which enough *brouillis* are being produced to load up a still for the second, the *bonne chauffe*. Too long a gap can have unfortunate effects. Between 1973 and 1975 there were three enormous crops and not enough vats to hold all the wine, so a great deal was reduced through an early *première chauffe*, and there was some oxidation during storage.

The second, *la bonne chauffe*, is the glamorous one. But the yield is minimal: the twenty-five hectolitres provides only 6.8 litres of spirit at Hennessy and 7.2 at Martell – though up to six hectolitres more can be redistilled. Its role is simple. "It simply selects and separates; it is not creative," says Jacques Rouvière of Bisquit Dubouche. As with the first *chauffe*, a small percentage, a *tête*, is drawn off the top before the brandy is allowed to flow into the *bassiot*. The point at which the *tête* is cut is not crucial. As Francis Gay-Bellile, formerly of the Centre Viticole, points out: "The first 0.5 per cent is used merely to clean out the *serpentin*, which is full of diluted wash. After that it doesn't matter too much. There is some difference depending on whether you start allowing the spirit from *la bonne chauffe* through after one or two per cent, but since the *tête* goes back into the next load of *brouillis*, the effect is minimal."

By contrast, the point at which the flow is diverted after the *coeur* has been extracted and the *secondes* are put on one side is a matter of considerable skill. The *bonne chauffe* starts flowing at about seventy-eight degrees of alcohol, and the legal maximum for the final spirit is seventy-two, but below that point the break is a matter of subjective judgement. The basic criterion is simple enough: the higher the degree of the final spirit, the more neutral and rectified it will be; the lower the strength of the last drops allowed through, the more essential aromas they will contain but the greater the danger of including noxious ingredients.

But many of the aromatic compounds liable to be excluded are essential in producing rich cognacs, for they include "congeners", a word covering all the impurities found in any spirit not distilled to 100 degrees of alcohol, at which level it would be rectified with everything else eliminated. There are literally hundreds of them, including aldehydes, polyphenols, and more or less aromatic esters, but there is no correlation between their quantity and their importance. Some, often present in tiny proportions, should be cherished, others eliminated, while others are of no importance to the quality of the final spirit. Nevertheless, the need for many of them can be exaggerated. In the early 1980s an international firm specializing in the creation of artificial substitutes for natural tastes concocted an ersatz cognac and smuggled it into one of the routine tastings conducted by the BNIC. It was duly approved. By no means outstanding, said the tasters, but perfectly acceptable. Nevertheless, an element of mystery remains. Michel Caumeil of Hennessy says simply: "We know how a man is made, but not cognac."

Using a high proportion of the *têtes*, and thus allowing more neutral spirit, can be a useful precaution in a bad year when the solids may turn out to be particularly nasty. In a good year you can afford to let through more of the nutrients. Even in a good year Martell deliberately cuts both *têtes* and *secondes* early as a matter of style, aiming to produce a dry, clear-cut, relatively neutral brandy that will absorb character from the wood in which it will be housed for so long. At the other extreme is Jacques Rouvière of Bisquit, who tries to extract as many of the secondary elements as possible. The decision is a delicate one: "Even half a degree makes a difference," says Rouvière. Some distillers believe that it is essential not to cut too many of the *têtes* in the Grande Champagne, since you want to include as much of the rich raw material in the wine as possible.

But there is more than one decision to make before the brandies are ready. If the discarded *secondes* are mixed with the wine, this strengthens the raw material used in the *première chauffe* from nine to eleven degrees of alcohol, so the *brouillis* comes out at around thirty degrees. This is useful if, like Martell, you are looking for a relatively neutral result, for some of the wine will be distilled four times. (It is also useful if you are using grapes that are more unripe than usual and therefore low in alcohol.) If the *secondes* are mixed with the *brouillis* then you get a greater depth of aroma, with the brandies extracting the maximum benefit from the original grapes.

For 200 years the end result has been much the same. In the words of Jean Demachy: "The liquor flows into the receptacle forming a thread, which thickens imperceptibly; and when this thread is roughly the width of a medium-thick pen, the distillation process is well established."[7] The cognac is now ready for its long years in wood.

[7] Jean Demachy, L'Art du distillateur des eaux-fortes, Paris, 1773.

3

Brandy + age + oak = Cognac

The thin trickle emerging from the *alembic charentais* is not yet cognac. It needs years of maturation in oak casks. These have always been used by the Cognaçais for maturing and storing their brandies, and over the centuries distillers and drinkers alike have increasingly appreciated the importance of the role played by the wood. The oak and the spirit react, both physically and chemically. With greater understanding of the complexity of the ageing of cognac has come an enhanced capacity for blenders in different firms to define their house styles more accurately.

For in Cognac style starts with the wood. From the outset *Quercus pedunculata*, the common oak, was chosen for casks, originally for its physical properties. In the words of Francis Gay-Bellile, these included:

> *its strength; elevated density of texture, which increases its strength; its hardness, which protects it from shocks and mechanical tension; its suppleness, which allows the curved lines of the cask to be formed by bending; its water-tightness, which prevents the liquid from leaking; its lack of permeability, which prevents the spirit from being diluted by the humidity in the atmosphere; and its light colouring.*

The French are lucky: theirs is still a very wooded country, and oak occupies one-third of all their woodland. Even today *tonnelleries* use less than a tenth of all the oak sawn in France (even though there is an increasing demand for the wood from winemakers abroad, especially in California and Australia). Only two types of oak, both French – the Tronçais and the Limousin – have ever proved suitable for ageing cognac. Increasingly, however, many distillers, anxious to minimize their expense, have returned to the alternative sources used by their predecessors, oak from Russia, the Baltic states (called Danzig) or the Adriatic (Trieste), and now from the USA. But none of the alternatives has provided the unique combination of physical and chemical qualities required to turn raw-brandy-from-the-Cognac-region into cognac.

The differences between the Tronçais and the Limousin are based on the very different terroirs on which they are grown. The Limousin forests, centred in the hills to the east of Angoulême (the name derives from the same root as Limoges, a city northeast of Angoulême), conform to the British idea of oak woods: they are small, and the trees widely scattered, thick, and sturdy. The wood is appropriately tough. In his detailed work on the making of cognac's casks, Jean Taransaud explains:

> The oak from the Limousin is a rough, heavy, hard and sinewy wood, with big fat grain up to 2.4 cm/1 inch in size. It is difficult to work and more porous than oak from the Tronçais, but it is renowned for its tannic qualities, and if its best recommendation to the merchant is its rate of evaporation, none the less it provides a much appreciated tannin for taming the harshness of cognac.[1]

Limousin wood, floated down the Charente, was the only oak available when cognac was just beginning its rise to fame. Tronçais, its only rival, comes from a man-made forest that was first planted in the middle of the seventeenth century, so its trees were not ready to provide oak until after the Revolution. The great French statesman, Colbert reckoned that the only way to combat the over-mighty warships of Holland and England with their "hearts of oak" was for France to grow its own. The Tronçais forest was the result. It is in the Bourbonnais, the very heart of France between Montlucon and Moulins, extending north towards Nevers and east towards Burgundy (Ravaz calls it "wood from Burgundy"). The forest itself is now a major tourist attraction, awarded two stars by the editors of the *Michelin Guide*. The trees are more crowded, and therefore taller and slimmer, than those grown in the Limousin – and thus unfamiliar to British eyes accustomed to naturally grown oaks. Today a great deal of wood from other forests is labelled as Tronçais, for it is now recognized as a type of wood rather than a geographical description. When Jean-Marc Olivier of Courvoisier went looking for *grains fins* ("fine-grained oaks") in other forests he found them notably in the Jupilles

---

[1] Jean Taransaud, *Le Livre de la tonnellerie*, La Roue à Livres Diffusion, Paris, 1976.

forest south of Le Mans, which was planted at the same time as the Tronçais itself.

The wood from Tronçais and Tronçais-type forests is darker than that of its rival, copper-coloured where that from the Limousin is a lighter yellow. To quote Jean Taransaud, "Mature clumps of trees provide an oak which grows thin and straight. The wood from it has a delicate and soft grain which is easy to work. It is particularly impervious to alcohol, very unporous. It has an excellent tannin, soft and slightly sweet, which permeates the cognac only slowly." The Tronçais is not only tighter-grained than the Limousin, it also contains less tannin and more lignin than wood from its rival and so imparts a less woody flavour to the cognacs. So Limousin is not entirely suitable for the cheaper cognacs, which are going to spend only a few years in wood; they are liable to absorb too much tannin and to become too *boisé* ("woody"). In the long run Limousin is more suitable for the same reason: it has so much tannin to impart that the cognac still has reserves to draw on after a decade or more in the wood.

The first Cognaçais to discover the forest of Tronçais was one of the Martell family. By the 1840s, according to letters preserved in the firm's archives, it was already a regular source of wood. He found it was better suited to the Martell style – even though more difficult to treat because harder – than that from the Limousin and was already used by winemakers on the Loire, of which the river Allier is a tributary.

But the tannins form under five per cent of the chemical make-up of the wood. Seventy per cent is cellulose, some of which is chemically inert. It is important mainly for the "backbone", the mechanical strength, it gives the wood, although the spirit does absorb some of the sugars in the hemicellulose as the molecules shrink during the ageing process. But more important than either is the lignin, which forms about twenty-three per cent of the oak and hence has a much more important influence on the maturation process than the better-known tannins. Luckily for the Charentais, oak contains only about 0.5 per cent of resinous matter, which would pollute the grapiness of the brandy with the turpentine taste so marked in brandies matured in casks of pine, which contain eight per cent of resinous matter.

The oaks used for Cognac's casks have to be at least fifty years old – most of them are centenarians. The only part that can be used is the section of the trunk from just above the roots to the lowest branches, to ensure that the planks and their grain are straight and free from knots and faults. But not all of even this limited selection is suitable: the heart itself is too knotty; the sappy wood under the bark is too rich in soluble organic essences, which would pollute the brandy. The drying, too, is special. The ready-cut trunks are piled up in the open air in stacks, which allow the air and the rain free access. The trunks dry naturally and slowly at the rate of a year for every centimetre of thickness. Most of the planks are 5–6 cm/1.96–2.36 inches thick, so reputable cooperages tend to dry their oak for considerably longer than the statutory minimum of three years – most of them use planks dried for five or six years.

The wood needs to mature, but the drying also has a chemical role to play. Lengthy exposure to the air and the rain washes away some of the more bitter tannins in the wood; others are broken down into more palatable tannins; and a mould develops that works on the lignins in the wood. Enzymes split the big (and tasteless) lignin molecule into four smaller ones, all of which taste of vanillin. The acid and the alcohol in the cognac dissolve the vanillin-lignins. These emerge with the vanilla aroma that is so essential in the finished cognac.

The fuss about air-dried oak sounds absurd. It is not. With the help of the cooperative that markets the Prince de Polignac brand, the Station Viticole compared brandy stored in oven-dried oak with the same spirit stored in the air-dried equivalent. After a year in the oven-dried oak the spirit was bitter and astringent, fuller of acids and tannin than if the air had been allowed to do its work unaided.

The cognac cask itself has always been special. Its shape was not unusual – the bulge in the middle, making it easier to roll, was a feature of other regions as well. Nevertheless, it was instantly recognizable by the hoops made of thin strips of lathe laid around most of the sides of the cask, only the wood in the middle remaining visible. The staves of today's casks are circled only sufficiently to enable them to be rolled more easily. The size of the cask is crucial, since it determines the extent to which the brandy will be exposed to the wood: the smaller the cask, the woodier the cognac. As with the size of the alembic, balance has to be achieved. In the past the *barrique de cognac* held over 205 litres, although the brandy was housed in *tierçons* which held over 500 litres. But now virtually all distillers have standardized on smaller casks. By trial and error they have found that casks holding around 350 litres provide the correct balance.

Not surprisingly, *la tonnellerie* (the craft of the cooper) has always been important. In his book Taransaud proudly styles himself *maître tonnellier de Cognac* – and one little affected by modern production techniques. Because they are such substantial users of casks, the major firms became involved with some of the biggest *tonnelleries* in France. Hennessy took over the Taransaud family business in the 1950s, though forty years later it was sold to Henri de Pracomtal, the firm's former managing director. For a long time Rémy Martin owned Seguin Moreau which it claimed was the largest cooperage in France and became a major supplier of casks to the Australian wine industry. But it too was sold off in the 1990s. Today only Martell owns its own cooperage, buying its own wood.

The firms' previous self-reliance was explained by the horror stories they all have to tell of the leaks that developed in casks bought from outside, defects that ruined the quality as well as reducing the quantity of the spirit. The slightest flaw in the cask can mean that the precious contents drain or become infected. Charles Walter Berry, the wine merchant who was probably the leading expert on cognac in London between the two World Wars, said that "a split stave will cause a woody taste".[2]

Despite the size of the workshops, the casks are still made in the traditional way; the wood has to be cleaved along the line of the grain, not sawn across. Although some of the staves can be relatively mass-produced, the actual fabrication of the casks remains the task of individual craftsmen, each with his own rhythm of work.

Even though the wood is so dense, the casks so carefully made, and the bungs so tight, there is inevitably some evaporation when cognac is stored in wood. Indeed the art of the cooper and the distiller is to ensure that the evaporation is controlled, so that the necessary reactions between wood, air, and brandy can proceed at the appropriate pace. The spirit evaporates at very different rates depending on the humidity of the chai, a loss described by the locals as *la part des anges* ("the angels' share"). Strictly speaking, anything called a chai ought to be partly underground, as it is in Bordeaux. In Cognac the word is used to describe any warehouse used for storing spirit.

The ageing process is both physical and chemical. Robert Leauté, ex-technical director of Rémy Martin, divides the maturation process into

[2] *In Search of Wine*, London, Constable, 1935.

five stages. In the first year the cognac loses its "boiler taste" and takes on its first colouring, a pale yellow tint. In the next couple of years the spirit starts to absorb some woodiness and ceases to be merely a raw spirit. In the two subsequent stages covering the next seven or eight years the woodiness diminishes, the cognac mellows, a hint of vanilla starts to creep in. From around its twelfth birthday the cognac gets more complex and harmonious. More prosaically, the spirit also gets progressively weaker, at the rate of up to one percentage point a year in the first ten years in cask but much more slowly after that – a brandy with fifty years in cask behind it will still be about forty-six degrees of alcohol. The balance is a delicate one: if the chai is especially humid, then the loss of alcoholic strength will be much greater, whereas an unusually dry warehouse induces unnaturally fast evaporation of what remains a strong spirit. Maurice Fillioux of Hennessy reckons that a cognac left for twenty years in an especially dry chai will retain the youthfulness of a ten-year-old. The same period of time spent by brandy in an unusually damp chai will add five years to its physical age.

The traditional brandies sipped by the British aristocracy were bought soon after distillation and shipped immediately to London or Bristol and stored for decades in damp cellars in the docks. This produced the classic taste of what were erroneously called "early-landed, late-bottled" cognacs. The two are not the same, since virtually all cognacs are "late-bottled", in the sense that they are bottled only just before they are sold. The brandies matured in Britain were pale and delicate. This was much to the taste of old-style English connoisseurs. One of the breed, Maurice Healy, described such a cognac as "of almost unearthly pallor and a corresponding ethereal bouquet and flavour". By contrast they were – and are – not overly highly rated by many French blenders, who find them flabby; and certainly they are not sturdy enough to last more than twenty or thirty years.

Scientists now perceive the controlled evaporation involved in the maturation process as a continuation, albeit at a much slower rate, of the processes begun in the alembic. The evaporation is only part of the most important reaction involved – that of the oxygen in the air outside the cask and the wood of the cask itself. The wood allows the oxygen to seep steadily through to the spirit, and its metallic elements act as catalysts. This slow oxidation ensures that the aromatic elements in the spirit are preserved, although they would be lost in a speedier chemical reaction. The wood itself is profoundly affected by the spirit and gradually drained of the elements which enrich the cognac – inevitably, the longer the cask has been used, the more neutral its wood and the less important the role it plays in the chemical changes to the cognac as it ages.

The tannins play an important role, as they do with maturing wines: they bring colour to the spirit, which is colourless when it emerges from the alembic, and at first they increase its bitterness. But after a few years the molecules are enlarged and the flavour has mellowed. The lignin brings with it an aroma of balsa wood and, when it breaks down, results in the vanilla and cinnamon overtones detectable in some cognacs. These processes are slow. Tannic matter really starts to build up only after eight years in cask; and while the aldehydes reach their peak after a mere thirty years (they have absorbed one of them, vanillin, within five), the volatile acids build up over the fifty years a truly old cognac spends in cask before it is transferred to *bonbonnes*. Of course in a glass container it does not develop further or at least to any great extent, so the oldest cognacs are essentially frozen in time. The Fillioux believe that cognacs should generally be left a mere thirty-five years in wood – others think it could be up to sixty years. In fact it all depends on the age and cleanliness of the wood to ensure that the final brandy will not be too woody.

The tannins and the lignins dissolve at different rates, so after five years only ten per cent of the lignin in the cask has been absorbed in comparison with twenty per cent of the tannin; after ten years only sixty per cent of the tannin is left but eighty per cent of the lignin. The conventional wisdom that cognac takes up to fifty years to absorb all the tannin in the wood is challenged by Michel Caumeil, who reckons that after twenty or thirty years virtually all the tannin has been absorbed, so that the only role of the wood is a physical one – it continues to allow air through for oxidation.

But age does not automatically bring quality with it. After fifteen or twenty years some cognacs – not all, by any means – become maderized and the fatty acids in the cognac are oxidized. But after twenty or so years the best acquire the very particular *rancio charentais* which develops in different stages, ending with overtones of leather and cedary cigar boxes. Charles Walter Berry (who did not like it) described *rancio* as "a special character of fullness and fatness in some Brandies; rankness (*rance*, *rancio*)". The richness, he implies, reminds some tasters of Roquefort cheese; indeed there is a sort of mild cheesiness in the nose, a sense of hidden depths, far removed from the foxy *goût de terroir* of young, inferior brandies but nevertheless a reminder of the earthiness of the spirit's origins. For me *rancio* is much more exciting, infinitely appetizing, exactly like the essence of a fine fruit or Christmas cake, which combine a certain nuttiness with the richness of dried and candied fruits.

Chemically, *rancio charentais* derives from the oxidation of the fatty acids in the spirit, producing the ketones that feel so rich and fat on the palate. But this is only one of many such reactions. The scientists are still busy analyzing the chemical reactions and their results on the palate. One team under Dr Heide detected 334 ingredients in cognac: twenty-four acetals (ethylates of aldehyde and alcohol), twenty-seven acids, sixty-three alcohols, thirty-four aldehydes, twenty-five ketones, seventy-seven esters, nineteen ethers, three lactones, eight phenols, and forty-four "diverse substances". The scientists have still separated and analyzed only seventy of these, either because they form an important part of the mix or because they strongly influence the taste. The two are not the same: with Michel Caumeil I sniffed certain entirely neutral ingredients present in some quantity, and others – like some ethyl compounds – whose smallest whiff is strongly reminiscent of rotten fruit. But these considerations are for the perfectionists. The vast majority of cognacs are sold before their fifth birthday, before they have time to develop any of the complexities of a great cognac. The decision as to what is worth keeping and what is good merely for immediate sale is largely in the hands of the blenders in a few major firms. In Cognac the market reaches right into the cask.

4

The Personality of Cognac

Between the distiller and the drinker comes the blender and the firm under whose name most cognacs are sold. Most of the blends will be unremarkable, and most of the merchants – there are still over two hundred of them – resemble their eighteenth-century predecessors; they are largely brokers, intermediaries between the growers and foreign buyers. Most have stocks, but these are largely "tactical", held for a few years, relying on growers – and wholesalers like the Tesserons – for most of the older brandies they require. Only a handful are big enough – the classic cases are Hine and Delamain – or enjoy a sufficiently high reputation to be able to afford a "house style" of their own and hold a balanced stock extending back through the decades. Nevertheless, like great craftsmen the world over, the blenders in all the better houses have a clear idea in their heads and in bottles in their tasting rooms, rather than on paper, of the essential qualities historically associated with their name.

The obvious comparison is with the merchants in Champagne. They too have lovingly cultivated house styles; they too usually depend on raw materials bought from hundreds of individual growers. But most of the major Champagne houses rely on their own estates for a substantial proportion of their raw material. By contrast, in Cognac the ownership of estates seems largely irrelevant. Three of the biggest merchants – Martell, Hennessy, and Rémy Martin – own vineyards of their own, but these account for an insignificant percentage of their requirements.

Since the late 1970s an increasing number of grower-distillers have begun to sell their own cognacs. In many cases this is because they can no longer rely on selling their brandies to the Big Four firms – Hennessy, Rémy, Martell, and Courvoisier – which account for over three quarters of sales of cognac. But some are simply looking for independence. The classic case is Frapin, with its 315 hectare/778 acre estate in the heart of the Grande Champagne, which sold its cognacs to Rémy Martin until the 1980s and since then has had increasing success with its own production. Frapin is one of the very few producers with enough cognacs from different vintages to be able to provide a reliable blend at the lower levels; most have to rely on their better brandies.

Not only are none of the major firms remotely integrated but none of them buys grapes; all buy wine and new brandy. They all have to buy in parcels of old cognacs when they are mixing their finest blends, for not even Hennessy or Martell can guarantee an adequate supply of every one of the hundreds of cognacs they require for their blends. Obviously, all the "serious" firms keep a tight control over the brandies they buy, mostly through contracts with hundreds of supposedly "independent", but closely supervized, growers. Some of them, like Hine, Courvoisier, and Delamain, do not distil any of their own cognac but rely entirely on growers from whom they buy young cognacs. Neither Hine nor Delamain buys newly distilled cognacs at all.

The blending is the key, and very private it is too – Maurice Fillioux never allowed any of the directors of Hennessy to attend. Maurice was the sixth generation of his family to act as chief blender for Hennessy and his role is now taken by his nephew Yann, who is responsible for two out of every five bottles of cognac sold in the world. The problem, he says "is to be able to guarantee the style and constant quality in the quantities demanded" – and this inevitably limits the possibilities. For the object is not so much to isolate a single star but to find cognacs which will mix to provide the firm with the constant blend which is the overriding object of the exercise.

Choices are made every year when the blenders taste every cask in their chais. Many will have been destined for the house's VS from the time they emerged from the still, the destiny of others decided at the age of five when, say the Fillioux, "one can start to talk of a cognac rather than of a child". The casks are marked with elementary signs. At Hennessy they range from BB – perfect brandies 20/20 – down to a mere 12 which means simply "correct". The analysis can be pretty brutal: I noticed that two brandies from the Petite Champagne were dismissed as "simply grape jam" and "tisane".

All the blenders are playing with a number of variables: the type of oak they are using; the age of the casks; the length of time for which they mature their different "brands"; and, crucially, the area from which they buy their cognac. At least three, Rémy Martin, Hine, and Delamain, sell only brandies from the Champagnes. For their VS (formerly Three-Star), VSOP and, in many cases, their Napoléons and XOs, all the other merchants inevitably rely on brandies from the Bois and the Borderies and over recent decades of continuing oversupply they have become much choosier as to which corners of the Fins Bois they use. None buys from the west of Cognac, and they buy very little, if any, cognac from the Bons Bois. Recently two firms – Leopold Gourmel [q.v.] and Château de Beaulon [q.v.] – have headed the fight to prove that fine, elegant, floral, long-lived cognacs can be made from chosen spots in the Fins Bois. Beaulon is on the Gironde Estuary; Gourmel relies on estates in the heart of the Fins Bois de Jarnac.

A number of the bigger and more serious houses have a secret weapon: using brandies from the Borderies which are very special, "nutty", intense, and capable of ageing for several decades. "They are well-rounded after fifteen years," says Pierre Frugier, formerly chief blender at Martell, which uses a great deal of the brandy in its Cordon Bleu. "We pay the same for cognac from the Borderies as we do from the Petite Champagne," says Maurice Fillioux. "I can always distinguish a cognac from the Borderies – there's that little something. To talk about violets, as some people do, is a little poetical; to me the essence is of nut kernels." This "nuttiness" so characteristic of the Borderies forms an essential part of the better VSs and VSOPs. Indeed, the brandies from the Borderies are tailor-made for VSOPs, which include brandies of between five and ten years of age. Some purists claim that the whole idea of VSOP is unnatural, that the age range is too old for brandies from the Bois, too young for those from the Champagnes (though Rémy Martin has made its fame and fortune by refuting this particular old wives' tale).

In theory, brandies from the Grande Champagne and even from the Petite Champagne are so intense as to be almost undrinkable before they are ten or more years old. But Rémy Martin disagrees. "They don't mature more slowly. They are simply more complex, and therefore it is more interesting to age them longer," says Robert Leauté, ex-technical director of Rémy Martin, and indeed his successors make an excellent VS from the Petite Champagne. Impressions of the aroma and taste of Champagne cognacs revert to the vine, to the flowers and twigs as well as the fruit of the grape, resulting in the preservation, in a uniquely concentrated form, of the natural qualities of the raw materials, nature transformed by man.

Not all cognacs, even from the Grande Champagne, have the capacity to age so vigorously and gracefully, for there are obviously some bad brandies made in the Champagnes. Although the growers now all know how to distil good cognac, some of them are still careless. The Station Viticole imposes some form of discipline, since all the cognacs have to be sampled (given the *agrément*, or permission to have the appellation) before they can be sold to the public, and this eliminates the truly worst brandies. Yet, broadly speaking, the buyer has very little legal protection. The houses are not allowed to give the exact age of their brandies and the *Compte* system (the system for describing the age of cognacs; *see* p. 211) is only now creeping up to ten years of age. As a result the buyer of a cognac where the firm hints that it is a centenarian can be sure only that all the brandies in it are at least ten years old. Moreover there are plenty of inferior, well-aged cognacs on sale, for unscrupulous blenders who can fabricate a "venerable" Grande Champagne cognac with some undrinkable, albeit genuinely aged, cognac plus a generous dose of caramel and oak shavings to increase the flavour of age. The reputation of the firm selling the cognac is inevitably a better guarantee of quality than the legal descriptions.

House style starts with the cognac itself, for there is a marked contrast between firms which rely primarily on the spirit and those, notably Martell and Delamain, which concentrate on the effects of the wood – Alain Braastad, the former chairman of Delamain, says bluntly that the newly distilled cognac accounts for a mere twenty-five per cent of the quality of the final product. By contrast, Laurent Robin of Louis Royer, "not wanting to rely on the wood and the progress of ageing for the quality of the result", is "looking for the richest possible raw material". However this need not be related to the wine. Olivier Paultes of Frapin found that richer, more aromatic wines did not necessarily produce richer and more complex brandies than wines that were more neutral.

Factors in their search for their own style inevitably include not only the source of the brandy but also the type of oak used and the age of the casks. A high proportion of Rémy Martin's cognacs are destined for VSOP brandies, to be sold within six, or at the most ten, years of distillation. So it is looking for a type of wood which will speed the maturation process, and naturally uses Limousin oak. Martell uses Tronçais because it is looking for precisely the opposite qualities: the wood has less tannin and is denser and therefore less porous, so ageing is slower and less wood is imparted to the cognac. Indeed, the secret of the dry Martell style, originally destined for the British market, was that the cognac itself and the oak in which it was aged were both directed towards a target which is ascetic in theory, but in practice, fills the mouth with a balanced fullness.

The same considerations apply to the age of the casks. Most firms keep their better cognacs in new wood for up to a year to provide an initial "attack" of tannin before transferring them to older casks to prevent them from becoming too woody. At the Tesserons, where the average is three months in new wood, the length of the stay depends also on the quality of the casks. Like many distillers Yann Fillioux is wary of overly long contact with new oak – for him nine months is a maximum time. Otherwise "the cognacs are marked for life" and if the brandy is to be kept for fifty years or more it has to be kept in old oak from the start. But, cask-wise, old age starts young. "New" generally means a cask less than three years old and "once it's twenty years old," says Yann Fillioux, "it is above all a neutral container".

The only exception is Delamain: none of its cognacs has ever seen any new wood – the cognacs it buys have been lodged in wood which is at least seven years old and it keeps the casks for at least sixty years. At the other extreme the equally reputable house of Frapin keeps its best cognacs in new oak for up to two and a half years, depending on the amount of colour (and hence, by inference, the tannin) the spirit has absorbed. Both are exceptions: Delamain is seeking a light, almost ethereal style; and the cognacs that the Frapins use for their Château de Fontpinot brand all come from a particularly favoured corner of the Grande Champagne, so they can respond to the strength of the new wood.

All the houses are aiming at a standard product from grapes that inevitably vary from year to year. If the year has been especially wet or the grapes are unusually ripe, the cognacs could be flabby, so Rémy Martin, for instance, stiffens their backbone by a longer stay in new wood. In very dry years the opposite applies. Bisquit uses old oak for Champagne cognacs and new wood for a third of those from the Bois. There is a regular routine as the brandies are gradually transferred to older and older casks.

But the pace varies for, as Alain Braastad of Delamain says, "Every cask has its own personality because of the very different qualities of the wood in which it is lodged." All the blenders agree with him that while the brandy is above forty degrees of alcohol, the wood still contributes something to the final result.

So, of course, do the chais in which the brandies are housed. These are a cross between a commercial warehouse and, in the case of the fabled *paradis* housing the oldest cognacs, a living museum. Originally they were located on the banks of the Charente, so that the casks could be loaded on to the *gabares* (the barges that shipped the cognac down the Charente). This was another lucky accident. Initially the Cognaçais probably did not realize the contribution made by the dampness of the riverside atmosphere to the quality of the cognac. So the north bank of the Charente in Cognac, and both banks at Jarnac, are still lined with handsome stone warehouses, inevitably blackened by generations of *Torula compniacensis*, the famous fungus that thrives (as who would not?) in the rich, damp air of warehouses full of casks of maturing brandy. In the eighteenth century some distillers had problems with a lack of water, but Delamain's stills – like its chais – were located near the river and so never had to stop.

The old sites had two problems, fire and flood, neither entirely conquered even today. In December 1982 the Charente flooded. Casks of brandy bobbed about like life rafts, and the dark stains left by the receding waters can still be seen halfway up the walls of Louis Royer's chais on the banks of the river in Jarnac. Rémy Martin was particularly badly affected because it ended up with casks half full of old cognacs with loose bungs floating down the river. In the end the flood lasted a full month, though they had two days' warning.

Fire is an even more serious hazard. Vizetelly remarked that if Cognac "were once to catch fire at any point, it would explode like a mountain of lucifer matches struck by lightning, and would blaze afterwards like an ever-burning *omelette-au-rhum*, intended to be gazed at but never eaten". Rather more limited conflagrations are a regular occurrence. Yet when Hine built a new chai in 1973 everyone laughed at the use of sprinklers. Then both Martell and Rémy suffered from blazes and people stopped laughing.

Despite the disadvantages of a riverside location, both Martell and

Hennessy still rely on their old sites. Rémy Martin did not inherit any historic chais and now owns a number of rather unromantic sprawls in and around Cognac. In Jarnac, Courvoisier dominates one bank of the river, although its stocks have never been as large, in relation to its size, as those of other major firms.

The blenders clearly have an immense palette from which to work. Typically, Hennessy has 700 growers under contract. Rémy Martin buys from 500 individual growers who provide particular qualities to add to the basic cognacs bought from twenty *bouilleurs de profession* (professional distillers), who themselves draw wines from 1,200 growers. All of them have been trained, often over several generations, to distil their brandies in the specific fashion best suited to the house's requirements. At least once every year (twice at Hennessy) the blenders taste the thousands of individual casks they have in stock. Historic contracts with the growers offer the immense advantage of records indicating just how cognacs from a particular holding have developed in the past, making it easier to know which are capable of long maturation.

At a certain point even the most venerable are ready for blending and mixing with distilled water to bring them down to forty degrees of alcohol, followed in most cases by "adjustment" with a little caramel. Both are delicate operations. Only a few of the oldest cognacs are weak enough to be sold without dilution; the younger the blend, the stronger the basic spirit. To bring a three-year-old down from perhaps sixty degrees to forty degrees is a delicate business. "The dilution can never be too brutal," says Michel Caumeil, who compares it with landing an aeroplane – after all, there are four hundred ingredients in the cognac which have to be blended with the water. The need for delicacy is increased by the fact that when brandy is blended with water, molecules of fatty acids clash and the result is the sort of cheap, soapy, and often obviously sugary cognacs found in all too many French supermarkets.

The decision is irreversible: "Once a cognac has been cut," says Caumeil, "it can never go into one of our best blends." But even the meanest spirit cannot be brought down from its cruising altitude (or undiluted strength) in one go. The process occurs in several stages, each of them separated by a period of months. Many firms dilute immediately to around fifty-five to sixty degrees. If you dilute immediately to below fifty-five degrees the cognac is too weak to attack the wood directly: it has to be stronger to extract the tannins. "At Hennessy we prefer to keep the brandy's character," says Maurice Fillioux, so they mix it a year before the brandy is to be sold. At Martell they taste even the distilled water. Obviously the slower the dilution the better. To slow the process some of the more scrupulous merchants use *petits eaux*, cognac diluted to fifteen degrees.

Since the arrival of the appellation system the merchants have not, in theory anyway, been able to tamper with the cognacs. They can add one part of caramel per thousand and eight grams of sugar per litre, and that is all. Because the sugars from the hemicellulose in the wood gradually infiltrate the cognac after twenty years, Hennessy, for one, finds that it has to put only two grams of sugar, a quarter of the permitted level, into each litre – the Tesserons say that they have only two parts in 10,000 in their cognacs. The sugary syrup softens the young cognacs – it "rounds" them – while the caramel, neutral to the taste, merely standardizes the colour. Some merchants disguise the characterlessness of their cognacs with relatively heavy doses of caramel, but with most you can tell the age not only from the rawness of the alcohol and the burning sensation it leaves on the palate, but also from its depth and complexity.

Most of the houses add a little caramel to bring each cask up to the level of the darkest individual element in the blend. Because the Chinese and the Japanese equate darkness with age, so the blends sent to the Far East may well be darker than those sold in Europe or the USA. There is another widespread habit that is frowned upon: artificially ageing the cognac by tipping oak chippings – *le boisé* – into the casks and thus boosting their tannin contant. This "turbo-charging" is disapproved of for reasons that go back to the basic rhythms of ageing. It speeds up the process of ageing too much, it swamps the spirit with a harsh, heavy coating of tannin which is in theory natural, but because of the intensity and the suddenness of the oakiness, emerges as an artificial woodiness on the palate. Even less well publicized is the alleged use of artificial flavours imported by a handful of unscrupulous houses from Dutch fragrance manufacturers.

Nevertheless, purists concerned with the level of caramel in today's cognacs are hankering after what they feel was a golden age. In fact it was literally golden in character if not in quality, thanks to the far heavier doses of sugary syrup common in the past when the merchants enjoyed complete freedom as to the additives they could employ. Then they were particularly aware of the need to darken their brandies. Many British drinkers especially were keen on rich "brown brandies", partly because of a fond delusion that a dark brandy was an old brandy and partly because they were powerful enough to be diluted, then with soda, now with ice. In those not-so-far-off golden days prune juice, sweet, dark and a trifle nutty, was a great favourite, as it is even today with the brandy producers of Jerez, and if more nuttiness was required, almond could be added. Henry Vizetelly, the Victorian journalist, was shown a special locked storehouse and was offered a sample "from an enormous cask of the burnt-sugar syrup, which 'brownifies' the brandy (English customers admiring a gypsy complexion), and which syrup is not nice at all; and also a glass of softening syrup, made of one-fourth sugar and three-fourths eau-de-vie, which sweetens and smooths the cordial for lickerish lips, and which is so delicious that you would not have the heart to reproach your bitterest enemy if you caught him indulging in a drop too much".

Even the normally puritanical Tovey approved of such additions:

> The old Cognac houses are very particular in the quality of their colouring, and prepare it with great care; it is important, too, that it should be old, and it is made up with Old Brandy. Consequently good old colouring imparts a fulness and roundness to Brandy which is not to be met with in the coloured spirit, although the latter may merit the preference in character and finesse.[1]

But firms still adjust their blends for specific markets. For the Far East they produce richer cognacs which can be diluted through mixing with ice without losing their flavour – the Japanese, for instance, were unhappy at the dry intensity of Martell's cognacs. And there's a new phenomenon, the many blends designed to be drunk when smoking cigars. To cut through the rough smokiness of the cigars these have inevitably to be heavy, rich, dull, caramelly, and often unbalanced as well. I tend to agree – but then I'm not a smoker – with David Baker of Brandy Classics, the specialist importer, that "you might just as well put cigar blends in your gravy browning".

[1] Charles Tovey, British and Foreign Spirits, Whittaker, London, 1864.

Whatever their style the brandies are left to enjoy each other's company for several months before being refrigerated to –9°C and filtered (generally centrifugally) to ensure that they do not throw any deposits even if they are left on tropical docksides or in icy Alaskan warehouses for weeks at a time. For a house style has to be capable not only of being applied on an industrial scale but also of surviving the many accidents that can happen between the Charente and the drinker. But whatever you do to it, mature cognac is the purest and most complex liquid distillation – in both senses of the term – of the heart of France, *La France profonde*.

part II

1

Not by Brandy Alone

The traveller is made aware of Cognac's most famous product well before reaching the town, for the roads all around are lined with endless placards bearing the names of famous brands and rather rougher signs promoting the innumerable individuals who sell their own cognac (and the local apéritif, Pineau des Charentes) directly to the public. But the main road from Saintes to Angoulême merely skirts the old town, visible only as you cross the bridge over the Charente. So the casual visitor is tempted to believe that the town centres on the Place François 1er. In fact, this unremarkable junction is the centre of the new town that grew up outside the town's walls only in the nineteenth century. The new town is agreeable enough, but not easily distinguishable from a hundred others throughout France.

The historic heart of Cognac lies in the old town which clusters behind the Château de Cognac in a semicircle on the steep southern bank of the Charente. Many of the buildings in this picturesque and still unspoilt huddle date from the sixteenth century; others are up to a couple of centuries younger. But all of them – houses, offices, and warehouses alike – have been blackened into uniformity by the activities of *Torula compniacensis richon*. The facades of the buildings along the quay have been preserved and cleaned by Hennessy, which has bought many of them. But the Hennessy writ stops a few hundred metres down the river at the rue Saulnier ("Street of the Salt Harbour"), named in the thirteenth century after the commodity that first made Cognac an important commercial centre. It is still cobbled, though recently, like so much of the old town, it has been cleaned and "gentrified". Halfway up the street on the right is the Maison de la Gabelle, an imposing double-fronted structure, recognizable by the amiably battered and grotesque gargoyles on each side of the door. It is a key to Cognac's story, for the *gabelle* was a tax on salt in the Middle Ages, when it was a basic necessity for preserving meat and fish for consumption during the winter, and the *gabelle* was an important element in the revenues of many impecunious monarchs.

Further up the street is a rather less imposing building, formerly the offices of the cognac business owned by the Gauthier family, a typical example of the houses that for hundreds of years housed the homes and offices of such families. Like its neighbour, it is double-fronted, the two halves separated by a covered corridor leading from the street to the yard behind the house. On the ground floor one side was devoted to work: in the front was a general office behind a private office for the firm's partners. The dining room was on the other side of the corridor below the living room, the *grande chambre,* and the bedrooms. The horses were stabled behind the house, and, despite its compactness, the other corner of the yard housed a still, which fell into disuse only after World War II.

The street, the Maison de la Gabelle, the Gauthiers' house, all emphasize the continuity in Cognac's story, the thread of international commercial awareness that marks this apparently sleepy little town, and thus makes it unlike the typical French town it appears at first sight. Cognac dates back over 2,000 years and was probably named after a pre-Roman chieftain called Comnos or Conos. The -ac ending, meaning a town in the local dialect, the *langue d'oc*, is common in the area – though the nearness of the frontier with the *langue d'oil* is shown by the presence only a few miles to the north of towns like St Jean d'Angely with the -y ending characteristic of the northern tongue.

Historians have always assumed that such towns were originally someone's home. This is not invariably true, although no one has yet queried the derivation so far as Cognac is concerned. The only query lay in the spelling of so apparently simple a name. In Latin, it was called variously Compniacum, Compinacum, Compnacum, and Coniacum. More recent variants include Coingnac, Compniac, Cougnac, Congnac, Coegnac, and as late as the eighteenth century, when the town was already world-famous, Coignac or Cogniac. Today, although there is an agreed spelling of the name, it can be pronounced in two ways, for many inhabitants use a long "o", as in "cone" rather than the shorter vowel usually employed.

Its importance was originally geographical. In the words of a modern geographer, Cognac had "the advantage of being a crossroads on the river axis of the Charente linking Limousin and the sea, near the threshold of Poitou and the estuary of the Gironde",[1] an axis that Alain Braastad of Delamain calls the "Charente motorway". But it was more than a mere crossroads. As M. Lartaut puts it: "On the site of a sheltered stretch of the Charente in the chalky soils between the broad pastures of Jarnac and Merpins, it was first a fortified town, a religious centre, a stopping point." In Roman times it was in a rich Gallo-Roman province with important towns such as Saintes and the major port now being excavated at the Moulin du Fa at Talmont south of Royan. Nevertheless, for most of antiquity the region was relatively marginal for it was the Mediterranean which was the centre of Greco-Roman civilisation. But in later Roman times the European world became increasingly centred on the Atlantic coast from southern Spain and Portugal up to the Low Countries, Britain and northwest Germany. This change ensured that the Charentes and the Gironde estuary were at the heart of the most important trade route in Europe.

The river Charente was navigable as far as Cognac and its importance was recognized as early as the eleventh century, when the town was first fortified. The Cognac we know today started to emerge when northern sailors discovered the quality of the region's salt. It faced competition from other saltpans scattered right down the Atlantic coast but they found it very *conservatif*, especially well suited to preserving fish and meat. Indeed, its qualities became famous throughout northern Europe as the Flemish, the Scandinavians, and the Germans from the Hanseatic ports all spread its fame. The Hanseatic merchants even set up special fishery stations in Norway to use the salt.

In theory Cognac should have been at a definite disadvantage compared to towns nearer the sea. But it was on a tidal river at the limit of sea-going navigation, and from the twelfth century on it enjoyed two crucial advantages. It enjoyed a *monopole saulnier* (the right to insist that every cargo of salt passing along the river had to be trans-shipped in the town) granted by King John in 1199; and because it was in the western part of the Angoumois its merchants had only to pay a quint, a single tax of twenty per cent, on the salt they traded, whereas their unhappy brethren in Saintonge and Aunis nearer the coast had to pay the *quart*

---

[1] M. Lartaut, *Norois*, Paris, 1963.

de sel, a levy of twenty-five per cent due whenever the salt changed hands.

The salt trade ensured that the Cognaçais, like the inhabitants of other riverine towns – including Bordeaux and Nantes – were used to trade. Although it was La Rochelle, rather than Cognac, that concentrated on the international market, Cognac made its living – and a very good one it was except during times of war – from shipping salt throughout western France. But both communities were totally untypical of France's social and commercial structure. Unfortunately, the town enjoyed no such advantage when the type of trade shifted in the second half of the twelfth century. In 1152 Eleanor of Aquitaine, heiress to the whole region, married Prince Henry of England, who mounted the throne two years later as Henry II and ruled a vast Anglo-French Empire for the next thirty-four years. The marriage led to an amazing change in English drinking habits, as virtually the whole population took to drinking the wines from the new dominions, and above all from Bordeaux, and made the city's fortune until the English finally departed three centuries later. Not surprisingly "Aliénor" remains a heroine of regional history, a heavily romanticized legend still fondly recalled in many an after-dinner speech. But the importance of the alliance has rather blinded historians to three other crucial developments: new ports, a new type of ship, and new social relationships.

The most famous new port was La Rochelle on the coast. The new type of ship, the cogue, was first developed by the Flamands. They displaced over 1,000 tons, and so they were far more efficient than the much smaller vessels they replaced, which could carry only a tenth as much cargo. The cogues could sail as far up river as Tonnay-Charente, down river from Cognac, where they were loaded with wine – and later with brandy and paper – thanks to the region's plentiful supply of wood and water from its numerous rivers. Paper remained by far the most important product in the region and the one most coveted by the Dutch. Indeed as late as 1960 there were nearly fifty paper mills in the region.[2] All these products could be conveniently shipped to Tonnay along the Boutonne, the Sèvre, the Seudre or the Charente itself in much smaller barges – the famous *gabares* used by the Cognaçais to transport casks of brandy until

[2] The only remnant is a much-visited reconstruction at St Fleurac.

the 1930s. In the early thirteenth century the region was even described as a "terrestrial paradise".

Almost inevitably, these changes ensured that the pattern of feudal relationships normal throughout France was broken, and a new legal framework emerged; the Roles or Judgments of Oléron, named after an island just off the coast, formed the basis for maritime law affecting shipwrecks and other nautical problems throughout western Europe. But the changes worked right throughout the whole region. In Robert Delamain's words:

> These two products, salt and wine, which foreigners sought out in the ports of the coast of the Saintonge, created in the rural mass of the Charentais basin a mentality adjusted to commercial practices, a mentality which was highly unusual at a time when the whole economy elsewhere was confined within the limits of the seigneurie in which lords and peasants alike were forced to find within the domaine the wherewithal to clothe and feed themselves.

Bordeaux and La Rochelle became rival suppliers to the English trade. Bordeaux concentrated on its famous light red wine, claret, but the wines shipped from further north were mostly white. And whereas the merchants of Bordeaux jealously preserved their monopoly, and thus effectively shut out from the international trade the *Haut Pays* ("High Country") up river, the whole of the Charente basin, extending more than eighty kilometres/fifty miles inland, benefited from the demands of the English market.

As late as the sixteenth century, when the English had been chased from France for a century or more, we find the expression *vin de Cognac*. Although it was not as important or as expensive as *vin de Ritsel* (wine from La Rochelle), Cognac itself retained some of the importance it had acquired earlier from the salt trade. Nearer the sea the vines had spread over land also suitable for grain, but the Cognac region was different. The late Professor Enjalbert compared Cognac with the area around Reims, now famous for its Champagne. In both regions the word "Champagne" was used originally to describe a landscape similar to the original Campania north of Rome, a fair, fertile, rolling countryside. Unfortunately for the Cognaçais the winemakers round Reims were the first to use the word as a brand name and thus to confuse generations of brandy drinkers. In both regions the vine was originally largely confined to the slopes and plateaux above the rivers, while grain remained dominant in the more fertile "Champagne" valleys. Around Cognac vines were first planted instead of the *bois* (woods), which had only partially been cleared for growing grain and which later proved a natural source of the wood required for distillation. The vines then spread to the Champagnes – the chalky hillsides round Châteauneuf overlooking the Charente valley – which had continued to grow cereals throughout the Middle Ages. In 1576 a local historian,[3] emphasized that the "Grandes Champagnes de Segonzac" produced great quantities of fine wines which were shipped down river all over the world. A century later these slopes emerged also as the source of the best wine for distillation.

In earlier centuries Cognac and its surrounding countryside had owed its special position less to geographical advantages than to royal favour. The town had been granted its first charter early in the thirteenth century by the hapless King John ("Jean Sans Terre" to the French), the heir of "Aliénor", and soon afterwards his widow reunited the town with its natural hinterland, the county of Angoulême. It was during John's reign that a château was first built to guard the bridge over the river, and it remained important – it was a favourite home for the Black Prince. Early in the fourteenth century Cognac was separated from the feudal lordships that still governed most of rural France, whereas until 1789 Jarnac, a few miles further up river and its main potential rival, was dominated by its feudal lords. In consequence, and much to the resentment of its inhabitants, Jarnac has generally played very much a secondary role in the story. For King John had inadvertently set off the train of events that ensured that the famous brandy would be called cognac and not "jarnac". In fact the finest brandies have always come not from a round either of these two towns but from the slopes above the little town of Segonzac in the heart of the Grande Champagne. But the way the major firms have suppressed the different appellations over the centuries has denied to "the capital of the Grande Champagne", as it calls itself, its rightful place as the Mecca of the region.

The Charente was reconquered by the French far earlier than Bordeaux, the last redoubt of the English occupation, which was aban-

---

[3] Corlieu, *Receuil en forme d'histoire*, Jeanne Laffitte, Marseille, 1976.

doned only in 1453. In the short term this created problems for the locals, since they lost their most important market and their region remained a battleground through the later years of the Hundred Years' War. But in the longer run it was the Bordelais who suffered worse from their dependence on a single outlet. The alternative buyers of the Charente's wines, who filled the gap left by the English, were the same northern countries that had earlier taken their salt from the Cognaçais, and above all the Netherlands. They provided a far greater continuity than had the English; and whereas the Bordelais' wines did not become a force in the French market for centuries, the Charentais, once reunited with their fellow countrymen, managed to sell their wine at home.

Three centuries after King John, a lucky accident ensured that cognac was again singled out for royal favour. François I, the very model of a Renaissance monarch, was born in the town in 1492 and naturally showed his gratitude to his birthplace. After he ascended the throne of France twenty-three years later, he immediately exempted the inhabitants from all of the many taxes, forced loans, and other levies imposed on the rest of the county of Angoulême to sustain the French army in its numerous wars. The citation emphasized how loyal the town, very much on the frontier of two provinces, had been through many assaults and sieges by the country's enemies.

François I's attachment to Cognac ensured that the town retained its privileges – and its inhabitants their feeling of being special, part of a wider world – during the tumultuous century that followed his death. In 1544 there was a revolt, brutally suppressed by the royal forces, against the *gabelle*, the dreaded salt tax. The Angoumois then became one of the heartlands of French Protestantism and thus, inevitably, a major battleground in the religious wars that dominated the last half of the sixteenth century; one of the crucial battles was in Jarnac itself. The Protestants and their work ethic took root and provided a further boost to the inhabitants' commercial-mindedness.

The upheavals continued during the first half of the seventeenth century, culminating in the Fronde, the civil war between the feudal barons and the young King Louis XIV, who inherited his throne as a mere baby in 1643. Again Cognac was involved. Again it was lucky. It staunchly held out on behalf of the king against the assaults of one of the leading Frondeurs, the Duc de Rochefoucauld, and was duly rewarded for its loyalty. The mayor was ennobled; the inhabitants were exempted from taxes for twenty years and were granted the right to hold four fairs a year, each to last three days. These provided an unequalled meeting place for the local farmers and merchants. As the century wore on, the fair-goers began increasingly to bargain, not over wine but over a new product, eau-de-vie.

2

The Triumph of "Coniack Brandy"

Distillation for medical purposes had long been widespread in both Spain and southern France, a legacy of the long occupation by the Moors, experts in this as in so many other arts and sciences. *Chimistes-apothicaires* in all the major French towns were also distillers. According to Savary's *Dictionnaire universel*, the *marchands-épiciers-droguistes-apothicaires* distilled and sold the best spirits in Paris, but the *vinaigriers,* the *limonadiers,* and the *distillateurs d'eaux fortes* also had the right to sell spirits. The first distillers to sell their wares commercially and not merely for medical purposes were probably from Armagnac, about 350 km/200 miles to the southwest. The Armagnaçais enjoyed the same natural advantages as their northern competitors: they had ample stretches of marginal scrubland suitable for vines; they had plenty of wood to fuel the *bruleries,* and they could transport the resulting spirit, largely by river, to the well-established port of Bayonne. But they lacked Cognac's long commercial tradition and thus the merchant class required to act as middlemen between the local growers and distillers (who later combined the two functions) and the foreign buyers. It was this long commercial tradition which proved crucial in establishing Cognac's brandies on the European market.

The first date we have when brandy entered international trade is 1517, when a *barrique d'eau ardent* was shipped from Bordeaux, but the first records of sales of eau-de-vie come from La Rochelle. In 1549 *quatre barriques d'eau-de-vie bonne et marchande* ("four barriques of eau-de-vie, wholesome and fit for sale") were traded, and in 1571 a certain Jehan Serazin was described as *a marchand et faizeur d'eau-de-vie* ("merchant and producer of eau-de-vie"). By the end of the century the trade was important enough to be considered suitable for the grant of a monopoly, a favourite means for impecunious French monarchs to raise money throughout the ages. In 1604, according to Pierre Martin-Civat,[1] one Isaac Bernard paid an unknown sum for a monopoly of the distillation and sale of all the eaux-de-vie made in the provinces of Tours, Poitou, Languedoc, and Guyenne – effectively the whole of western France. Inevitably, this extremely wide grant was largely ignored by the Flemish as well as by native merchants, who dodged it by carrying brandies by road as well as by sea. Nevertheless, the monopoly was confirmed four years later, and it was not until 1610 that Bernard had to surrender it. This was largely because of the opposition of the powerful merchants of Nantes, although the list of merchants who had broken the monopoly was a long one – showing just how widely the trade had already spread. From then on the cognac community was not hampered by any of the monopolies that restricted so many other French businessmen.

Within fifteen years the brandies involved had been transformed into a unique spirit: "cognac" or, as it was more usually termed, "coniack brandy". The Cognaçais were also still dealing in the region's wine, for the rival products, wine and brandy, coexisted for over a century. It was largely a matter of horses for courses. The wines were not bad – a medical textbook written by the Prince de Conti's doctor in 1603 claims: "The wines of Aunis and Anjou, which are white, excel all others in goodness", and an agricultural handbook published a quarter of a century later echoes the same point: distillation had simply become more profitable. Just as vines had formerly been concentrated on the uplands as against the river valleys, so wines suitable for drinking continued to be produced wherever they could command a premium price, as they could in the Borderies. The sweet white wines produced in the Borderies from the Colombard grape were much prized by the Dutch until the second half of the eighteenth century, largely because the sweeter the wine the more suitable it was for transporting long distances. Indeed wines from the Champagnes sold for a mere two-thirds of those from the Borderies. After an appalling frost in 1766, however, these lost their market to competitors from Sauternes and switched to producing wines for distillation. But the Borderies were the only real – and tiny – exception to the rule that, by

[1] Pierre Martin-Civat, La monopole des eaux-de-vie sous Henri IV, 100 ème Congrès Nationale des Sociétés Savantes, Paris, 1975.

the end of the seventeenth century, brandy was triumphant. Robert Delamain quotes a letter written by the intendant – the governor – of the province to Louis XIV in 1698:

> *Wine is the major product of the Angoumois, but the most important vineyards are in the Cognac district. The red wines find an outlet in Poitou and the Limousin. Very little is sold to foreigners who do not find them stout enough to stand the journey. But when the white wines are converted into brandy, which is their normal fate, the English and Danish fleets come to look for them, in peacetime anyway, at the ports of the Charente and drink them up, to the great advantage of the province.*

Luckily for Cognac, like La Rochelle and above all Bordeaux, the town's inhabitants were accustomed to trade and had that vital necessity, easy access to the Atlantic and thus to the Channel, the North Sea, and even the Baltic, thus providing them with natural markets. The virtues of Cognac's brandies had been noted as early as 1617, when a bill of sale at La Rochelle mentioned brandy that was guaranteed to be from Cognac. Five years later we find brandies from Cognac paying nine livres in tax as against 8.5 for those from Bordeaux and between seven and 7.5 for those from Spain or the south of France. In 1678 "coniack brandy" was first mentioned in the *London Gazette*, the official English journal. The wars between Britain and France that occupied much of the next thirty years did not prevent cognac's rise to fame – indeed, the scarcity bred of wartime difficulties seems merely to have enhanced the drink's attractions for a fashion-conscious market.

The success of "coniack brandy" was largely due to two very different foreign influences, the Dutch and the aristocratic drinkers of Restoration London. Then as now the Dutch wanted cheap drinks and found that the wines from the Charente provided inexpensive as well as suitable raw material. The inhabitants of the northern Netherlands had freed themselves from Spanish rule in the 1570s and almost immediately dominated European trade; their supremacy lasted for over a century and affected every supplier who came into contact with them. Inevitably the Charentais had to follow the demands for the new product, brandy.

The Dutch were dominant: in the 1720s they took over half of the brandy exported from the district round La Rochelle. They needed the spirit to compensate for the impurities in the water carried by their sailors during long spells at sea, and there was an increasing demand for spirits both at home and from the markets they supplied throughout northern Europe. The Dutch thirst for brandy is easily explained: a distilled spirit, eight or nine times more concentrated than wine, was obviously far cheaper to ship and could simply be cut with water by the buyer to provide the equivalent amount of liquid to quench sailors' thirst. But the original trade involved the shipment of wine, not brandy, to the Netherlands as raw material for some of the many distilleries built there in the late sixteenth century. These were originally called *wijnbranders* (literally, "wine burners") and the product therefore brandywijn or *brand-vin* ("burnt wine"). Although these "burners" used a wide variety of raw materials, wine was officially favoured: the Dutch government discouraged the use of the obvious alternative, grain. Even before 1600 there were complaints that the distilleries tended to make corn far too expensive for the poor, a concern that formed a recurring theme in the story of brandy. In the early eighteenth century the French government discouraged the planting of vines in order to provide enough grain to feed the population.

But cognac's emergence as the superior form of a routine drink would have been impossible without the existence of a market sufficiently rich and fashion-conscious to pay a premium price. Fortunately for Cognac, in the last forty years of the seventeenth century the drinkers of the café society of London after the restoration of the dissolute Charles II had developed a marked taste for luxury beverages. These included sherry, port, claret aged in wood, and the first bottles of sparkling Champagne, all of which they introduced to the world. The first decade of the eighteenth century saw the emergence of "coniack brandy". Indeed the first mention of a specific eau-de-vie de Cognac came from 1710.

In January 1706[2] an advertisement in the *London Gazette* proclaimed that thirty-four "Pieces of Old Coniack Brandy" were available for sale at the port of Southampton. Clearly, this was no ordinary brandy: none of the other spirits advertised was "old". The distinction is equally clear in other advertisements. "Bordeaux and Nants" brandy was nine shillings a gallon, a full shilling less than "Old Cogneac, fit for drams" – implying

---

[2] Britain was still employing the old calendar under which the year started on March 25. By our reckoning it was January 1707.

that it alone could be drunk neat. "Bordeaux brandy" clearly had rather a bad reputation: one lot of "Entre-Deux-Mers brandy" is described as having "a much better flavour and Proof than generally Bordeaux is".

But our clearest picture of the emerging cognac market comes from a series of advertisements placed five years later by two rival suppliers in the City of London, William Cowper, "wine cooper" of Crooked Lane, and Major Thomas Bird, who owned a warehouse in Pudding Lane. They were getting their supplies from the same sources, ships supposedly seized as prizes and located either at Leith, the port of Edinburgh, or in Guernsey. They agreed on the difference in price between "coniack" and other brandies but on precious little else. Cowper undercut the Major by a shilling a gallon and even offered better terms to bigger buyers. The Major hit back: "Some others in Print," he thundered, "pretend to sell neat brandy they call French at a cheaper rate. To prevent the abuse in fetching theirs for his, he gives a printed receipt therewith of the Price and Quantity" – but only if you bought a gallon.

Major Bird promptly lowered his best old Cognac to nine shillings and sixpence a gallon. – sixpence a gallon less than his previous price, though still sixpence dearer than his rival's. The Major's charge removed Cowper from the scene, and he continued to advertise his cognacs for four years at steadily increasing prices. By September 1711 he had apparently exhausted his stocks, and because none was available on the market except for "one small parcel and that sold from sixteen to seventeen shillings a gallon by reason of the Duty of seven shillings a gallon laid by the late Parliament and not any hopes of having more till a peace", he was reduced to selling brandy from Portugal (which paid much less duty) at a mere twelve shillings a gallon.

It was not only the British buyers who distinguished between cognac and lesser brandies. There were at least two local witnesses to the rise of cognac: Jean Gervais, a local magistrate who wrote a much-quoted description of the area in the 1720s[3], and Etienne Munier, a well-known engineer whose description, written half a century later, remains a major source of information about cognac in the later eighteenth century.[4] "The

[3] Jean Gervais, *Mémoire sur l'angoumois* (reprint), SAHC, 1964.

[4] Etienne Munier, *Essai sur l'Angoumois a la fin de l'Ancien Régime*, Bruno Sepulchre, Paris, 1977.

brandy from Cognac is accepted as the best in the world," wrote Gervais. "The region of Cognac is famous for its brandies," echoed Munier, adding, "The quality of Cognac's brandies being superior to all others, they will always be preferred if the price is the same."

The original brandies which made Cognac famous clearly came from the "Champagne" areas to the south and southeast of the town and from the Bois to the north and northeast. Munier did at least define Champagne: for him the name encompassed "a mere seven or eight parishes, to wit, Angeac, Segonzac, etc, where the earth is soft and powdery, destined preferably for the cultivation of white grapes". This intense localization, which applied also to the other drinks made fashionable in London at the time, was a major novelty in what one can only call a "Restoration revolution". Until the drinkers of Restoration London had defined the precise qualities they were seeking, vines had been planted where the wine could be marketed and not because the soil or the climate was particularly suitable.

The distillation of "Coniack brandy" is still a contentious subject. For a start it has led to one of Cognac's most enduring, most widespread, and most misleading legends: that the secret of the double distillation which resulted in cognac was not because the wines were more suitable for distillation but a happy accident, the product of the musings of a local soldier-poet, the Chevalier de la Croix Marron. He had written a long poem called *La Muse Catholique*, which ran into two editions, published in 1607 and 1614 respectively. In a preface to the first edition, dedicated, as usual, to a great local lady, he remarks how he has been distracted from his Muse by "a thousand different notions on as many different subjects . . . I have distilled the springtime of my spirits" – the pun is the same in both English and French. He then proceeds to dilate a little on this conceit. Unbelievably, a whole school of thought has been erected on this idle notion, this short, allusive, whimsical play on words. The fullest account of the idea was published only a few years ago by the late Pierre Martin-Civat, a local antiquarian. This provoked a savagely effective exposé from Alain Braastad, a grandson of Robert Delamain, who shares his grandfather's antiquarian interests. But this had little effect: the legend is even enshrined in the standard work on the legal definition of cognac.[5]

[5] Marguerite Landrau, *Le Cognac devant la loi*, L'Isle d'Or, Cognac, 1981.

The idea that the chevalier discovered the secret of cognac remains the officially authorized version, as in *Le Cognac et les aléas de l'histoire*, a book by Jean-Vincent Coussie published in 1996 by the Bureau National, Cognac's official ruling body. Even Robert Leauté, then the technical director of Rémy Martin, repeated that the chevalier "perfected the eau de vie through double distillation", in a lecture he gave in 1990 to the American Society of Enology and Viticulture. I find the continued existence of this *canard* ridiculous and demeaning since it replaces the truth, that their product is superior, by a silly myth.

The key to the superiority was that the wines from the region were so acidic, and so suitable for distillation, that their inherent qualities did not have to be filtered out by repeated distillations. In the seventeenth century lesser spirits were distilled not once (as the legend assumes) but several times. Only the grapes grown around Cognac were capable of producing a superior, drinkable spirit after only two *chauffes*. Raw materials – not just grapes – from everywhere else in France had to be distilled again and again to remove their noxious impurities. In the process, of course, they became nearly rectified; they lost the qualities inherent in the raw material. Only the grapes from Cognac produced spirit which, because it had been distilled no more than twice, retained the flavour of the original grape.

Using a mere two *chauffes* to produce a spirit which would be agreeable to drink was clearly a delicate matter. The situation was summed up by one highly influential authority, Jean Francois Demachy, by training a pharmacist, who became director of the central dispensary of the French army. Demachy's work, his three-part *L'Art du distillateur d'eaux fortes* (which was even translated into German), provides a unique, encyclopaedic view of the problems facing distillers in the eighteenth century. Demachy was firmly convinced that only the best would do. Some chemists, he said scornfully, believed that if you rectified second-grade brandy, you got as good a result as with a double-distilled, first-rate eau-de-vie. It might be as dry, he said, but "connoisseurs do not make the same mistake". The distillers themselves agreed. They too understood that only the first quality "combines an exquisite bou-quet with all the lightness and dryness it is possible to imagine". This is a contrast because in Demachy's time many second-rate spirits could not be used even for chemical purposes, let alone drinking, but were suitable only for use in varnishes because of their disagreeable smell.

By Munier's time the conditions for producing the very best cognac had been precisely defined, though the basic strength was a few degrees below the present-day level of seventy degrees of alcohol – and the brandy produced to the west in Aunis was recognized as being weaker than that produced round Cognac itself. The key to the quality, then as now, was the separation of the *coeur*, the heart of the distillate, *eau de vie bonne et forte* as it was termed, from the richer, lower-strength and generally second-rate *secondes*. Indeed "double brandy" – double tax not double distillation – was undiluted with *secondes*. The key cut-off point was not between *coeur* and *seconde* – which occurred at about fifty-seven degrees of alcohol – but at about forty-six degrees, below which the brandy was really rather nasty and contained what they called "phlegms", what we would term undesirable congeners. Christopher Glaser, chemist to Louis XIV, had frequently advised what he called "cohibition", which Professor Forbes defines in his standard work on the subject[6] as distilling "several times, each time adding the distillate to the residue in the *cucurbit* (the distilling vessel) and redistilling again". Demachy assumed that even after several *chauffes* they would have to use oil extracts to hide the disagreeable tastes from the "phlegms" left. He devoted a whole volume to the issue of how to distil the eaux-de-vie resulting from the first *chauffe* into *esprit de vin*, which the French merchants sold to their local customers at sixty-seven degrees of alcohol. The Cognaçais already separated "single" which meant basic spirit, "simple" from 46–57 degrees. Then there was the rectified *esprit de vin* – where three or even four distillations brought the strength of a brandy used to beef up lesser spirits to above eighty degrees. Smaller distillers were forced to weaken their brandy by topping up their still with wine between *chauffes*, whereas a bigger distiller with two or more stills had brandy to hand to top up the level.

The Cognaçais immediately realized and exploited their advantages. They did not need to devise any new apparatus; they merely followed the best of existing technology, which was largely Dutch. They were lucky because they were perfecting their product during a century when a great many people interested in science – aristocratic amateurs as well as pro-

---

[6] A. Forbes, *History of Distillation*, Leiden, 1970.

fessional technicians – were compiling books on the subject. None of them advanced contemporary understanding of the chemistry of the distillation process; they merely helped the ordinary distiller to improve his product. The Cognaçais, however, were practical folk, not chemists. So was Demachy, who believed that "habit and the experience of the Bouilleurs is more useful than would be the rules and tables" established by mere theorists. Not surprisingly they made no impact on the art or science of distillation – indeed, are not mentioned at all in Forbes' book. In 1766 the Royal Agricultural Society of Limoges offered a prize for the best treatise on the subject, but even then the criteria were strictly practical: "on the best way to distil wines taking into account quantity, quality and saving of costs". Apart from this one show of intellectual initiative they relied on their incomparable raw materials. Reasonably enough, the Cognaçais have not felt the need to change the formula which made them rich and famous, so the distillation of cognac, by and large, remains just as it was in the eighteenth century

Predictably, the quantities and strengths of the *brandywijns* were both expressed in Dutch. The *velte* (amounting to just over seven litres) was a basic measurement of quantity, and the barrique (the contents of a cask) was reckoned not in French *pintes* but in *veltes*. Both barrique and *pinte* varied greatly in size, although in time the cognac barrique was standardized as twenty-seven veltes, about 205 litres. Similarly, the strength of the spirit was expressed in relation to standard Dutch gin (*preuve d' Hollande*), about forty-nine degrees of alcohol. *Preuve de Londres* (London gin) was about fifty-eight degrees, that of cognac about sixty degrees. The basic spirit, much scorned by connoisseurs, was "three-six", double *preuve d'Hollande*, because three parts of water were mixed with six of alcohol. "Three-seven" was even stronger because seven parts of alcohol were used instead of six, while "three-five" was slightly weaker.

Nevertheless, there were still problems associated with defining the right qualities and above all the strength. In his *Dictionnaire universel du commerce*,[7] the standard source of information on scientific matters at the time, Jacques Savary wrote that eau-de-vie should be "white, clear, with a good taste and, as they say, '*d'epreuve*' – that is, when it is poured into a glass, it produces a little white head, which, as it dies down, forms the

---

[7] Abbé P.L. Savary, *Dictionnaire universel du commerce*, Paris, 1823.

circle which brandy merchants call the *chapelet* if all the brandy has lost its phlegms, and where there is not too much humidity remaining, in which case the *chapelet* is uninterrupted".

Indeed distillers used to apply the rule of the *trois perles:* distillation of proper brandy was supposed to be complete when three bubbles formed on the surface of the brandy when it was shaken in a sample glass. Although accurate measurement of the strength of a spirit became possible only through the work of Gay-Lussac in the nineteenth century, the first practical hydrometer to provide some indication of strength was invented in 1725, and by the 1760s most distillers – and the crucial London trade – had proper alcometers. But the authorities were slow to recognize them and many distillers remained what were called *distillers à perle*.

None of this helps to solve what has emerged as a major bone of contention, the role of the Dutch in the distillation process. Professor Cullen, author of two books on cognac in the eighteenth century[8] is not alone in believing that "the key importance of the Dutch in the brandy districts" was not their technical help but "a thirst for spirits in a rich and growing home market which progressively outran traditional grain-based supply by the late seventeenth century". Some historians, like Cullen – who provides no evidence for his view – and the local Alain Braastad, deny any technical dependence since the stills used in the Charente, like those employed in other parts of France, were simple copper pots. Nevertheless, it was the Dutch – followed by the British – who were the first to produce spirits, mostly gin, on an "industrial" scale. By contrast, tradition has it that the Dutch imported copper from Sweden, built the stills, and when the Cognaçais began to distil their wines they used the same Swedish copper as the Dutch. Copper remained a major cost for the distillers since their stills lasted a mere twenty years. In 1624 an agreement is recorded between two Dutchmen living in the Charente to build a distillery at Tonnay-Charente to distil wines shipped down river. Another indication of the importance of Dutch technology is that at the end of the seventeenth century stills imported from the Netherlands were twenty per cent more expensive than their locally made equivalents. The

[8] Professor Louis Cullen, *The Brandy Trade under the Ancien Régime,* Cambridge, 1998; *The Irish Brandy Houses of eighteenth-century France,* Lilliput, 2000.

Dutch influence was also boosted by the marriage in 1643 of Philippe Augier, probably the most important Cognac merchant of his time, with a member of the Dutch Janssen paper-making family. Augier's father-in-law persuaded his son-in-law to move from Châteauneuf to Cognac, and probably helped him with distillation.

The biggest problem for the cognac producers was the burden of taxes, a problem which also darkened the scene in the last twenty years of the twentieth century. As early as 1640 a special royal tax was imposed on brandies, and twenty years later eau-de-vie was taxed as an ordinary drink. During the eighteenth century the whole Cognac community had to pay taxes. The peasantry were hardest-hit, but the nobility and clergy, who were normally exempt, naturally protested most loudly. In 1713, at the instigation of the arch-priest of the small town of Bouteville, the curés of the Grande Champagne launched a bitter complaint. In 1744 a group of aristocrats joined in. They complained that their major source of income was in the form of wines suitable only for distillation, so they were hit by an anti-fraud tax dating back to 1687, which supposedly affected only merchants. The "tax farmers" (notorious entrepreneurs who had bought rights from the monarch) argued that it applied also to the landowners, since brandy was not a natural agricultural product but resulted from art and industry and was therefore liable to the taxes levied on manufactured articles. They had to pay even on the large quantities of wine destined for their own consumption, and were victims of their own success: their vines were productive, and taxes on wines were based on the quantity produced. The specific "farm" that hit the locals hardest was that of the *courtiers-jaugeurs*, licensed intermediaries who took a fixed percentage on every transaction within the area. The problem was worse in La Rochelle than in the Angoumois (which included Cognac), where the *courtiers-jaugeurs* had been bought out and the distillers could transport their precious cargo free of duty.

The problem extended to the British market. To the British taxman "brandy" became "spirit" above sixty-six degrees, and the duty doubled (even higher duties were imposed in the 1750s). In France duty doubled above sixty degrees (when the spirit became an *eau-de-vie double* instead of *simple*) and tripled for *esprit-de-vin* of above eighty-six degrees. The reduced-strength spirit had then to be strengthened to just below sixty-six degrees with some *esprit-de-vin* for sale to Britain. When the spirit reached London the importers would add six *veltes* of the stronger *esprit de vin* – and when a New Yorker was buying he asked for "brandy fortified to the London standard".

The tax system as a whole struck especially hard at a largely commercial community like Cognac. A cask of wine or brandy paid up to ten times its value in internal duties on a journey through France to Paris. Royal greed extended even to Cognac's vital – and officially encouraged – export business. The town's brandies had to pay a substantial tax when they passed through the ports to leave the kingdom. These dues trebled during the eighteenth century, and they were increased further in 1782, with the Cognaçais paying double the amount levied on the Rochellais, a bias which led to a major protest.

Foreign countries were already exploiting the revenue-producing potential of these luxury imports. Even a free-trade city like Hamburg levied heavy import duties on wines and brandies. In Britain, French brandy had been a tempting target since Elizabethan times, and in wartime brandy was always among the first things to be prohibited. An attempt at a commercial treaty in 1713 merely exposed the depth of the opposition backed by the politically powerful rum lobby.

Nevertheless, the Cognaçais enjoyed increasing success. In the 1720s the Dutch were still buying twice as much cognac as the British, but during the century the Cognaçais reduced their dependence on Holland and on Ireland, both highly price-conscious markets. For the key decade in which cognac was officially recognized as superior was the 1720s. The first edition of Savary's book, published in 1723, did not include any separate entry for cognac, whereas the *Supplément* published seven years later contained a complete analysis of the subject, including the simple encomium: "Brandy from Cognac is better and more highly regarded than any other." The 1720s were also important because of the consequences of the financial disasters associated with John Law, the Scottish economist who dominated French financial policy for some years after 1715. These included domestic economic depression and a devaluation of the French currency, both of which greatly encouraged exports.

By then the products of the region were divided into three levels. This was headed by "Champagne brandy". Judging by the buying books of the merchant Jacques Augier, their production was confined to the Champagnes and the Fins Bois north of Jarnac – indeed maps of the time show this region as "Champagne". Then came "Fine cognac" from the west near Pons and the north around Saint Jean d'Angley, which was said to be "inferior to Cognac by ten to fifteen per cent in strength and flavour", for the Cognaçais admired strong brandies. By the time of the Revolution the buyers had gone further than asking for brandies from a specific region, and were asking for "pale", "perfectly without colour as white as water" or "not too high coloured". Others preferred brandies that were "capital and full of rich flavour".

Only too often the richness was somewhat artificial. In the early nineteenth century Auguste Hennessy worried that Martell's cognacs were richer than Hennessy's because of the "syrups" they used, which he guessed came from prune juice – an additive much used today by the brandy makers of Jerez, most obviously Osborne.

By the Revolution some of the brandies were being sold at a later age. After the 1760s brandy for London was usually described as "old", meaning three or four years old – in 1768 James Delamain advised a London importer that "what we usually ship for said market is from three to ten years old".

Taste was not the only reason why the brandies destined for the London market – and to a much lesser extent to be sold to drinkers in the rest of Britain and in Edinburgh – were inevitably the best. Heavy duties increased the pressure, by contrast with Ireland with its lower duties. But the Londoners knew what they wanted and it was the best. As James Delamain wrote in 1788, "the great connoisseurs are in London and do not have their equal anywhere else". By the 1720s quality-conscious buyers, virtually all based in London, were demanding what was called "champaign brandy, some of the finest in the world" and one of Hennessy's partners, John Saule, instructed his London agents that "you must never blend brandies from the champagnes with other cognacs". There were over sixty London importers – indeed John Saule bought one, Yeats and Brown – and the existence of the City's financial markets helped the always cash-strapped Cognac merchants. By the 1770s London was the largest single outlet for the best "champaign brandy". But the importers were a canny lot, objecting to the dominance exerted by Martell during much of the second half of the century and encouraging newcomers to compete.

But the Irish were more important clients than the English, although the brandies they bought were described as "best cognac" one down from that required by Londoners, but still better than those sold on other markets. In the eighteenth century Ireland had almost as many inhabitants as England and usually lacked the – albeit irregular – surpluses of grain which enabled the English to produce rival spirits, normally gin, and also lacked the regular trade with the Caribbean which provided another competitor, rum, for the English market.

During the eighteenth century the merchants based in Cognac who supplied the English and Irish markets were using not La Rochelle, but Tonnay-Charentes, halfway between Cognac and the Bay of Biscay. La Rochelle had no direct riverine connection with Cognac, but at Tonnay sea-going ships could load brandies not only from Cognac but also those from Saint Jean d'Angely which had been carried down the Boutonne, as well as brandies from Pons down the Seudre. Tonnay had started to emerge as a convenient point at which to tranship brandies and other products from river barges in the seventeenth century – possibly during the long siege of La Rochelle in the late 1620s. During the eighteenth century Tonnay took a great deal of trade from La Rochelle, and unlike La Rochelle it was within the Saintonge region so was not liable to the duties levied in transit further west to the Aunis. For, unless the brandy was made within the same province, it had to pay three duties. Not surprisingly brandy shipped through La Rochelle, and inevitably produced from the inferior vines grown near the coast, got a bad name. In Flanders until quite recently, second-grade brandy was called "Rochelle", with the name "cognac" reserved for the best brandies. The third grade in Flanders included the brandies destined for northern France which came from the west of the region, especially the islands off the coast. At Tonnay the merchants could do their own shipping without using expensive middlemen and they were free of duties if they were held in an entrepôt for export. Not surprisingly by 1789 Tonnay dominated the region's foreign trade.

Paris was a different matter. Until the 1970s the city was always a major market for cognac, and in the eighteenth century sales in the capital were at least as great as exports and sometimes much greater; indeed the trade could be profitable enough to cause exports to be restricted. The trade was not new: during the late seventeenth century Nantes was a bigger supplier of brandy than the cognac region, largely because it was closer to Paris – and it is a tribute to the quality of even the second grade brandies of the Cognac region that they were so successful in the Paris market. This even though cognac, unlike the wines of Burgundy and Champagne which could be transported to Paris directly by river, had to be carted overland to Chatellrault in carts that were hauled by six oxen, which could carry a mere six barriques. At Chatellrault they could be loaded onto barges on the Vienne and Loire rivers to Orléans, the entrepôt for Paris.

These cognacs came from the east and north of the cognac region and were sold either by merchants based in Jarnac – where Delamain was a major force – or the *Aigriers*, merchants based at Aigres in the very north of the region. The brandies were basically weaker than those destined for export so had to be beefed up by rectified spirit, which of course reduced transport costs.

In Paris there were two markets. One was workers often on their way to work – the tradition of the "café cognac" which lasted until well after World War II. The other was financiers and those round the Court who from time to time would order "Champagne brandies" of up to eleven or twelve years of age. According to Savary, by the 1740s Cognac supplied forty per cent of the brandy from the region and Saint Jean d'Angely twenty-five per cent, the same percentage as La Rochelle and the islands.

La Rochelle fought back, albeit unavailingly. In 1751 the town's merchants tried unsuccessfully to reduce the strength of the eaux-de-vie coming from up-country to the level of their own (inferior) products. But the Rochellais were not the only competitors. Thirty years later the Cognac merchants complained that they had lost their markets in the Baltic to rivals from Spain and other parts of France, who sold inferior brandies which were often mixed with the "real stuff" and passed off as pure cognac.The opening of the Canal du Midi made it much easier for unscrupulous merchants to substitute cheaper and inferior products from Southern France. The tax system did not help. According to Demachy, merchants would try to smuggle *esprit de vin* into Paris disguised as *esprits odorants* from Montpellier, which paid a lower rate of duty. They would add a drop or two of essential oil, or even rub the cork with it, and try to convince the officials in that way. Some fraudsters did not bother to distil a second time but disguised the basic liquor with lavender oil and water.

But the biggest outside influence was Bordeaux. The brandies it sold could never provide competition for any market which demanded quality. Brandy was always a secondary product compared with wine, useful mainly for using wine which had, quite literally, passed its sell-by date and was liable to turn into vinegar, whereas the wine used in Cognac was specifically suitable for making brandy. So the spirit had to be rectified to a high alcoholic strength by passing it through the stills a number of times. For the same reason the brandy was lodged in any casks that were handy. Nevertheless many clients – especially the Dutch – were buying purely on price. So by the 1640s Bordeaux was exporting sizeable quantities of brandy. It was also enormously important as a source of credit and as an entrepôt – brandies were transported overland from Pons to the port of Mortagne on the Gironde estuary. Bordeaux was also the entrepôt for the – much smaller but better – quantities of brandy from the Armagnac region to the south also made from the Folle Blanche grape used in Cognac.

Many of the buyers were smugglers, for the heavy British duties inevitably led to a lively smuggling traffic throughout the century. In Rudyard Kipling's words, "Brandy for the parson" (together with that other highly taxed item "Baccy for the clerk") was a staple of the smugglers' cargoes. In the late eighteenth century Adam Smith concluded that smugglers were the biggest importers of French goods into Britain (and vice versa), for by then the traffic had been institutionalized. "Like drugs today," writes Professor Cullen, smuggling "seemed to offer an apparently easy method back to riches and success" – especially as the Irish authorities were not keen to prosecute them. In 1774 one Dublin brandy dealer explained to Richard Hennessy that "the private traders have hurted our trade here very much".

Despite all the folklore connected with the smugglers, they were probably not as important an element in the cognac trade as in the trade in inferior brandies. The smugglers naturally needed the sort of swift turnaround available only in Nantes and above all Bordeaux, which also offered immediate delivery of large quantities of – necessarily inferior – brandies.

The two major centres for brandies being shipped irregularly were Guernsey and Dunkirk; indeed in the early eighteenth century, after the long wars between France and Britain, the Guernsey dealers were the only group with any real knowledge of the brandy trade in Britain. But these were not necessarily cognac, for forty-three per cent of the brandy listed as "prizes of war" in the London press in the first decade of the eighteenth century was described as "Spanish brandies".

Smugglers were only one of many variables in a trade which fluctuated because of a wide variety of factors. They included the tax situation abroad as well as in France, while harvests varied wildly in both quality and quantity, and the buyers were quite happy to switch to competitive spirits. A number of wars throughout the century interrupted trade or forced sales to go to a neutral port like Dunkirk, Ostend, Hamburg or Rotterdam, sometimes getting there overland via Paris. Prices rose after the outbreaks of war in the 1740s, the 1750s, and 1770s. Nevertheless, the effects were sometimes surprising. The outbreak of the Seven Years' War in 1756 provided Jean Martell with enough of a boost to enable him to give up dealing in beef and tallow; and he recorded that consumption of brandy in London and Dublin had tripled during the war. The worst effects came during the War of American Independence though, surprisingly, in 1782 the merchants complained that their trade was virtually confined to England – then, of course, at war with France.

An even more important factor was the availability of alternative spirits. In Ireland, then a crucial market, bad harvests (and thus reduced supplies of grain for distillation into whiskey) during the late 1750s were enough to send the price of cognac soaring, though any shortage of rum also provided an opportunity for the Cognaçais. The shortage of grain lasted well until the late 1760s.

3

The Cognac Community

In Cognac, and to a lesser extent in other brandy towns like Jarnac, there was a distinct "agro-industrial" community that grew the grapes, made the wine, and distilled and sold the brandy. From a number of contemporary sources we get the picture of an astonishingly modern capitalist society hampered by few of the feudal restrictions usual in pre-Revolutionary France. The biggest barrier was religious. In 1685 the Revocation of the Edict of Nantes put an end to a century of legal toleration and forced the Protestant community to scatter. Many Protestants went abroad to join the "Huguenot Mafia", which provided local merchants with a network of contacts throughout Europe. These included Europe's leading bankers, who were always prepared to lend money to their co-religionists. Those who remained were forced to abandon the many official and professional positions they had held and to rely on trade for their living. This change, boosted by their connections outside France, was enormously helpful for the region as well as for themselves, and ensured their continuing dominance of the trade.

Even the Martells, staunchest of Protestants, had to go through symbolic Catholic marriage ceremonies to ensure that their children would be recognized as legitimate. Nevertheless, throughout two generations of active persecution the Protestants defiantly held secret services in lonely country barns. The Cognaçais remained sympathetic, and the soldiers sent in pursuit of the preachers at the behest of the Catholic clergy often found it impossible to arrest them, though their whereabouts were known to hundreds of the local peasantry. For the Church, like the aristocracy, had a far weaker hold on the region than on most of rural France.

In the second half of the eighteenth century the Protestants began to benefit from an implicit toleration. The only memorials to their previous sufferings were the solitary cypress trees on the families' estates, each marking the tomb of one of the faithful. Yet their ambiguous position could still be exploited. As late as 1767 the dowager Countess of Jarnac, who had the monopoly on baking in the town, wrote a ferocious letter from her Paris home to James Delamain, Jarnac's leading merchant, who had dared to encourage the locals to build their own bread oven. They were related by marriage, but the breach of her rights so infuriated the countess that she exploded: "Remember your religion is that of neither the State nor of the king. Your profession is a noble one, since it is free . . . your father-in-law was born a vassal of our forefathers, not even a vassal, for only the nobility is entitled to this title."

Despite the persecutions, the majority of merchant families remained intact during the terrible years. They dealt mainly in cognac and in wine from the Borderies but, to earn a living, often traded in other agricultural products. The merchants were also dealing in other manufactured products, especially the paper for which the region was already famous. The merchant brokers enabled mill owners and distillers alike to sell their products; and in both instances they acted as what we would call "freight forwarders", assembling small lots to be transported in bulk. In return they sold imported implements – and Dutch stills. In 1750 Guy Gauthier sold almost as much tanned hides, walnuts, and clover seed as he did brandy, and Jean Martell also bought leather, goatskins, and sheepskins. But they were still acting for principals based elsewhere. The three-cornered relationship born of the earlier Dutch dominance persisted, with the ultimate buyers located in London, Dublin, Hamburg or, most often, Ostend, where Richard Hennessy learnt the business.

These "real" merchants described themselves as those from Cognac, Jarnac, and Pons, for Cognac, in Munier's words, was emerging as "the major township and trading centre of these provinces" (Saintonge and the Angoumois). By his time *preuve de Cognac* had replaced *preuve d'Hollande* as a measure of a spirit's strength, just as the name of cognac had become the standard by which all other brandies were judged. Cognac was still a small town, with only about 2,000 inhabitants, but was increasingly recognized as important. It even enjoyed a superb postal service: there were four services a week to Paris, and letters took a mere four days to get there. Those to England took only ten days, even in wartime. The cognac business itself had become increasingly institutionalized. Only a handful of merchants were actually based in Cognac, but a lot of business was done. Savary described in his *Dictionnaire Universel* how "on Saturday each week a brandy market was held in Cognac. All the merchants and distillers meet to buy and sell."

The families were already international. Guy Gauthier – who, although a Protestant, acted as a spokesman for the people of Cognac in Paris – settled his son in the City of London after an apprenticeship in Holland; his brother worked in Barcelona, and two other members of the family at Port-au-Prince in Haiti, in the West Indies. The market was a big one. Every year Cognac produced *200,000 barriques de vins propres à bruler* (casks of wines suitable for distilling) from which emerged 13,400 *pipes* (each of three barriques or about 600 litres), adding up to eight million litres of eau-de-vie. In bad years the yield was somewhat less, since then it took six, rather than five, barriques of wine to make one of eau-de-vie.

During the century a handful of merchants managed to acquire sufficient capital to mature their brandies before shipping them, though most brandy – except that destined for London – was shipped within the year following distillation and only the best Champagne brandies were kept back for over two years. Nevertheless as early as 1718 Augier shipped two *pièces* (228-litre barrels) of cognac between eight and ten years old. By the second half of the century they were stocking their brandies and not necessarily selling at the first opportunity.

But whereas in Bordeaux it was the merchants who held the stocks, in Cognac the landowners made the running. As Munier noted in 1779: "When the brandy has been distilled, the rich landowners often store it until they can get a high price for it. I have seen some who have converted into brandy and hoarded in their cellars the several years' vintages which they have sold in one fell swoop at the right moment, making 12,000 to 15,000 *livres* on the transaction." These were still relatively young brandies. In the 1780s Richard Hennessy noted that shrewd operators with enough capital had bought up most of one year's production and were not prepared to sell until they saw if the next vintage would be good or not. They made money also by storing the brandies, although they did not have to keep them for long. Brandy was called "old" once it had spent a year in cask, and the oldest Hennessy brandies shipped were generally no more than four years old (although he occasionally sold brandies ten or even eighteen years old). Prices were set by geographical origin as well as by age, for during the century brandy from the "Champagne" region grew in value by comparison with less-blessed vineyards nearer the coast.

By then, too, customers' tastes had started to vary. The northerners like the Dutch and Germans wanted colourless brandies, while British buyers tended to want coloured brandy. Molasses or caramelized or burnt sugar were used not for colour but for sweetness, but the buyers were not fooled. As Sam Turner wrote to his partner James Hennessy, "your house I think overloads them with syrop and know that this will never assist to cover a foul spirit".

Nevertheless the market was a relatively small one with only three major forces, Augier, the oldest firm, Martell, and Delamain. Jean Martell, who founded the firm, was a member of a leading commercial family in Jersey, a major centre for smuggled goods. So it was natural for him to seek his fortune in Cognac, where he arrived in 1715. He started as a broker, buying casks of cognac and wines from the Borderies for buyers mainly in the Channel Islands, but also in Normandy, Picardy and Holland. He made an unpromising start. His arrival coincided with the short-lived boom engendered by John Law's fallacious and ruinous economic policies. The price of wines and spirits soared and then, inevitably, slumped. Martell was caught in the boom-and-bust and was forced to liquidate his first partnership. But he repaid his debts and enjoyed considerable success when he started up again, greatly helped by successive marriages to the daughters of two major Cognac merchants. He married first Jeanne Brunet and then, after her death, her cousin, Jeanne-Rachel Lallemand, a direct descendant of Jacques Rousi a pioneer seventeenth-century Cognac merchant.

She provided the young hopeful with a secure position within the merchant hierarchy of the town. So there is an uninterrupted line from Jacques Roux to Jean Martell's direct descendants, the Firino-Martells, who owned one of Cognac's largest businesses until 1988. Martell provided an early example of a theme which recurs in the history, that he made his way by marrying the daughter of a powerful local figure. *Il se fait gendre* is the local way of putting such a union; the nearest Anglo-Saxon equivalent I can find is the old Hollywood crack, "the son-in-law also rises". But such in-breeding was inevitable in a small community conscious of its foreign origins, its different religious allegiances, and its separation from the native aristocracy and gentry.

Martell was not the first son-in-law in the cognac business. That honour should probably go to Phillipe Augier, who in 1643 founded the oldest cognac firm and got his start in life by marrying the daughter of a rich banker and paper merchant from Angoulême. In the 1720s Augier was in trouble and Martell took a – temporary – advantage of the trade he was conducting through Guernsey (it did not help that he was from the rival neighbouring island of Jersey), but by the end of the decade the London merchants were buying direct from Cognac, with a disastrous effect on Martell's business, and his failure to establish himself in the domestic business did not help. So the dominance of the firm through the following 250 years owes more to Rachel Lallemand's brother Louis Gabriel than to the founding figure.

Louis Gabriel transformed the business into a major local firm. He was a ruthless businessman who took over on Martell's death in 1753, stamping it with what Cullen calls the family's "overbearing and narrow influence . . . the future of the Martell business was secured not because it was a Martell house but because it was a Lallemand one".

The other major force was Delamain, the result of another *gendre*, for Marie Ranson, the descendant of another Protestant and founder of probably the oldest firm in the area, married James Delamain in 1763. Delamain was a Dublin-born Protestant and got his job because of his Irish contacts – a position naturally reinforced by his marriage to Marie Ranson and the immediate partnership it entailed. He was one of the rare outsiders in the cognac business, but a man of authority who used his position as a freemason to make contact with the leading lights of the region. By the 1760s his was probably the biggest firm, with twelve stills. The trade with Ireland was dominated by him and Martell. He was also a genuine original – he was, for example, the first man to introduce potatoes to southwest France.

Until the Revolution, Hennessy, today the region's biggest firm, was a negligible factor in the business. This was largely due to the personality of the founder Richard Hennessy, whose portrait still dominates the company's publicity. Misleadingly he is portrayed in military uniform, though he served for only a few years while waiting for a permanent commission. He left the French army in early 1753 after a five-year wait for a commission – a length of service that one of his Irish connections made out to be twice as long. This exaggeration was later exploited by his son James to prove that he was not a mere foreigner but the son of a man who had served in the French army for ten years.

Richard was an ineffective fellow, a small-time wheeler-dealer who entered the trade only at the relatively late age of forty-one. He was prone to fits of depression and relied for his livelihood on a series of fluctuating partnerships. Nevertheless he was much loved: "few men", wrote the generally disapproving Cullen, "can have been loved as much as Richard . . . he was warm and kind also able simultaneously to retain the friendship of his contemporaries and of young people". He was described as "a younger son in trade with little resources" and was lucky to be the only survivor of a number of young Irishmen who settled in the region in the late 1760s and early 1770s. As one of the Irishmen who formed the link between Cognac and Bordeaux – the firm of Exshaw was the last relic of the Dublin–Bordeaux nexus – his major asset was not his business acumen but his connections with influential families in Ireland.

His "career" was typical of the way many of those involved in the cognac trade drifted from Ostend to Bordeaux and then – in his case in 1765 – to Cognac. He stated bluntly: "It was the only town in the province with a market dealing in brandy." In 1776 he returned to Bordeaux and during the 1780s enjoyed the profits from a major distilling business in Bordeaux, in partnership with an energetic Irish go-getter called George Boyd. Hennessy's major contribution was to bring with him a distiller from Cognac during a period marred by the death of his beloved wife, Nelly, and two of his sons, both from scarlet fever (characteristically he was defrauded by the woman he employed to look after his remaining offspring). Unfortunately after some years their distillery was undercut by smaller competitors and Boyd's arrogance and "hazy bookkeeping sense", in Cullen's words which led to disaster and left a financial mess on his death in September 1788.

But the merchant classes were not the only ones to benefit from the lack of feudal overlordship, for the peasant landholders shared in the general prosperity. Many of the feudal rights had been transformed into fixed-money rents, so the peasants could pocket most of the profits from any increased sales. The most burdensome feudal relic was the *ban des vendanges*, the *seigneurs'* right to decide the date of the harvest, which was used to force the peasants to harvest the nobles' grapes before their own.

The region's prosperity was concealed from writers because so much of the evidence left to us is in the form of complaints, directed mostly at the taxman, which give the impression of grinding poverty. Even Etienne Munier, himself a royal official, was misled. He grossly underestimated the yields and hence the profit available. Other witnesses were equally gloomy. In an obviously anonymous publication, A *Sad Picture of Rustic Folk*, published in 1786, the author explains that those who could not afford to distil their wines were forced to drink them, "thus giving their children bad habits from an early age; and as it was natural to serve up worthless wines which would otherwise have been lost, they naturally took advantage of the excess". Modern sociologists would call the result a cycle of rural deprivation, leaving as legacy a great many widows, deformed children, and other signs of misery. It would be fairer to say that there were large pockets of poverty and misery in what was, by eighteenth-century French standards, a prosperous and socially cohesive area. Even in 1789 the peasants directed their complaints against the tax collectors rather than the nobility.

For centuries everyone in the Cognac area had known that grapes were the most valuable crop, so the clergy and the nobility, as well as humbler tenants, farmed the land themselves and did not follow the usual habit of leasing it to sharecroppers. Jean Gervais remarked: "Formerly only the rich bourgeois and the better-off cultivated their own vines; nowadays virtually every peasant and simple rustic fellow has planted them for himself, which keeps them busy and means they give up working for others, so that the remaining day-labourers, sought by everyone, prefer to work for those who can pay them to excess"[1] – thus putting pressure on small or inefficient farmers. For the peasants were fully alert to commercial opportunities, even at the expense of farming techniques. As Munier put it: "In the Angoumois the peasants do not form a class apart, since they apply themselves indiscriminately to every type of cultivation. This over-extensive appetite is perhaps the cause of the bad farming methods in the Angoumois."

[1] Jean Gervais, "Memoire sur l'angoumois", 1725; reproduced in the *Bulletin* of the Société Archeologique et Historique de la Charente, 1864.

The *fureur de planter*, the mania for planting vines, spread throughout southwest France after many of the crops had been devastated by the great frost of 1709. The subsequent famine merely increased the authorities' concern about possible starvation, and they repeatedly tried to stop new plantations and to induce landowners to pull up their vines. But no one took much notice. The growers had more immediate worries such as the plagues of noxious worms, insects, and other pests which periodically afflicted them, and the growing shortage of the wood required as fuel for the stills. Father Arcère, an eighteenth-century historian from La Rochelle, recommended the use of coal, which provided a more uniform and reliable source of heat and could be imported from England (in peacetime anyway). One merchant even imported coal as ballast when ships were returning from England, but the Charentais were conservative and remained faithful to the cheaper, local wood for another hundred years or more.

Many of the peasants had their own stills, although there were also precursors of today's *bouilleurs de profession* ("professional distillers"), some of whom had mobile stills. Throughout the century the more important distillers also used to speculate on the future price of cognacs. Old brandies had been worth more than new since the 1720s and speculation became even more profitable when the market soared in the 1780s following the end of the American War of Independence. Claude Masse, writing in 1712 about the previous century, claimed that the "merest peasant, once he was comfortably off, distilled his own wine and the merchants find a ready sale for the wine in its new form. And it is this which decided everyone to plant vines so that very little land remained uncultivated."[2]

The 1780s were good years for the region. The 1782 tax increases were rescinded two years later, the American War of Independence ended in 1783 and a Free Trade Treaty with Britain, which came into operation in 1786, provided a new impetus for the cognac trade. Exports (and prices) rose rapidly; even more important, the Treaty launched the Cognaçais on to a new pattern of trade. But that did not stop the inhabitants grumbling. The woes of generations exploded in the famous *Doléances* of 1789, the endless pages of complaints that provided such a dense background

---

[2] Quoted in Delamain.

to the Revolution. Typically, the citizens of la Valette, a small town near Angoulême, had hoped that:

> having paid their Tailles, their poll taxes, taxes on utensils and equipment, forced labour, subsidies for waifs and strays, personal dues, the first, second and third portions of the "twentieth", having paid their labourers, the priest and the landlord, and after we have endured bad weather, like hail, frost, rot and drought, we had hoped that what remained of our crops could be gathered into our barns and cellars. But far from it. Our friends the tax collectors are beating at our doors demanding that we pay over three livres for every barrique of wine we produce.[3]

But the Revolution was to prove a mixed blessing.

[3] Doléances de la Senechaussée d'Angoulême pour les Etats Generaux de 1789.

4

A Revolution, not a Disaster

In 1789 the Cognaçais had worse things to worry about than a mere revolution. The previous winter had been memorably harsh, the worst since 1709. The wine had frozen in the cellars; stocks of grain were almost exhausted by early summer; the harvest that year was a mere twentieth of the average level and famine was averted only by a timely loan from Messrs Augier and Martell. But otherwise business continued as usual until the Revolutionary Terror of 1793–4. In 1791 the merchants of the district, Augier, Veuve Martell, Allemand, Arbouin & Zimmerman, Hennessy & Turner, Ranson & Delamain, and Guerinet & Robin, reasserted their traditional stand when they swore to use only brandies from the Saintonge and the Angoumois and not to imitate their competitors by mixing the local produce with brandies from the south of France or from Spain. For in the stern words of one eighteenth-century patriarch to his son: "you will not sell under your name anything other than cognac . . . you must not mix your cognac with any other product". Most importantly, middlemen – especially those in the major entrepôt, the free port of Dunkirk – were not averse to blending cognac with lesser brandies.

During the troubled years the cognac trade came to be regarded as a "sheltered sector" so far as revolutionary problems were concerned, with the local revolutionaries hesitating to go after the merchants. Nevertheless, they had to be adaptable. M. Augier had been elected a deputy in 1789 but, like so many others, was left stranded by the increasing extremism of the Revolutionary tide, when Irishmen who could not prove that they had been naturalized were imprisoned.

The longer-term effects were much greater. It was during the Revolutionary period that Cognac developed into an independent commercial centre no longer dependent on Bordeaux. The major firms were transformed from being brokers with some stocks to being proper merchants, employing managers, accountants, and maîtres de chai in charge of distilling, stocking and blending the brandies. Key employees like these often handed down their role to their children, though today the position of the Fillioux family as hereditary distillers to the Hennessys is the only relic of the tradition established in the early nineteenth century, though until the 1980s the Chapeau family fulfilled the same role as hereditary chefs de caves at Martell as the Fillioux.

Moreover, even though they were of foreign, enemy, origin, it was during the Revolutionary years that the Martells and the Hennessys in particular became part of the local establishment. For the Ancien Régime disappeared in more senses than one, and some in the trade could not cope with the uncertainties. The Revolutionary shocks were too difficult for a member of the older generation like James Delamain. He was already fifty-two years old in 1789 and had been caught short by the speed of Revolutionary events – in 1792 his patron, the Comte de Jarnac joined the emigrés and his business never recovered. This put an intolerable strain on his relationships with his children – in 1797 he is recorded as believing that his family had failed. He died in 1817, and in a story which was to remain a recurrent theme in the history of the trade he left ten children who went their own way, though by 1824 the name had been resurrected by one of his sons in partnership with a member of the Roullet family.

But it was during the Revolutionary period that Martell, already a major force, particularly in the London market, and Hennessy emerged as the dominating forces in the business, a position they were to hold until well after 1945. Indeed the commercial history of cognac in the century and half after the Revolution consisted largely of successive challenges to their duopoly, challenges which have often seemed invincible in the short term but have rarely lasted more than one generation. For, as the novelist Jacques Chardonne points out, even the most important merchants owed very little to inheritance: "wealth does not last long in this business". The duopoly was founded not so much on their cognac business as on the commercial risks and opportunities they grasped between 1789 and 1815 which enabled them to build up the capital required to concentrate on brandy. Not that they had a duopoly that early: shipping documents show that in the mid-1790s the long-extinct firm of Laberge was as big as either, and that together the two halves of the Delamain business were almost as big. Yet all the time the business was concentrating. In the 1790s probably only ten of the fifty or so merchants were exporters, the others merely suppliers.

The Martells were largely untouched by the Revolution. Jean Martell Jnr and Jean Augier commanded the local national guard and Martell was well enough placed to defend one of his salesmen against accusations of the local Revolutionary committees. Moreover, they benefited from the Revolutionary wars. In particular Theodore Martell was involved in large purchases of foodstuffs for the land armies. He was not alone; the Broussard family held the valuable monopoly to supply spirits to the Napoleonic navy.

This was not a new business. Throughout the eighteenth century the French army and navy were both considerable buyers at a time when Rochefort, just down river from Tonnay, was growing in importance as a naval base and arsenal, and the ships provisioned there required large quantities of cognac to sustain the sailors and prevent scurvy.

More surprising was the sudden blossoming of Hennessy's firm. "Citizen Hennessy" was considered safe enough to be charged by the local Revolutionary committee with the sale of brandy, but the key was a seven-year partnership between Richard's son James Hennessy and James Delamain's nephew Sam Turner. By 1796 Turner had emerged as the biggest shareholder in a three-sided partnership, with seven of the sixteen shares; James had five and the ageing Richard – he died in 1800 – the remaining four. As Cullen notes, "James Hennessy and Sam Turner were quicker to do business with the Revolutionary governments in the 1790s than any other house." James had learnt his trade in London, which he visited in 1789 as a mere twenty-four-year-old, building on the London connections of his father's partner, the late John Saule. In Cullen's words, James – who was a commander of the *Garde Nationale* – and Turner were "not put off by the challenge of transforming their business from orthodox trading to government orders" which became their major business. Their first coup was to act for a year on behalf of the Revolutionary government in exchanging their brandies against much-needed grain imported through foreign business channels. By the late 1790s they were living high on the hog – the socially ambitious Richard even became worried about his son's Irish brogue.

Turner – and Jean Martell – both spent the years between 1796 and 1799 in Hamburg, which had become the major entrepôt for shipments to Britain, by then at war with France; Otard admitted that virtually all its overseas trade was through the city. They all faced severe price competition from the cheaper brandies from elsewhere in France, although Hennessy and Turner claimed to take the greatest possible care when blending their brandies. Turner also found it useful to be in Hamburg to avoid accusations of royalism, but he stayed because it was crucial to the success of the business. It was also, and not coincidentally, a major financial centre, essential at a time of fluctuating financial problems in France itself. In the last years of the eighteenth century the peasants were naturally deeply distrustful of the *assignats* and other dubious notes issued by the Revolutionary governments. To buy their precious cognacs the merchants had to come up with gold or foreign currency. The partnership suffered badly when Hamburg's bankers collapsed from overstretch in 1799. Two years later Hennessy and Turner only were saved by a timely loan from the Martells, although even then they continued to have problems with their bankers in Paris and remained in hock to both the Martells and their bankers until 1805. Nevertheless, by 1813 James felt strong enough to end the partnership with Turner.

In 1795 the two families had been united through the marriage of James Hennessy with Marthe Martell, daughter of Frédéric Gabriel Martell. In her husband's frequent absences she proved as able a businesswoman as Rachel, Jean's widow. The marriage was something of a comedown for a clan which dominated the trade and had become accustomed to marry its female offspring with local notables. But it corresponded to the view of marriage normal in bourgeois France until relatively recently. As Auguste Hennessy put it, marriage "rests on considerations of [financial] interest rather than happiness". In a second link, James's daughter Lucie married her cousin Jean-Gabriel Martell in 1816. Though the mutual interests of Martell and Hennessy became stronger and stronger, they never hesitated to go their own way commercially.

The principal challenge to the duopoly came from a newcomer, Otard-Dupuy. This was a partnership of two growers who had accumulated comfortable stocks before the Revolution; it was also one of the earliest examples of growers-turned-merchants, though Jean-Baptiste Otard had social pretensions. He claimed, rather unconvincingly, descent from an old Scottish family which, like the Hennessys, had settled in France for religious reasons, for it was useful to pretend to have connections with Scottish Jacobite gentry. Unlike Richard Hennessy, however, Otard was sentenced to death by the Revolutionaries and escaped only through the timely intervention of his loyal friends. Jean Dupuy was a local, who brought a new market to the partnership they established in 1794: his uncle, Léon Dupuy, had pioneered sales to the newly independent United States. They were not the only pioneers here: the first recorded sale to New York was made that same year by Richard Hennessy to one Jacob Schieffelin (an ancestor of the family which remained Hennessy's agents for nearly 200 years). The American connection became valuable, not only because of the direct sales but also because the Americans were neutral, so their ships could be used to ship brandy in wartime to an equally neutral port for trans-shipment to England.

All the merchants benefited from the availability of cheap property confiscated from previous aristocratic or religious owners, but it was Otard and Dupuy who managed to buy up the finest corner site in all Cognac, the Château des Valois, on the river guarding the bridge across the Charente. The château was a fortress which had been reduced to acting as a prison and had naturally become vacant with the fall of the French monarchy. Ever since then it has provided an ideal warehouse – and a magnificent shop window for the firm's products.

Otard-Dupuy was not the only new firm established at the time. The other important newcomer was Thomas Hine, the descendant of a Dorset family, who had originally gone to France to complete his education – a link arranged through the Huguenot mafia. He settled in Jarnac, went to work for Ranson & Delamain, and soon married a daughter of his employer, James Delamain.

Another merchant to take advantage of the new situation was Rémy Martin II. His grandfather, Rémy I, had started as a grower and set up a modest merchant business. In 1759 Rémy I suffered a severe blow when his only son Pierre died. At the age of 64 he had to return to work to preserve his legacy, including his father-in-law's estates, for his six-year old grandson Rémy II. The first Rémy died in 1773, and Rémy II proved able to cope with the traumas of the Revolution. We know from his tax returns that he emerged a rich man from the upheavals of the 1790s.

But the Revolution had other important effects. It relieved the peasant landowners of their burden of feudal dues and institutionalized the tolerance unofficially granted to the region's Protestants over the preceding quarter of a century. More crucially, it removed the restrictions and taxes which had impeded the circulation of wines and spirits, and thus, for the first time, enabled the Cognaçais to blend brandies from different distilleries. The ability to blend meant that individual merchants could establish their own style of spirit, although this development was slow to emerge.

For the Napoleonic years were not lost. Sales to Britain had been boosted by the Free Trade Treaty of 1786 from below 50,000 hectolitres to over 60,000. When war broke out in 1793 sales slumped, but only to between 30,000 and 40,000 hectolitres. Exports and prices recovered somewhat, for even the new-style Revolutionary War did not mean the end of all trade with the enemy. Some elements of the former pattern of trade remained. An old-style shortage of grain in 1795–6 had its usual effect of increasing demand, and the Peace of Amiens in 1802 brought the usual result, a slump, which led to the bankruptcy of Casimir Martini, one of Cognac's leading merchants.

Even the period of blockade and counter-blockade which followed the outbreak of "total" war in 1804 included elements of sheer farce. Sales dropped, but because of excessive British tariffs, not on account of war – and even the licensing system merely complicated the traffic. The British blockade of French ports which followed the Orders in Council of 1807 should have put a stop to the traffic. Far from it: imports soared, partly because prices in France had dropped sufficiently to provide bargains for the British, who declined to deprive themselves of their habitual luxuries. In 1808 Sir John Nicholl, a British Minister, recognized that "we need a little wine and French brandy to rejoice and comfort ourselves". A system of import licences ensured that the British kept some control over the situation while still slaking their thirsts. As Jean Martell Jnr put it: "We only want freedom to get out, and the blockade will not stop us, above all if we have good letters of credit." Nevertheless, he had needed political protection at a high level in Paris to obtain the necessary export licences. The ban on purchases of French wines and spirits for the British armed forces in 1807, and later the total ban on French imports, was inspired not by patriotic fervour but by pressure from the "West Indian interest", the traditional lobby of rum merchants whose sales had been badly hurt by the success of French brandies. Imports soared in 1809 in anticipation of the ban, which caused a temporary slump but lasted less than two years until counter-pressure from the rest of the commercial community forced a relaxation. In 1812 things began to return to normal, a process that took nearly a decade.

Not surprisingly, as Frédéric Martell said, "It was with feelings of the greatest relief that the citizens of Cognac greeted the news of Napoleon's deposition." Peace brought a short-lived boom in prices and a steady increase in sales – from an average of 30,000 hectolitres during the war to over 80,000 in the late 1820s and over 100,000 in the following decade. Nevertheless, British customs duties continued to rise, and at their post war worst amounted to six times the value of the cognac itself, far higher than those payable by rival spirits like rum. So-called "British brandy", a cheap imitation of the real thing, enjoyed a considerable vogue, largely because it carried one-third of the duties imposed on the French equivalent.

The Restoration of King Louis XVIII not only restored the *status quo ante bellum*; it also reinforced the London connection. All three of James Hennessy's sons, James, Auguste and Frédéric, were automatically sent there to learn the business and Hennessy rapidly gained momentum, above all as Auguste took over. By 1815 Hennessy and Martell had emerged as real merchants, with proper accounting systems – even travel expenses, an important item, were properly checked – while Auguste talked of buying casks in their thousands. Nevertheless, even Hennessy had relatively little brandy over three years old and always relied greatly on purchases on what we would now call the spot market.

The period had left its scars. As one of Martell's colleagues put it: "What is becoming appalling for our region is the relentlessness with which our hapless brandies are being pursued; it is much to be feared that people will lose the taste for them, and it is very difficult for a trade which has been thus disturbed to get back on to its former tracks."

The Cognaçais, like their colleagues in Bordeaux, were almost totally dependent on sales to the British market, which took over four-fifths of their exports, so both communities were early campaigners for Free Trade. As one 1838 petition expressed it:

If the French government does not get a reduction of the exorbitant duties which disrupt our brandy trade, they will cease to be drunk at all, which will force the wine growers to pull up their vines. This does not mean to

say that they can plant other crops . . . the soil is too dry . . . the govern-
ment should not forget that it is a question of 200 million francs and the
ruin of 4,000 families . . . what distinguishes the Cognac trade from that
of other spirits is that no merchant here bothers with distillation: the
owners of the vineyards, in both the departments of the Charente, are at
the same time farmers and distillers.

The pattern established before the Revolution continued, with hundreds
of small farmers, few large holdings (except those being accumulated by
the merchants themselves), and even fewer labourers – a situation that
produced the usual crop of complaints about the lack of labour. One
authority estimated that there were 1,500 growers with holdings large
enough to produce a dozen barriques of wine. Most of them distilled
their production themselves in small stills which held only a single barrique of wine and cost a mere 500 francs.

The signatories to the 1838 petition emphasized that although their
traditional methods of distillation were both slow and extravagant, they
were essential to retain the natural qualities of the grape and justify the
price of Cognac: "These methods are the only ones that can be employed
without damaging these qualities." Distillers making lesser spirits from
grain could use larger, quicker, more modern stills, the continuous stills
named after their inventor, an Irish customs officer called Cooley. In
Cognac these produced inferior brandy. But at the back of the Gauthiers'
house in the rue Saulnier is the brick tower which used to house a steam-
heated continuous distillation apparatus. According to Guy Gauthier-
Auriol, it provided a much smoother product than any other type. Some
of the Cognaçais did experiment with a new-style apparatus, using a
second still by the side of the first, so that the distillation process could
be more or less continuous – the second still was emptied only once a
week to rid it of the accumulated lees.

Throughout most of the century the growers continued to hold the
bulk of the region's stocks of older brandies, and the richer among
them could choose whether to sell their brandy new, speculate by
holding it for a few months in case the next harvest was bad, or age it
themselves. In the early post-war years prices were still set in the traditional way. "Every Saturday," according to J.P. Quénot[1], "the day of the

---

[1] Statistique du Département de la Charente, 1818.

brandy market in the town of Cognac, the growers who wish to sell, the middle men who are buying to sell on, and the merchants from the whole region . . . repair to a small square in Cognac called Le Canton where most of the buying is done on the simple presentation of a flask in which the seller has put a small sample of the spirit which he agrees to deliver. The price at which most transactions have been concluded becomes the official market price, which the merchants use when calculating their selling price."

This mechanism gave the merchants a chance to increase their profits. The official price was for brandies from "la Champagne", defined as the whole of the arrondissement (the old name for a canton, and thus a sub-division of a département) of Cognac lying on the south bank of the Charente, as well as some from the neighbouring *arrondissement*. As in the eighteenth century those from the north bank were worth less, and those from the outlying regions to the west formed a third division. The less scrupulous merchants, said Quénot, "blend the different brandies and make their foreign buyers pay in relation to the full market price. To this considerable advantage they added the price of the cask, which they also make their suppliers pay, without allowing the amount when dealing with the growers."

The poet Alfred de Vigny had retained the vineyard near Blanzac that he had inherited from an aunt because he loved the place and its setting. The property did not matter to him financially – it was only after ten years spent restoring the property, Le Maine-Giraud, that he could claim that receipts had exceeded expenses. He was anxious to produce good cognac, using only wood to heat the wine and not the peat used by less finicky distillers, which naturally altered the taste of the brandy. He was a squirarchical figure, trying out his poems on the locals and even found-ing a library for them. He also kept a beady eye on the cognac market. Like many other growers, he normally sold to one particular firm (in his case it was Hennessy), but this did not stop him from speculating. "The price of brandy seems to me to be pretty satisfactory," he wrote to his estate manager in April 1854, "but as the season is inclement and M. Auguste Hennecy [sic] has informed me that prices will neither rise nor fall before the harvest, I will wait until you tell me about the late frosts people are afraid of before deciding." Four months later he had still not sold: "I haven't settled anything with M. Hennecy [sic], and you will not deal with anyone over my brandies, because the outlook for the harvest this year is unpromising."

But there was one group that did not accept the existing state of affairs. In 1838 Pierre Antoine de Salignac rallied some hundreds of the region's wine growers into the United Vineyard Proprietors Company, the Société de Propriétaires Vinicoles de Cognac. He launched the new firm as a direct challenge to the "Big Three" houses – Martell, Hennessy, and Otard-Dupuy – who, he claimed, monopolized the purchase of the growers' brandies (according to Quénot, six or eight houses controlled the trade). Salignac claimed, reasonably enough, that cognac owed its worldwide fame to its quality, and that this was provided not by the trademarks burned into the casks by the three firms but by the growers and distillers themselves. Their fight against the "Big Three" was soon successful: within a few years the United Vintners' brandy, with Salignac's own name prominent on the label, joined the "Big Three" and within a generation the cooperative effort had been entirely obliterated in favour of the family name.

In Charles Dickens' magazine *Household Words* his friend Henry Vizetelly[2] gave a lyrical description of the relationship of the growers with Salignac as he witnessed it during a visit in 1855:

When a peasant proprietor out in the country has burned his wine into eau-de-vie, if the markets put on an inviting aspect, he loads the chariot before his door with precious tubs, he then washes his face and hands, puts on a clean shirt and blouse, and takes his Sunday broad-brimmed hat out of the closet. He proceeds slowly on his way with stately step, and enters the narrow crooked passages which Cognac dignifies with the name of streets, announcing his arrival by a long succession of what you might take for pistol-shots, but which are no more than harmless cracks of the whip. He stops at the gate of the establishment, say of Messrs R & Co. His cargo is set down, taken in, rolled up an inclined plane, and measured at once by transfusion into a cylindrical vessel which has outside it a glass tube, to which a graduated scale is attached, communicating with the interior, and therefore showing exactly how full the measure is. That settled he walks off with the empty casks, goes on his

---

[2] According to Charles Tovey, Dickens himself was the author. But Dickens never went near Cognac, and the style is unmistakably Vizetelly's.

way rejoicing, leaving the rustic eau-de-vie to be converted into gentlemanly cognac brandy.

The idea was copied by other groups, and the growers from Barbezieux, for instance, were soon selling their brandies direct to the British market. Salignac, too, had his imitators. Jules Duret and the founder of the firm of Barriasson used their position as managers of growers' cooperatives to launch themselves as merchants. Salignac himself had the strikingly modern idea that cognacs, like the wines of Bordeaux, ought to be graded by their age and quality, arguing that cognac's principal clientele, the better-off classes in Britain, could afford higher prices. He was the only merchant who actually welcomed visitors like Vizetelly. More traditional houses, in the words of Charles Tovey, "would like the English consumer especially to retain the delusion that a special name branded upon the exterior of a cask has everything to do with the quality of its contents. They would not wish the world to know that any merchant in Cognac who has cash to go to market with can purchase from the farmers as good Brandy as another." In an understandable effort to retain their aura of mystery they did not even reply to Tovey's letters.

Salignac did not confine his ideas to the market place; they had an additional, political, dimension. This was not especially radical – Salignac was joined by two of the leading landowners of the region, the Marquis d'Asnières and Jules de Bremond d'Ars, and the three of them headed a rather reactionary, Catholic political grouping. In his election propaganda he accused the "Big Three" of exploiting the growers and making monstrous profits at their expense. He mocked the idea that they had opened new markets: they still depended, he said, almost entirely on British buyers and even used British ships, to the great detriment of the French merchant navy. He finished with a splendid flourish: "Stop giving yourself an importance which you lack. Your only claim to fame is to have profiteered at the expense of the growers . . . and the region has never forgotten the fact!!!!!"

His success in Britain – he increased sales by a half during the late 1840s – alarmed the older-established firms, but Hennessy at least managed to leap ahead through replacing its agents, Sandeman, with Twiss and Browning (who remained its importers for over a century). In Britain all the firms were pitching at two very distinct markets, the traditional aristocratic drinkers of "fine Champagne cognac" and a new class of much humbler drinkers who drank brandy and water as a precaution against the impure London water. As Auguste Hennessy remarked in 1849: "The fact is that the public originally took to drinking brandy and water for medical reasons, and, having found it both pleasant and effective, they are likely to continue."[3] Indeed brandy and water was a classic stimulant in Britain and – as *fine a l'eau* – in France as well. But drinking was largely concentrated in London, which accounted for around three-fifths of total sales. Because many ordinary drinkers were looking for cheaper spirits they also took to "British brandy", whose sales were roughly a third of those of cognac, which was also far more heavily taxed than native spirits, a problem which remained a theme in cognac's history in the twentieth century.

To Vizetelly, as to the Victorian middle classes as a whole, cognac was more than a drink: "We are therefore . . . obliged to a district which supplies stores for our medicine chest as well as for our cellar," he wrote. In the days before antibiotics brandy was widely prescribed: "There are countless aged persons and invalids, whose stomachs cannot bear either wine or beer, to whom pure brandy, or brandy-and-water, is an indispensable sustenance." The notion of "medicinal brandy", the half-bottle kept in the corner cabinet of even the humblest British home, was firmly implanted in mid-Victorian times and was the foundation of Martell's long and profitable dominance of the British market.

The Martells and the Hennessys were tempting targets, politically as well as commercially, for by 1815 they were what the French call *notables de Province* ("local worthies"). Indeed when James Hennessy died he left a fortune as considerable as any of the aristocratic wine merchants living on the Quai de Chartrons in Bordeaux. For the second quarter of the century saw a steady improvement in the region's fortunes. Judging by some 1846 tax returns, the Martells, the Hennessys, the Otards, and the Dupuys were the richest, but the Commandons, the Planats, the Augiers, the Gauthiers, and, in Jarnac, the Hines and the Bisquits, all had substantial fortunes. In 1838 their growing financial needs led to the foundation of the town's first bank.

Both families provided Cognac with mayors and deputies, and in 1824 James had replaced Baron Otard as a deputy. One member of the Martell

[3] Quoted in Tovey.

family even ventured, successfully, as far afield as Libourne, the con-stituency in the Gironde that includes St-Emilion. Salignac alleged that they ganged up on outsiders, supporting each other's candidatures against the growers even if they did not share the same political labels or beliefs. These varied, but both families tended to be what Continental Europeans term "liberals": like their constituents, they were secular, luke-warm or hostile to the Church's political pretensions; they naturally favoured Free Trade; and, in French terms, they sometimes strayed into a paternalist sort of radicalism. Auguste Hennessy, for instance, showed considerable courage in protesting against the seizure of power by the future emperor, Louis Napoleon, at the end of 1851. Nevertheless, per-sonalities, not policies, mattered most to what was still a highly restricted electorate. James Hennessy senior was extremely popular because he had been an early opponent of the reactionary King Charles X, whom he had helped to dethrone in 1830, so he was invariably elected. But when his son stood in his place he was defeated.

The political atmosphere gradually became less stormy after Salignac's death in 1843, but his commercial ideas remained valid and the firm con-tinued to prosper, first under Salignac's son and grandson, and then under the management and name of the Monnet family, for the growers still felt the need for a manager of distinction who would lend his name to their product. But the firm remained rather different – Jean Monnet remembered that some of the firm's more important "shareholders" came to dinner every Saturday: "well-off men, full of wisdom, close to the soil . . . the links between them and my father were closer than mere interest; there was also friendship and mutual trust".

During the eighteen years of the July Monarchy of Louis Philippe, so abruptly terminated by the 1848 Revolution, many merchants moved away from their cramped quarters in the old town. Some, like Auguste Hennessy, bought country houses and estates: by the end of the century some members of the leading families had become landed gentry rather more interested in their estates than in their commercial affairs. But others remained within Cognac itself, for during the first half of the cen-tury the town expanded beyond the cramped alleys of the old town. In 1800 it still covered the same area, 226 hectares/558 acres, as it had in medieval times, and the population, a mere 4,000 in 1840, doubled in the following twenty years. "Twenty years ago," Vizetelly pointed out,

"Cognac was only a village; the same dull, steady-going place that it had been ever since the dawn of time. Now, not to speak of the merchants, the peasantry of the *arrondissement* of Cognac are the richest in France." He contrasted the "narrow side streets which look as if they were hewn out of the rock itself", covered with vines which "seem to climb for the sake of reaching the summit of a natural cliff", with the many "great houses in the town surrounded by that symptom of wealth, luxurious gardens".

Some of these are now Cognac's municipal pride. The Museum,[4] for example, is housed in a mansion built by Jules Dupuy in front of the Town Hall, itself originally the town house of his partner, Léon Otard. All this activity gave employment to an increasing number of local builders and architects, and, more directly, to 300 *tonnelliers* ("coopers") in Cognac and Jarnac. As Vizetelly put it: "Arthur Young's[5] test of a town's prosperity is manifestly visible; public and private buildings are being erected and restored on a liberal scale." The town, like its principal product, was on its way.

[4] It is an essential stop for any visitor interested in Cognac the town, the drink, and the people who grew the grapes and distilled the spirit.

[5] A much-quoted eighteenth-century British traveller.

5

An Imperial Glow

The 1850s and 1860s, the reign of Emperor Napoleon III, signalled a golden age for the Charentais, for they, together with the Bordelais, were amongst the biggest beneficiaries in France of the Emperor's policy of Free Trade, unprecedented in French history. They remained loyal to their benefactor for a generation after his downfall, though they paid for their loyalty: much of the bill for the gigantic reparations imposed by the victorious Germans after the Franco-Prussian War of 1870 was met through a substantial increase in the taxes paid on spirits. At the beginning of Napoleon's reign British customs duties were still very severe. A first reduction in 1849 had only a limited effect because sales were hampered by the spread of oidium, a fungal disease that devastated all the vineyards of the southwest in the early 1850s. It was soon found that dusting the vines with sulphur provided a complete cure, and by the end of the decade the vineyards were back to normal. Although the price of new cognac more than doubled, an enormous harvest in 1858 restored stocks to their historic levels.

The Cognaçais were thus ready for the expansion that followed the signature of the Free Trade Treaty between Britain and France in 1860. The outbreak of the American Civil War that year had sabotaged the growth of a promising market, but the dramatic reduction in British customs duties more than compensated for the lost opportunity. Before the Treaty cognac had cost eight times the sixteen francs it fetched on the local market: afterwards it cost a quarter of the previous figure, putting the French product on equal terms with its British competitors. Before the onslaught of the oidium sales had risen to nearly 200,000 hectolitres. They dropped to a mere 110,000 in the 1850s and by 1860 had recovered only to 150,000 hectolitres. Within ten years they had soared to 450,000. Not surprisingly, Cognac is the only town in France to boast a Rue Richard Cobden, named after one of the men who had preached the gospel of Free Trade so effectively. The French negotiator, one M. Chevalier, lacks this mark of honour.

The prosperity was general, but although a number of new firms were formed, the trade remained highly concentrated. Between 1852 and 1870 the top dozen firms were responsible for over seventy per cent of the exports; sales in France were relatively unimportant. Hennessy alone accounted for nearly one-quarter of the total, and Martell just over one-fifth. The growers assembled under the Salignac banner supplied nine per cent and Otard-Dupuy 5.6 per cent while both Salignac and Bisquit-Dubouche had nearly five per cent each. Nevertheless, even the biggest houses were still under-capitalised family firms; their stocks were not enormous. In the 1870s the venerable house of Augier reckoned that it had the second biggest stock of cognacs, although this amounted to the equivalent of only about a million bottles of normal-strength brandy. Much of the region's production was exported immediately to be aged in wood in Britain, while the growers still held most of the older brandies – and thus remained in a strong position to bargain with their customers. In the late 1840s two-thirds of Hennessy's stocks were less than two years old, and only one-ninth more than five years old, a proportion that did not change dramatically in the following quarter of a century. The evidence is obvious to every visitor: the older *chais de stockage* ("storage cellars") are not large.

In some ways the trade remained set in its traditional ways. The railway line from Angoulême through Cognac to the coast was completed in 1867, but brandies continued to be shipped by barge to Tonnay-Charente – the river route was only abandoned after 1926, when the government stopped spending money to ensure that it remained navigable. Nevertheless, one relationship was totally transformed in the third quarter of the century: that between the Cognac houses and their British customers. The Cognaçais started selling their product in bottles under their own name and not, as previously, in anonymous casks whose contents were to be bottled and labelled with the name of the London merchants. These all-powerful middlemen also controlled other markets in the British colonies, especially India, an increasingly important outlet.

The revolution was a dramatic one. Until the late 1850s the merchants had been relatively helpless. Unscrupulous foreigners could – and did – import inferior brandies and have them stamped as if of French origin because they had passed through a French port. All this was stopped by the French law of June 23, 1857, by which trademarks could be registered and thus protected against interlopers. Within a few years every house in Cognac had registered several marks. The Tribunal of the Chamber of Commerce in Cognac, which started registering marks in 1858, is a rich repository of brand names. There are 16,000 in all, although only 3,000 are still legally valid, because they have to be re-registered every ten years.

The locals were anxious to establish trademarks because they could then personalize their products even further by putting them into bottles. Martell owns what is probably the earliest bottle of cognac – it dates from 1848 – but two relatively new firms, Jules Robin and Jeanne-Antoine Renault, also seized the chance early to make their name by bottling their cognacs. By 1855 the practice was widespread: at Salignac's "establishment" Vizetelly saw a man making thirty or forty cases (or, as he playfully called them, "volumes") a day. The Act of 1857, allowing for the registration of trademarks, provided a further boost. Between 1860 and 1875 the Martells were sending one-quarter of their sales in cases of a dozen bottles. In the 1870s the trade as a whole matched this proportion, but by that time half of Hennessy's sales were of bottles.

The next step was to identify the contents of the new-fangled bottles according to age. Planat and "Bellot et Fils Frères et Foucauld", for example, both registered "Old Brandy" as one of their marks. But this was merely a vague indication. According to family legend, it was Auguste Hennessy who systematized the idea. Noticing a star engraved on a window in one of the firm's offices, he devised a system by which one star meant a two-year-old brandy, two stars a four-year-old, and three stars a six-year-old. The term "old" meant more than six years old. Had the Hennessys registered the star system, they could have protected the idea, but they did not. But then the Hennessys have always been rather careless in registering their ideas for they also thought up the idea of using the letters XO to indicate an Extra Old cognac and failed to register the name – though even today their XO remains a standard by which others are judged.

The legislation opened the floodgates to the impressive ingenuity of the less scrupulous members of the trade. In 1870 Messrs J.L. Martel registered a splendid spoof label, virtually the same as that of the double-l Martells, boasting, truthfully enough, that their maison was "*fondée en 1870*". This was a dig at the real Martells, so proud that their venerable firm had been founded in 1715. The Hennessys also had to take action against a newcomer advertising itself as "J. Albert Hennessy & Co; Maison fondée en 1877; Old Cognacs".

Many labels boasted of their suppliers' successes at exhibitions. Jules Duret, for instance, had been awarded a *Medaille Première Classe* at the *Exhibition Universelle* held in Paris in 1855, the exhibition which set in tablets of stone the classification of the wines of the Médoc. So, in theory, Duret could claim to be a "Cognac premier cru". By contrast Martell felt that it could afford to be decidedly sniffy; it had "never submitted its products to any of the exhibitions, large or small, which have multiplied everywhere and which give rise to a veritable avalanche of awards sought by houses of the second rank". During the golden years Hennessy was clearly in front in the century-old two-horse race. The Martells were in the middle of a transition between the Martells themselves and the Firinos, who had married into the family, for the tradition of sons-in-law taking over continued as strongly as ever. Alexander Bisquit's son-in-law, Adrien Dubouché, himself had a son-in-law, Maurice Laporte, who duly added his grandfather's name to his.

The dominance of Martell and Hennessy forced lesser houses to find some distinctive mark to help in specific markets. Bisquit registered "La Presidenta 1848" to commemorate some long-forgotten event in the history of Guatemala, and Bonniot registered a "Fine Vieux Cognac" under the pseudonym of "Paul Dupont" (the French equivalent of "John Smith") that was "expressly bottled for India". Many other firms employed more than one name: P.A. Maurain had used "John Bellot", with a label, clearly aimed at Far Western thirsts, of a cowboy (or possibly a gaucho, for the Latin American market was growing rapidly) lassoing a buffalo. But my personal favourite was registered by Charles Rousseau, "Imperial Brandy Proprietors": it showed a dishevelled young lady, clearly the worse for wear, hanging on to some wreaths, in which she was entwined, as though they were life-jackets.

Commercial pressure also led to the first attempts to define the different parts of the Cognac vineyard. For at least a century the inferiority of the cognacs from the Saintonge and Aunis near the sea had been known and acknowledged by the lower price paid for them. But in the boom years it became increasingly necessary to define more precisely what had hitherto been a rather rough-and-ready series of categories. The initiative was taken by the Salignacs, who felt that their members were being cheated because the big houses used brandies from outside the choicest slopes. So, as Tovey put it in *British and Foreign Spirits:* "Salignac bound them to ship only the Brandy grown in a defined district (of which a map is prepared) well known to produce all the finest qualities." This was the first indication of a battle which remains central to the whole business: the dislike of the major firms labelling the geographical origin of their brandies, preferring to rely on their own names and thus reducing their dominance over the growers in a particular sub-region.

According to Hennessy in 1885: "everywhere in the world where we send our products they are known under the name of Cognac or eau-de-vie Hennessy, but we have never mentioned the term "fine Champagne" on our invoices . . . the different qualities of our brandies are the result of blends of different vintages". And only the merchant was allowed to know the proportions of the vintages and origins of the brandies in the blend.

The first map of the Cognac district had been prepared in 1854 by the cooperative at Saintes and naturally took the town as the beating heart of Cognac. Salignac's response was to commission a well-known geologist, M. Coquand, to carry out the first proper survey of the area in order to pinpoint the superiority of the Champagnes. Some years later the merchants of Angoulême followed suit but their map was so biased that Segonzac, the historic heart of the Grande Champagne, was placed firmly in the Bois. By the late 1860s there was a *Dictionnaire de crus* and a series of maps, drawn up by an engineer called Lacroix, defining and redefining the boundaries between the different *crus*. Unfortunately, he set a precedent by being too tidy-minded to cope with the fragmented geology and geography of the Cognac region.

The principal effect of the mania for classification was a proliferation of names for the enormous area covered by the Bois. At the summit, of course, were the "Premiers Fin Bois de Jarnac", while Tovey refers to a "fine brandy known as Premiers Bois". One much-liked cognac was marketed under the name of Château de Chassors, the heart of the area; and in the 1930s Charles Walter Berry, the leading English connoisseur of fine cognac, tasted and approved of a "fine Fin Bois". But the Premiers Fins Bois were merely top of a hierarchy, which naturally included Deuxièmes Bois, followed by Fins Bois, Bons Bois, Bois Ordinaires, Bois Communs, Bois à Terroir, and so on. Tovey listed "Champagne fine and common, Champagne de Bois and Eau-de-Vie de Bois, as well as that of Annis [Aunis] produced from the vines on the banks of the river". Robert Delamain claimed that some London buyers divided the region into no fewer than sixteen different *crus*. The distinctions made were commercially important, since a Champagne cognac could be worth forty per cent more than a mere Bois.

Not surprisingly, the distinctions gave rise to all sorts of frauds. The growers naturally blamed the merchants, but everyone was at it. In 1858 a report by the Sous-Préfet of Barbezieux firmly blamed:

> *an enormous number of the smaller distillers [who] buy a little wine and distil it at home. It is these fellows . . . who have given the local brandy trade a bad reputation. For most of them mix the local product with raw alcohols from the Nord and spirits from Languedoc. Unfortunately it is almost impossible to convict them of the frauds of which they are undoubtedly guilty.*

He was being a little unfair to the authorities' efforts. Tovey noted that in 1857–8 a number of growers were convicted of fraud and received long sentences which "had a very salutary effect, and contributed in a great degree to stop all adulteration and sophistication". But some merchants were forced to stress on their labels that the contents were "real" or "pure" cognac and it was the boast of one firm that all its cognacs had been produced in its own distilleries. As early as 1882 the leading London paper, the *Pall Mall Gazette*, was writing that: "Cognac in large quantities now enters England which comes out of potatoes and not out of grapes. Pure cognac can now be secured only through English holders of old stocks."

In Tovey's time these fraudsters could plead a lack of local grapes caused by the oidium. But the frauds continued in the 1860s and early 1870s, when the area growing grapes for conversion to cognac started to expand even faster than the market. Indeed, by the mid-1870s it formed the largest single vineyard in France. Thirty per cent of the *arrondissement* of Cognac was already planted with vines. So growth was concentrated in the woods to the north and west, in the Deux-Sèvres, and more especially in the Charente-Inférieure (now known as Charente-Maritime), where nearly 60,000 additional hectares (148,000 acres) were planted with vines in the third quarter of the century, all adding to the area of "Bois". In the peak year of 1875, production from the whole vineyard was more than double the 1850 figure. By the mid-1870s production had far out-stripped sales. One estimate, based on the figures given in Berrault's annual survey of Cognac, is that between 1861 and 1876 the region produced nearly eleven million hectolitres of cognac but exported under 4.5 million. The remaining 6.5 million represented no less than twenty-four times the exports shipped annually at the height of the Napoleonic boom.

The area's vineyards may have been the biggest in France but they were emphatically not the best-kept. Vizetelly had remarked how "the culture of vines for making eau-de-vie differs considerably from the management of mere wine-making vines. It is also more careless or slovenly in appear-ance." In the 1850s one commentator had remarked how loosely the rows of vines were planted, with enough room between them for an ox team to plough. The slovenliness of the vineyards and of their owners disguised their general prosperity. In the late 1850s Tovey shrewdly remarked how:

> Anyone who observed these people congregated together at the Cognac or Jarnac market or fair, would at once recognize them from their appear-ance as a class of men who, having had a difficulty in getting what wealth they possess, are determined to keep it, and are earnest in their endeav-ours to increase it. Although in their best apparel, they are ill-dressed and shabby-looking; the clothes they wear might at some time or other have been genteel. Some appear in dress coats, with outrageously large coloured silk handkerchiefs round their necks. The ill-fitted clothes show that the present wearers are not the original proprietors . . . one keen and subtle-looking man, whose clothes would not have fetched five shillings, was pointed out to us as a man worth eighty thousand pounds.

His observations were echoed by a later visitor, Charles Albert d'Arnaux, a well-known illustrator who signed himself "Bertall". In 1878, at the suggestion of Honoré de Balzac, whose novels he illustrated, he pub-lished La Vigne, an entertaining account of a visit to the Charente –

although it was inevitably rather patronizing, he being Parisian and they provincials and therefore, by definition, simpletons.[1] Bertall had arrived from Bordeaux, where the vines were grown in fastidiously tended rows, and the contrast was startling, given the proximity of the two regions – even today Bordeaux and Cognac, both dependent on the export of a luxury product derived from the vine, remain worlds apart. In Cognac, he noted, "The vines seem to grow haphazardly, like cabbages or beets in a field. Their branches wander at whim, without stakes, laths or ties, and the general impression of a vineyard is of a vast carpet of greenery, which is not dulled, as it is elsewhere, by the powdery grey tints of the stakes or posts intended to support the vine and its fruit."

This neglect extended to the wine-making. The growers did not even bother to de-stalk the bunches of grapes, which were crushed either mechanically or by the peasants' feet. It was all rather casual. But it did not matter much. As he pointed out, the wine was merely an intermediate product. What mattered was the cognac, especially the older stuff, and he was lucky enough to meet an owner of some of the best.

M. Curlier, a partner of M. Courvoisier, who was becoming a major force in the market, introduced Bertall to a grower, M. Saunier, rich and sage like those who dined with the Monnets every Saturday. "A small, grizzled man, completely tanned, baked and baked again by the sun; his face was wrinkled as a dried grape. His slim face, sharp and fine like a fox's muzzle, like some Norman countenances, is illuminated by small clear grey eyes, shining with intelligence and good-will." He was modestly dressed, and even his precious *pressoir* and still were "old, covered with a sheen resulting from long years of use". M. Saunier was not a superficially worldly man. He suspected Paris: he had only been there once and regarded it merely as the refuge for local ne'er-do-wells, one of whom had been shot as a Communard; another had been transported for his part in the same revolutionary uprising. This provincial outlook and modest exterior concealed a fortune (estimated by Bertall at two million francs) in old cognac, which M. Saunier was in no mood to sell. "Keep your money, I'm keeping my casks," he told M. Curlier. He was not alone in his wealth. Twenty years earlier Vizetelly had noted that "the peasantry

[1] His book was republished by Bruno Sepulchre in 1983 and quoted in his *Le Livre du Cognac: trois siècles d'histoire*, Hubschmidt & Bouret, Paris, 1983.

of the *arrondissement* of Cognac are the richest in all France. Some few are worth as much as sixty thousand pounds sterling."

He was not alone. In the words of Jacques Chardonne "their character, formed by continuous relationship with nature, its constancy and its caprices, remains unchanging . . . the Champagnauds [the inhabitants of the Grande Champagne] remain amongst their vines. They remain peasants, because that's what they want. But they are rich, and know it better than anyone. They send their sons to a grammar school and their daughters to the convent; they will become mothers, fine and discreet, capable of running a house they will scarcely ever leave."[2]

This general prosperity was about to be destroyed by the phylloxera louse. In 1871 and 1872 the plague had become firmly established on the dry uplands and in the valley of the Charente. It spread outwards from Cognac itself, speeded by a dry year in 1873 – the louse did not like water. Indeed, it could be exterminated by flooding the vineyards, but that year it first got a grip on the grapes in the Champagnes. By the next year it had spread to the Charente-Inférieure. Once established, the pace of its spread was frightening. On July 7, 1874 the *Sous-Préfet* of Jonzac declared that all was well. Ten days later he reported the first outbreak; by September a number of villages had been hit; and by the next year 1,250 hectares/3,000 acres had been ravaged. The relatively wet summers of 1876 and 1877 came too late to save most of the area's vines.

Ironically, the louse was almost welcomed at first, for the frantic planting of the 1860s had outstripped even the increasing demand of the British buyers. Within little more than a decade the situation had been completely reversed. As the table on p. 106 shows, the size of the vineyard, which had reached a peak in 1877 at over 280,000 hectares/700,000 acres, dropped by over three-quarters in the following six years and by the 1890s was down to an average of 47,000 hectares/116,000 acres, a mere seventh of its high point.

When Bertall visited M. Saunier the magnitude of the disaster had become all too apparent. Even in untouched areas he noticed the telltale signs that the "little louse" had begun its destructive work: "Here and there, unhappily, a few stains, yellow or earth-coloured, had appeared and darkened the carpet of greenery." Once the louse had taken hold the

[2] Jacques Chardonne, *Chronique Privée de l'an 1940*, Stock, Paris 1941

damage was appalling: "We easily pulled up a stump whose roots, frayed, blistered, destroyed, had retained neither their strength nor their life." These were not isolated outbreaks. On both sides of the road between Cognac and Jarnac they saw "a stretch five miles long and two miles wide, where the devastation was so complete that the roots were fit only to burn, and the harvest did not produce a single grape". Within a decade the stocks of growers like M. Saunier had been exhausted. Thousands of growers like him would never again know the prosperity they had enjoyed in the imperial years of the 1860s.

Size of Cognac vineyard

(Including vines destined for other purposes and vineyards not in production)

Date	hectares
1788	156,000
1877	282,667 – last year before the phylloxera
1880	233,110
1885	85,240
1893	40,634 – low point
1913	74,000
1926	77,000 – interwar peak
1939	63,431
1946	59,219
1959	64,114 – before new planting rights were granted
1976	110,331 – post-phylloxera peak. Start of arrachages
1997	85,495 – plan to adapt the vineyards
2001	80,487

6

The Biggest Disaster

"There are regions where the collective memory stops short at the war of 1914–8; others, like the Vendée, stop at the Revolutionary wars; so phylloxera serves as a full stop in the collective memory of the Charentais. There is before and after; before implies halcyon days, the Golden Age; after implies the hard grind of daily reality. For many years after the crisis, the word 'phylloxera' remained the ultimate threat hurled at naughty children, while many growers preserved a row of old vines 'out of friendship', in the same way that you keep a family souvenir".[1]

François Julien-Labruyère the author of these words knew what he was talking about. His family was affected, as he described in *A la recherche de la Saintonge*.[2] His great-grandfather was a notary who committed suicide because of his financial problems. For eighty years some growers ostracized the family because they had lost the money they had deposited with him – in the absence of a proper rural banking system the notaries acted as bankers as well as lawyers. The growers lost not only their new-found prosperity but their independence as well. Phylloxera completely upset the long-established balance of power between the merchants and the growers, who were forced to sell their precious stocks in order to survive. The crisis taught them a lesson which has lasted to this day, for many of them are still reluctant to sell their older brandies. Many of the older generation still feel that the longer they kept them, the more valuable they become. "We can wait" was, and remains, their slogan.

Many tried to sell their land but, not surprisingly, found that the price had dropped to a mere one-tenth of its former value during the first years

[1] François Julien-Labruyère, *Paysans Charentais*, vol I, Rupella, La Rochelle, 1982.
[2] François Julien-Labruyère, *A la recherche de la Saintonge*, Maritime, Versailles 1974.

after the onset of the plague. Others looked for jobs in other parts of France, for there were precious few available in Cognac at a time when the whole socio-economic structure was disrupted. In 1873, 2,000 coopers had been employed in 200 workshops in the town; ten years later there were ninety-three workshops employing a mere 321 workers. The growers could live off their stocks for a few years but had no financial reserves left to pay the costs of replanting, so most of them had to sell their precious stills and market the produce of their grapes as wine, not as cognac. The mobile stills they were forced to use could not be guaranteed to make spirits of the delicacy and quality required by the buyers.

The merchants were better off, though not much. Hennessy's profits fell to nothing and it took the rest of the century to recover to the levels of the 1870s. Boutelleau, the family firm of the novelist Jacques Chardonne, was saved only by the removal of his father as manager and the support of its bankers. Not surprisingly, the old fear that once customers lost the habit of buying a specific drink they would not easily be recaptured proved true, partly because phylloxera sent the price of cognac soaring and made it, for the first time, purely a luxury beverage.

The Cognaçais, like the Bordelais, tend to pin all the blame on the pest. Preoccupied with their own troubles, they ignore the world slump which afflicted other luxury industries at the same time. A wave of protectionism, set off by the tariffs imposed by the French government in 1892 – which undid all the good work done by the Free Trade Treaty thirty years earlier – helped to prolong the slump effectively until after World War II, just as it did in Bordeaux.

Phylloxera transformed the shape as well as the size of the Cognac vineyard, for it was simply not worth replanting the outer areas. The most dramatic example was in the far north of the vineyard, in the Deux-Sèvres, which had nearly 24,000 hectares/59,000 acres under vines as late as 1882. Twenty years later the figure was down to 6,300 hectares/15,500 acres, and today the department has virtually no vines at all. These outlying areas, which in any case had never produced very good cognac, soon found their true vocation as dairy farms. By the end of the century the number of cows in the region had trebled and Charentais butter, in particular, had become renowned through the efforts of a number of pioneering agricultural cooperatives. The rest of Cognac had to struggle to return to the only product it knew, but progress was slow.

Replanting in the very special conditions of the Charente was a painful and costly process. Elsewhere in France the growers rapidly took to vines grafted on to American rootstock immune to the louse. But in the Charente a stubborn lobby fought for more than a decade to avoid this solution, pinning its faith on chemical remedies, notably the injection of sulphur-based compounds into the soil. These chemicals were both expensive and unsatisfactory, since they never completely eradicated the pest and the treatments were seemingly endless. In 1877 a group of growers headed by André Verneuil of Segonzac, one of the region's most heroic figures, sent the first of a series of missions to the USA to discover rootstocks suitable for grafting on to the Charente's precious Folle Blanche and Colombard vines. It was ten years later that they finally discovered the solution in Texas, where a pioneer viticulturalist, T.V. Munson, had found a suitable wild vines species, *Vitis berlandieri*. His nursery at Denison on the Red River was discovered by a mission headed by Paul Viala, the professor of viticulture at France's leading vinous academic institution at Montpellier. The Cognaçais were properly appreciative. The town is twinned with Denison and in 1988 a plaque was erected in the Station Viticole in Cognac dedicated to the memory of Thomas Volney Munson.

Fortunately for the Charente, the old habits of communal solidarity had not died out. The merchant families, who alone had the funds, found that, if properly handled, the American rootstocks would thrive even in the Champagnes, although at first it had been thought that the grafted stocks were unsuitable for the soils because they were liable to be choked by the chalk in the soil, a malady described as *chlorose* ("chlorosis").

At first the vines were grafted in the vineyard. But the growers found that they could not graft the plants themselves and had to buy their vines at the special nurseries which sprang up all over the *département*, many of which were run by dubious characters who sold inferior, albeit higher-yielding varieties. But soon more reputable specialists took over, most of them based, now as then, at Nercillac north of Cognac, where the humidity of the river valley provided particularly suitable conditions. In 1889 they even set up a viticultural research station, the first in France, to help with the reconstruction. It was run by a young man, Louis Ravaz, a pioneer of scientific viticulture and a leading missionary for grafted vines, who was only twenty-six when he was appointed.

When the Charentais did come to replant, they did so in an unprecedentedly scientific fashion. Cultivation was rationalized. Where previously the vines had been planted higgledy-piggledy but often very close together (with only one metre/thirty-nine inches between the rows), the new vineyards left enough room for a horse, or ox-drawn plough. Before phylloxera, planting was simply a matter of bending a branch into the ground and letting it take root. This was clearly impossible with a grafted vine. The Charentais found another variety, the St-Emilion, which came to dominate the area as the Folle Blanche had done before the plague. But the St-Emilion produces cognacs that are less floral, less aromatic, less characterful, than those distilled from the Folle Blanche. Moreover, the change widened the contrast in quality – and thus price – between brandies made in the Fins Bois and those from the Champagnes. So the region's products, like its economy, suffered a transformation unique in France, for elsewhere the same varieties were planted to replace those destroyed by the vine louse.

We can appreciate the pain and expense involved from a description of Malaville, a village in the Grande Champagne, written by the local school-teacher in 1901.[3] He painted a depressing picture. Forty years earlier Malaville had had 800 inhabitants: by 1901 the number was down to 633 – and as elsewhere in the Cognac region, many of these were newcomers from other parts of Poitou, filling the gap left by former inhabitants who had fled to the towns. Whereas vineyards had previously been worth 4,800 francs a hectare, by the turn of the century many were on the market at between 600 and 900 francs. The pay of domestic servants had fallen by half, "in addition to their keep, grudgingly allowed". The growers were no better off: "Innumerable growers in this corner of the Grande Champagne first tried, alas without any success, to replant the varieties which had brought such prosperity to our region." Even in 1898 over half the area which had been replanted with grafted stocks belonged to a handful of major proprietors. The smaller growers started up only at the very turn of the century. Only by then had they found how to graft plants for themselves, thus saving the (to them) immense cost of new vines.

³ J.A. Verdon, *Une commune rurale vue par son instituteur d'alors: Malaville en 1901*, Annales GREH, 1982.

The government did not help. The French Revolution had done away with many dues and duties on the production and transport of alcoholic drinks, but they were far too tempting a target to escape the taxman's attention for long. The first post-Revolutionary retail tax on spirits was introduced in 1824; it was sharply increased in 1860 from sixty to ninety francs per litre of pure alcohol then boosted again, to 156 francs. A tax increase in 1871 greatly helped to pay reparations to the Germans. But the biggest blow came in 1900 when the tax was increased by a further fifty per cent. As a result, the total tax burden borne by a bottle of spirits, including the local taxes payable in major cities, amounted to six times its original value. In a report to the *Chambre de Députés* in 1902 M. Clementel, one of Cognac's stoutest defenders, remarked: "The regions worst affected by the increase of taxes on spirits must surely be the Charente and Armagnac. The quality of the spirits they produce and their cost of production obliges the distillers from these regions to demand unnecessarily high prices, which effectively puts an end to their sale in France." Not surprisingly, throughout the twentieth century the Cognaçais were deeply convinced that they were being unfairly discriminated against. In the bitter words of Jean Lys, in his thesis[4] on the cognac business: "Spirits are products that have to pay dearly for their right to be consumed."

Virtually the only grower to be able to break free from the historic dependence on the merchants, which was the norm throughout the region, and exploit the superior quality of brandies from the Grande Champagne on a major scale was Pierre Frapin, the biggest landowner in the heart of the Grande Champagne, with a vineyard of over 300 hectares/740 acres. His granddaughter Geneviève Cointreau has traced the family back to the thirteenth century, and found a direct relationship with the great fifteenth-century novelist Rabelais, as well as estates in the Champagnes dating back to the seventeenth century. It needed unusual personal qualities, including pride in his brandies and what his granddaughter calls a desire to *valoriser ses propriétés* – add value, make the most of his land, and the fine brandies it produced. Nevertheless, he did not put all his brandies into his own brand; he remained as a friend and supplier to the Hennessys, and also sold to Courvoisier.

[4] Jean Lys, *Le Commerce de Cognac*, Université de Bordeaux, 1929.

Frapin is remembered by his grandaughter Geneviève as "a man of natural authority". But behind the mask of authority was someone who enjoyed taking risks, a fearless horseman. And when motor cars arrived in the Charentes he soon became notorious for his fast and reckless driving – he used regularly to cover the nineteen kilometres/twelve miles between his vineyards and Cognac in precisely twenty-two minutes. From the start he multiplied the stakes by going out of his way to distinguish himself from "*les Messieurs de Cognac*". His brochures, in excellent English, emphasized that "The Frapins' vineyards are in the very heart of the Grande Champagne, the finest growth in the Cognac region." Fortunately Frapin's stocks were sufficient for him to be able to advertise that his cognacs were "*authentique, extra*". They were indeed: within five years of founding the business he had won a major prize at a fair in New Orleans. This was only one of two dozen awards lavished on his brandies a success that was echoed in the recognition of the quality of the brandies produced by his neighbours on the sacred slopes above Segonzac in the late twentieth century.

7

The Good Name of Cognac

For a quarter of a century the Cognaçais were preoccupied with fighting phylloxera. When they finally emerged from their ordeal it was only to find that their markets had been largely usurped by a wave of "industrial", mass-produced grain spirits, some of them even daring to take the name of cognac. There was *cognac du Cap* from the Cape of Good Hope, *cognac d'Australie*, and many others. "Fraud stalks the land, powerful and unashamed," wrote a local author at the time; "it sows confusion in the mind of the consumer and the inferior quality of its products depreciates the market value of genuine cognac."[1] These spirits were so dangerous that, for the first time, a strong temperance movement sprang up in France. Unfortunately, its supporters did not distinguish between "healthy" drinks like cognac and "poisonous" ones like absinthe, a lack of discrimination which induced the state to increase taxes on spirits of all descriptions.

Cognac's competition came not so much from other *bouilleurs* ("distillers") but from large-scale, systematic commercial fraud. As Professor Alglave wrote in a legal thesis at the time, "fraud is not proportionate to the amount of the tax, but to the profits that can be made from each fraudulent act".[2] The imitators, including a fair number of locals, had moved in as soon as the phylloxera had struck. In the short term the fraudsters were of some benefit to Cognac – although no one in the town was ever going to admit the fact. Yet the wave of fraudulent cognacs which swept the world in the 1880s at least ensured that the customer base for brandies alleged to have come from around the town was not lost.

[1] Henri Boraud, *De l'Usage commercial du nom du Cognac*, Bordeaux, 1904.

[2] Quoted in Maurice Neon, *De la Crise viticole en Charente*, Paris, 1907.

These imitations filled the gap in the years when there was not enough of the real stuff. But by the end of the century production was returning to normal: the frauds had outlived their usefulness and were damaging the market, not only because of their poor quality but also by their sheer size. In 1900 the world was probably buying fifteen times as much "cognac" as the 5,500,000 cases actually being produced in the Cognac region itself.

The worst offenders were foreign, and therefore hard to prosecute. A local court condemned one German who set up under the name of "Albert Bucholz, Cognac". And Martell, together with Moët & Chandon, Benedictine, and Grande Chartreuse, managed to pursue one delinquent, whose premises in Barcelona were found to contain copies of their labels, "bold and widespread forgeries, carried out with rare skill". The fraudster, M. Rapau, fled to Bordeaux and was duly sent down for a year. But in most countries the Cognaçais were helpless. In Italy, for instance, the French found that they could sell little or no cognac. By contrast, the Italians themselves exported fifty times as much so-called cognac as they imported. In the words of an official French diplomatic report: "The Italians lowered the reputation of our product by the low, inferior quality of what they sold and by the price war against which we could have struggled only by selling diluted industrial alcohol under the name of cognac."

The worst offenders of all were the Germans. As early as 1892 the Cognaçais were complaining about brandies "chemically fabricated in Germany, employing essences of every description including those most harmful to public health". The German government actively encouraged imports of wine rather than brandy, which paid twenty-seven times the amount of duty levied on wine (fortified wines paid even less, half the duty on ordinary wines). So German merchants, then as now, would import fortified wines (vins vinés) into Germany strengthened with industrial alcohol or even grape brandy. Once it was over the frontier, the Germans promptly renamed the product "cognac", for the customs documents that accompanied it were clearly marked with the name of the area it was produced. In another widespread fraud, shiploads of industrial alcohol were sent from Hamburg, touched at a French port, and returned duly baptized.

The Cognaçais fought back, in the law courts at home and abroad, and in the field of international diplomacy; they even fought against the lexicographers. Not unreasonably, the town council protested against the definition of cognac in the great dictionary of M. Littré: "A brandy from Cognac, and thus by derivation, an excellent brandy." Although the Cognaçais blamed foreigners for most of their troubles, unscrupulous merchants from all over France would also set up postboxes in Cognac with their names on them, arrange for someone to re-direct the letters addressed to them, and thus establish legal residence. By 1889 it was reckoned that 179 firms were operating this one type of fraud alone.

The growers and the merchants, either individually or through the Chamber of Commerce, hoped that the French courts would prove an adequate defence, basing their case on a miscellany of laws. Article 1382 of the Civil Code stated firmly: "Anything done by anyone which causes an injury to anyone obliges the guilty party to make amends"; and the Cognaçais hoped to follow the Champenois, who had turned a law of 1824 to their advantage by extending the protection it provided to the name of their region to its best-known product. But the judges let Cognac down. In 1886 a court in Bordeaux ruled that one M. Perpezat, a Bordeaux-based merchant, could label his offerings "Old Brandy Perpezat et Cie Cognac". The Cognac region, it said, extended to Bordeaux because merchants based in that city sold it. After that it was relatively useless for a court in Douai to rule that cognac was a "special spirit, whose qualities derived from the soil which produces it", condemning a local man on the grounds that the "special soils" did not extend all the way to the Pas de Calais.

For a short time the tensions produced the sort of conflict between growers and merchants which affected most French wine-growing regions (including Champagne) in the years before World War I. As in the rest of France the growers in Cognac were wholeheartedly in favour of the government's attempts to stamp out frauds. In Cognac the growers even demanded an export tax combined with a state monopoly for the sale of spirits in France itself. The merchants were naturally wary of the tax on exports and the effective nationalization of their domestic trade, an attitude the suspicious growers took as additional proof that they benefited from the sale of fraudulent spirits. The merchants then brought up reinforcements: they recruited the thousands of workers involved in ancillary trades, from glass to cooperage, who depended on the cognac trade, and organized their own mass demonstrations against the proposals.

The growers in Cognac, however, bore only a superficial resemblance to those involved in radical demonstrations elsewhere in France. They were not only farmers, they were also distillers, *bouilleurs de cru*. So, of course, were millions of other French farmers, who in other regions constituted the wine-growers' worst enemy. For these other *bouilleurs* were using lesser raw materials, like pears, apples, grain, potatoes or beetroots, to produce rough, raw hooch to be consumed at home or supplied illicitly to cafés throughout France. By contrast even the humblest peasant in Cognac was distilling a noble (and expensive) spirit designed for a discerning, generally foreign, buyer. So, in the long run, the Cognac growers were bound to break ranks with growers elsewhere and support the merchants. They were also naturally opposed to the over-generous rights granted to the *bouilleurs* in non-wine-growing regions, who in 1902 accounted for over three-quarters of the spirits produced on a domestic scale in France. These "back-yard distillers" formed a political lobby that was sufficiently powerful to block the controls introduced by successive governments until the 1950s. The growers even launched a magazine called, significantly, *Le Vrai Cognac*, and in 1925 another called *le Paysan*.

For the region still enjoyed a proper community spirit. In 1909 the Minister of Finance, one M. Cochéry, had proposed that every bottle of cognac should carry a guarantee bearing the name of the merchant who had supplied it. In theory the measure was designed as a weapon against frauds, but everyone in Cognac took it merely as a tax in disguise, since the state would have taken ten centimes merely for stamping each bottle as authentic. The proposed "guarantee" triggered off a splendidly dignified mass protest led by Edouard Martell, James Hennessy, the Mayor of Cognac Gaston Briand, a leading grower, and M. Roullet, the President of the "Syndicat de defence du commerce des eaux-de-vie de Cognac".

All French producers, not only the Cognaçais, quickly realized that domestic legislation could never provide adequate protection. At the Universal Exhibition of 1878 the French raised the subject of international protection for trademarks. A first congress on the subject in Paris in 1883 proved ineffectual, but seven years later the Convention of Madrid was signed by a number of major powers. Article IV, in particular, provided legal protection to "regional trademarks for products derived from grapes", which included products manufactured from grapes like cognac and Champagne. The Treaty, including the precious Article IV, was speedily ratified by the French and applied when prizes were awarded at the 1900 Paris Exhibition. The precedent was followed by the St Louis Exhibition of 1904 – the one immortalized in the famous Judy Garland film *Meet Me in St Louis* – where the judges ruled that cognacs were a class apart, not to be compared with lesser spirits.

Unfortunately for the French, not many authorities were as understanding as those in St Louis. The two major empires of Germany and Austria-Hungary ignored it, and even the British played them false for a while. A judge ruled that the Convention did not apply in Britain because the Treaty had not yet been ratified by Parliament. The French naturally assumed that the ruling was biased and that His Majesty's judges could be relied upon to bend the law to protect local interests – those of the producers of British brandy, that historic enemy of the Cognaçais. But in the long run Article IV served its purpose. Eventually even the Germans had to give in. One of the few effective clauses in the Treaty of Versailles stipulated that the Germans should conform to the Convention of Madrid.

But even Article IV could never have worked without proper protection at home. This was more difficult for the Cognaçais than for the producers of other threatened products because their brand name was the same as that of the town itself. In the end it was that old enemy of the growers, the *Aides*, that came to their rescue. The *Aides* was a system devised in the seventeenth century to extract as much revenue as possible from the movement of goods of all kinds through France. "If it moves, tax it" was the motto, and as a result every ship- or cart-load carried with it a movement order, an *acquit* certifying that the proper dues had been paid. The *Aides* multiplied the cost of brandy as it was carried through France in the eighteenth century, yet 150 years later served as the basis for providing Cognac with proper legal protection. Ironically, the legal mechanisms now welcomed by the growers were precisely the same as those against which they had revolted in 1789. They had complained bitterly about the obligation to declare the quality and strength of the spirits they were going to distil; now they accepted the requirement as a guarantee against imitations.

Mere changes of constitution have little effect on the French bureaucracy, and the *acquit* emerged in a new form in 1872 at the dawn of the Third Republic as a *titre de transport* ("permission to move").

Unfortunately for the Cognaçais this form did not specify the geographical origin of the goods. Since then the growers and French legislators have worked long and hard to refine the definitions of the *acquits* and the mechanism protecting the producers from fraudulent imitations. More detailed versions of these *acquits* now pinpoint the place and conditions of production of all the proudest products of the French countryside – not just wines and spirits but also foods like Roquefort cheese as well. All these regulations are designed to protect the producers; the idea that they originated in an attempt to protect the consumers is a useful myth which the producers are clearly not going to deny.

It took nearly half a century to surround Cognac with a complete protective system. The first effective legislation, in 1905, was designed to suppress frauds committed when describing any agricultural product. Adulteration was defined as adding alien substances or omitting essential ones. But the legislation was so general that it took thirty-five more years to complete the legal framework. The first loophole found by the region's less scrupulous merchants was that authorized warehouses or cellars could house brandies made from lesser grapes grown in nearby regions like the Vendée or the Gironde. This gap was plugged by a new law which came into force in 1909. It was this piece of legislation which, over 200 years after the superiority of "coniack brandy" had first become apparent, belatedly gave legal recognition to *Eau-de-vie de Cognac*. This was enshrined in the famous *Appellation d'Origine*, the guarantee not of quality but of geographical provenance.

In 1919 these *Appellations d'Origine* were provided with greater protection by a law making it a criminal fraud to pretend that any imitation which did not meet the standards historically associated with the product – *les usages locaux loyaux et constants* ("local, honest and habitual usage") – could be prosecuted. These were further refined a couple of years later when it was ruled that only caramel, oak shavings, and 3.5 per cent of sugar could be added to the spirit. And in 1929 cognac's special status was recognized when it was allocated its very own *acquit jaune d'or*, its "golden identity card", to distinguish it from lesser wines and spirits; this accompanies even the smallest quantity of cognac when it moves on to the public highway. Fraud at the vineyard itself was supposedly prevented by regulations forcing growers to declare the size of their holdings and, before every harvest, the quantity they were going to ferment and distil. A law passed in 1900 ensured that every still was registered and duly hallmarked.

It took the whole miserable postwar period to refine the legal description of cognac. This was no mere legal technicality. Throughout the 1920s Hennessy – and, to a lesser extent, Martell and Bisquit – were battling against Chinese imitations. They paid informers and even thought of hiring private detectives to increase the number of prosecutions they brought in the law courts. Some agents preferred to take on lesser-known brands because they were less likely to be imitated. Appropriately enough, it was the question of ageing that took the longest to regulate. In 1924 the Australians had protested against the only evidence the merchants could provide of the age of their brandies – a certificate signed by the mayor of Cognac. After the end of Prohibition the Americans queried the authenticity of brandies being sold as five, ten, twenty or even 100 years old, and in the 1930s a system was devised to ensure that the age of every lot of cognac was registered.

Another major gap in the regulations was even more basic: double distillation. It was only in 1935 that a decree was issued confirming that "real cognac" had to be distilled twice. This was designed to counteract a legal ruling which had greatly upset the Cognaçais. In 1930 the Fédération des Viticulteurs Charentais, worried by the increase of continuous stills, brought a case to prove that double distillation was required to produce true cognac. But the local court decided that brandies could be called cognac even if distilled only once, provided that the wine came from the correct region. The decree went on to say that cognac must be distilled only to seventy-two degrees Gay Lussac to prevent distillers from producing high-strength brandies which would lack the flavours extracted at lower strengths. This measure put an end to the irregular forms of distillation used even by reputable firms since the continuous still had been developed in the early nineteenth century.

There was one curious exception to the rule. It applied only to brandies distilled on the French mainland. Distillers on the Iles de Ré and d'Oléron were allowed to distil once only; but they were permitted to call their result "cognac" and nothing more. They could not use any of the sub-appellations, not even Bons Bois, and recently they too have been forced to distil all their cognac twice.

Double distillation was one instance where the law was merely providing backing for the historic norm. The same applied to the 1936 definition of the varieties of grape that could go into a bottle of cognac. In 1927 high-yielding hybrid varieties had been banned, and nine years later the varieties were divided into those that could form the bulk of the production and "supporting" varieties. To no one's surprise, only three principal varieties were allowed – Folle Blanche, St-Emilion, and Colombard – and five others – Sémillon, Sauvignon, Blanc Ramé, Jurançon Blanc, and Montils – which could form only ten per cent of the total.

During the 1930s the Cognaçais defined their boundaries more precisely. A commission of inquiry was appointed which included such well-respected local figures as Robert Delamain and Gaston Briand. In contrast to other parts of France, where the process was accompanied by the most frightful squabbling, they soon agreed on boundaries between the sub-appellations, Grande and Petite Champagne, Borderies, Fins Bois, and Bons Bois. The lack of argument was not just a tribute to the members of the Commission but also a recognition of their generosity. Like Lacroix eighty years earlier, they followed the administrative boundaries rather than the more refined definitions established by Coquand or Ravaz. In theory, as Robert Delamain put it, all the legislation did was to "purely and simply legalize the map of the different *crus* then in use". Unfortunately the new legislators accepted the generosity of the law of 1909 which had harked back to the far greater acreage of vines before phylloxera, and in the case of the Grande Champagne were based on administrative maps, for the appellation covered the whole canton of Cognac, which included the rich soils of the Charente river valley. So they naturally left room for argument – particularly over the Petites Champagnes d'Archiac. These are on the wrong side of the river Né to be called Grande Champagne but can produce undeniably finer cognacs than the alluvial plain of the Charente which was included in the Grande Champagne because it was in the canton of Cognac.[3]

Boundaries were one thing; age posed another set of problems. In 1933 a group of merchants suffering from the effects of the slump passed off brandies from the 1930 and 1931 vintages as "Grande Champagne

---

[3] "Fine Champagne" was also defined, as a cognac containing at least fifty per cent spirit from Grande Champagne.

1811". The locals took immediate action, but only on July 4, 1940 did the civil court at St Jean d'Angely confirm that age was an essential element in the legal description of cognac and that cheating would be subject to the same penalties as other frauds. Amazingly, this crucial judgment was handed down just after the Armistice, when the roads of France were choked with refugees and, supposedly, the whole of France's administrative mechanism had ground to a halt. By the time the Germans arrived at Cognac all the conditions defining cognac had been established, first by trial and error, human effort, and happy accident over several hundred years, then belatedly by French legislation.

8

Struggle

The aftermath of phylloxera placed enormous commercial and financial demands on the merchants. They needed to recapture the markets they had lost, while only the bigger ones had access to the bank credit required to improve their estates and to buy and hold the stocks formerly stored by the growers. Fortunately banks flocked to Cognac in the last twenty years of the century, led by the then privately owned Banque de France, which established a branch in the town in 1882. The credit was vital. Before the plague Hennessy had held in stock only enough cognac to supply its customers for six months. After 1880 it held enough for up to six years' sales. Sales had dropped, but by only twenty per cent – from an average of 290,000 hectolitres in the 1870s to about 250,000 in the following decade, a drop far less severe than the slump in production.

They then, quite literally, built round their stocks, erecting the first major industrial buildings the Cognaçais had ever seen. By 1892 the *Revue Periodique Mensuelle* found it natural to include a survey of the Martell establishment in its series on major industrial undertakings. It informed its readers that Martell's still-room was fifty metres/164 feet long and that each of its four stills held six hectolitres – six times the previous average, for phylloxera seems to have heralded a major attempt to replace "domestic" scale stills with "industrial" ones. Martell, said the article, had been forced to become a distiller in its own right. It had to defend itself against "frauds on the part of unscrupulous growers; and that is why its purchasing service is so sophisticated and why Martell possesses a laboratory so well equipped with apparatus and instruments" – a far cry from the informality of Vizetelly's day, less than forty years earlier. The business had suddenly become modern and capital-intensive. The three-storey *chai au coupage* ("blending hall") was dominated by fifty immense cylindrical tuns, each holding 175 hectolitres. On the top floor the line of thirty-six tuns could hold 6,300 hectolitres and was connected by 300 metres/985 feet of piping. This "gigantic hall" was unique in Cognac.

The Martells and their competitors did not abuse their power – although Martell and Hennessy found that they were able to fix the annual price for each year's vintage and expect it to become the norm, a duopoly broken in 1954. They could have gone much farther and bought up the whole vineyard, but they did not. They extended their estates, to be sure, but they never aimed to be more than substantial country gentry. The principal reason, according to the late Maurice Hennessy, was that Cognac's leading families were aware of their civic responsibilities to the electors on whom they depended (the Martells, for instance, were ardent defenders of the rights of the *bouilleurs de cru*, the growers who distilled their own cognac). They obviously felt they had a leading role to play in the region, but they did not want to own it. Politically, indeed, the region remained loyal to the Napoleonic tradition. Until his death in 1907 the electors of Cognac remained faithful to Gustave Cuneo d'Ornano, an absurd, moustachioed, theatrical but effective Bonapartist loyalist, although this does not seem to have had any very specific connotation. Chardonne for one claimed that "I have never understood what it meant to be called Bonapartist in Barbezieux." He was succeeded by Maurice Hennessy's father, James.

As the description of its "factory" shows, Martell was staging something of a comeback. It had bought stock so aggressively that sales were not reduced by phylloxera. Its new installations were also required to increase the proportion of its sales which were despatched in bottles. According to some rather dubious 1894 export figures Hennessy was still outselling its great rival three to one abroad, but Martell was already selling ninety per cent of its output in bottle, as against a mere half for Hennessy, and was also stealing a march at home. Martell painstakingly built up its distribution network throughout France, and until the late twentieth century was a major force in the domestic market. For both at home and abroad the Firino-Martells were prepared to get down to the grinding hard work of selling. The late Jacques de Varenne of Augier remembered going around Liverpool with Michel Firino-Martell. As he says, Martell "was quite prepared to knock on doors, and every evening we would go round the pubs to see if they sold his cognac". In lean times the Martells' reputation for being rather dour and plodding, for acting as *l'epicier du coin* (the corner grocer), served them well.

By contrast, the Hennessys had acquired some rather grand metropolitan habits during the golden years. "James Hennessy thought it was really rather vulgar to bother with the French market," says Alan de Pracomtal, his great-nephew and the former chairman of Hennessy. As a result the Hennessys were virtually unrepresented in their native country except in the smarter bars and restaurants. They invested elsewhere, building a substantial block of flats looking out on the Seine near the Pont de l'Alma. Craftily they donated the small triangle of lawn between the building and the river to the authorities to ensure that it was never built on, thus guaranteeing the view of the river for family members, some of whom still live there. Even before he succeeded d'Ornano, James spent much of his time in Paris. When his wife died in 1910 he turned his back on the house and the town associated with her and spent only a few days each month in Cognac. In the later half of the nineteenth century both the Hennessys and the Martells moved from living "over the shop", as it were, to living in country estates near the town. At the extreme, Jacques Hennessy, who owned nearly half the family firm, lived exclusively in Paris where he died in 1928, not having left the city for the previous twenty years. According to Janet Flanner (Genet of the New Yorker) "For eighty-nine years he inhabited Paris as a bachelor and bon viveur . . . he never took any exercise, never walked if the effort took him away from carpets . . . His eyesight remained remarkable: he never wore spectacles, claiming to be able to distinguish naturally between a blonde and a brunette."[1]

The merchants' attempts to impose themselves on the outside world were greatly helped by a revolution in the art of bottle-making. Until nearly the end of the nineteenth century bottles were hand-blown by men whose lungs and throats routinely suffered permanent damage from physically blowing thousands of bottles from molten glass. "Beside every glassworks they built," wrote Max de Nansouty in 1901, "they had to layout a cemetery which was never idle." The hero of the revolution was one Claude Boucher, a Cognaçais of humble origins, who invented a machine

---

[1] Janet Flanner, *Paris was Yesterday*, Angus & Robertson, London, 1973.

for blowing glass. Previously the only machine-made glass bottles seem to have been inferior, moulded varieties.

Boucher remains a local hero, although not all the firms bought from his newly established factory. In the 1890s the Martells brought their uniquely shaped bottles all the way from Montluçon, 320 kilometres/200 miles away, and contemporary enthusiasm did not extend to his social position. As Jean Monnet remarked: "Although he had literally revolutionized the glass industry, and thus the marketing of Cognac, in local society he always remained within the ranks of the suppliers." Monnet knew what he was talking about. His grandfather had been a small grower – Maurice Hennessy remembered how well he played the fiddle at village weddings – and it had been his father who had climbed into the ranks of the merchant class. And climb it was: "Cognac society was divided into two very distinct classes: on the one side there was the merchant class, and on the other everyone else, which in practice meant mostly suppliers."

Boucher's invention provided a colossal boost to the merchants' efforts to impose their brand names on the world. This was symbolized by the confrontation in Britain between Martell and the Gilbey family, then far and away the dominant force in the market with 2,000 licensed agents throughout the country. At the end of the 1860s the Gilbeys tried to force Martell to supply cognac for their own "Castle" brand. Martell refused, and for several years the Gilbeys contemplated his plight with some smugness. But by the 1880s they were forced to stock his cognac, not under their name (and thus on their terms) but under his, even though in the meantime Sir Walter Gilbey's favourite daughter had married into the Hine family. Martell, Hennessy, and the other Cognaçais were benefiting from a worldwide trend towards brand names which, in the 1880s, established the major brands of Scotch whisky and Champagne as well as of cognac.

The threat from blended Scotch whisky, containing as it does so high a proportion of cheaper "industrial" grain whisky, proved to be merely a foretaste of the problems created for cognac in the 1970s and 1980s. At the time it was naturally perceived as serious, leading even the lordly Hennessys to advertise their wares for the first time – the firm also had to sell in lots of a mere ten cases, a far smaller quantity than the minimum quantities on which it had previously insisted.

But there was another, parallel, trade in bulk brandies: at least one firm boasted that it had installed special equipment for creating and designing brands in buyers' own names – a practice which foreshadowed the "buyers' own brands" now sold by retail chains the world over. These are sold largely on price, whereas before the introduction of buyer's "own brands" were those sold by the smarter wine merchants, who were emphatically not competing on price.

Business remained poor, and the Cognaçais had to search for markets all over the world – Berrault's annual provided exchange rates for dozens of currencies from Turkey to Uruguay. Hennessy was already established in China and was the first firm to set up in Japan as early as 1868. Most youngsters from Cognac families spent their youth tramping around the world diversifying their sales, and their efforts did bear some fruit. Jean Monnet found it perfectly natural to be sent to London at the age of sixteen for a two-year apprenticeship before embarking on a prolonged tour of Canada when barely out of his teens. Even Jacques Chardonne, a most unsuitable salesman, was sent to Britain and Germany to sell the cognacs of his family's firm, Boutelleau. Monnet had already learned to think of the world as a string of clients to be visited: "If that took us to Singapore or New York that was scarcely felt as a privilege attached to our profession because it was our primary responsibility." It was a good education for a statesman in addition to the training in languages and modern politics absorbed at the family table. Monnet again:

I went to Egypt where I learned other forms of persuasion. I would accompany our Greek agent from village to village. We visited the wholesalers, who bade us sit down, we drank coffee while they busied themselves with their own business. We learned that you had to wait for the appropriate moment. At a certain point Chamah, the Greek, decided that we must bring the matter to a head. At that point he would write in his notebook the quantity which he considered it reasonable for our customer to take, a figure which was never discussed. He had simply respected local customs. Later, in the East, I rediscovered the importance of time, which made me wonder sometimes whether Cognac was not in fact closer to Shanghai than to New York. In China, you had to learn to wait. In the United States you had to learn to persist. Two forms of

*patience to which cognac, itself the result of a certain length of time, pre-
disposes you so well.*

Before World War I a number of countries – Belgium, Holland, Sweden,
Denmark, Canada, India, Argentina and, to a lesser extent, the USA,
Russia, Norway, and Egypt, had all become substantial customers. But the
bulk of the exports went to two contrasting outlets, France's numerous
colonies, which took nearly fifteen per cent of the total, and Britain,
which took forty per cent. The colonials bought cheaply in cask, while
the British imported virtually all their brandy in bottle – and the major
exception, the early-landed brandies destined for long years in the docks,
was among the most valuable. Not surprisingly, fifty-five per cent of
Cognac's total export receipts came from Britain. Half-bottles of Martell
Three-Star could be found in millions of humble British medicine chests,
while the cognacs of Hennessy, like those of Hine and Delamain, were
largely confined to the aristocracy, who otherwise drank the cognacs sold
by their traditional wine merchants.

As markets grew more difficult, so the merchants' search for novelty
grew ever more frantic. By the turn of the century there were half a dozen
more or less standard qualities: One-, Two- and Three-Star, VO, VSO,
VSOP, and WSOP. The 1907 catalogue of the Army & Navy Stores in
London lists eight cognacs from Martell alone: X, XX, XXX, VO, VSO,
VSOP, ESOP ("guaranteed over forty years in cask"), and Extra ("guaranteed over fifty years in cask"). But this was not enough. In the museum in
Cognac there are bottles of every shape designed to take the buyer's fancy,
many of them on maritime themes in the shape of ships or sailors. The
merchants registered dozens of trade marks involving various combina-
tions of "Grande", "Fine", and "Champagne" brandies, as well as a rash of
dire-sounding mixtures, like "Le Coup de Jarnac", described as "Liqueur
hygenique à base de fine champagne". More logical was "Brandy Bark", a
"tonic elixir containing as chief ingredients genuine champaign brandy
and royal yellow bark". This was almost certainly that new wonder drug,
quinine. So "Brandy Bark" was probably the prototype of that modern
fad, brandy and tonic.

Other companies looked for specific markets: labels were registered
for a cognac to be sold in railway buffets, a "*Cognac des dames*", and
"pocket bottles" (each containing "Five glasses of excellent Cognac").
Other brands were topical. In 1876 Bellot's "National French Brandy

Company" had commemorated the 100th anniversary of the Independence of the USA. Ten years later Gabriel Marchand rushed out a new label designed to appeal to supporters of the popular insurgent General Boulanger; and in 1889 the anniversary of the French Revolution and the construction of the Eiffel Tower were duly acknowledged.

But one of their most powerful marketing tools and one of the most surprising, was the name of Napoleon. The imperial name was seized on as a guarantee of legitimacy, a pledge that the brandy was indeed from Cognac. The name started to spread in the first decade of the century, when the trade was still convalescent, when the Army & Navy Stores still felt itself obliged to say that all its brandies were "guaranteed grape spirit from Cognac district". The successful identification of the drink with the emperor is rather puzzling: for a century Napoleon remained an arch-villain in Britain, and he had never been a particular hero for the Cognaçais, whose affections had been exclusively lavished on his nephew, Napoleon III. Since the onset of phylloxera came soon after the deposition of the ruler associated with Cognac's Golden Years, it would have been natural to use his name, and not that of his uncle. Yet the connection was made with the first emperor, and it served its purpose. Even today the name provides a splendid sales weapon, especially in the Far East where the name of Napoleon is better known than that of cognac itself, and is especially associated with the image of virility and strength for which the drink has become profitably renowned in the East.

The weapon was used at three levels. The name was freely attached to any dusty old bottle of brandy. Even today the London salerooms still offer for sale bottles of so-called "Napoleon" brandy. These are usually labelled 1811, the "Year of the Comet", which remains embedded in the subconscious of the world of cognac. By now the cognacs are naturally rather awful. One was described to me as being like "the water you've washed your leather boots in".

The Napoleonic magic was sufficiently powerful to cover bottles labelled with the names of his first wife ("Imperatrice Josephine"), his house ("Maison de l'Empereur") his tragic offspring ("Le Roi de Rome"), and even events associated with the Emperor. One rather tactless label even celebrated "La Grande Armée", the army he led to its frozen fate in the Russian winter of 1812, although the contents of the bottles might well have come in handy on the army's retreat from Moscow.

Some merchants piled it on. A bottle of 1928 "Bonaparte" cognac from Croizet was "guaranteed to be the distillation of the fermented juice of fresh grapes produced in the Cognac area", and it is indeed a smooth and delicious cognac. These "Napoleonic" bottles were almost certainly phony. One clue is provided by the alleged date of bottling: this is often given as the first decade of the twentieth century, ninety years after the date the brandy was allegedly distilled. During the years 1900–11 the merchants bottled up any brandies they still had in stock and slapped "Napoleonic" labels on them, for at the time any old cognac was called "Napoleonic" after Napoleon III, in whose reign it had been distilled.

At a much humbler level the name Napoleon was, and is, attached to a particular quality (oddly enough not the best), the one above VSOP. But it was, indeed is, Courvoisier, which has benefited most from the identification. For nearly 100 years the firm has used the name and the picture of the emperor, in a brilliant and sustained piece of image-building. To be fair, it was perfectly reasonable, for Courvoisier did have a genuine Napoleonic connection. The firm's founder, Emmanuel Courvoisier, was a native of the Jura, near the Swiss frontier. He had based himself in Paris, cultivating the business available at Napoleon's Imperial court, even supplying the emperor himself. His partner, Louis Gallois, was the builder of one of the first warehouses for wines and spirits which transformed Bercy, a dreary suburb on the eastern outskirts of Paris, into the centre of the French trade in basic wines (la grosse cavalerie: figuratively "plonk", literally "the heavy mob"). Their sons transferred the brandy business to Jarnac, and in the 1840s Courvoisier's son bought out his friend and partner. He retained the Napoleonic connection by supplying spirits to the court of Napoleon III. The business passed to his nephews, the Curlier brothers (it was a M. Curlier who had shown the Parisian artist Bertall around in 1877). In 1909 the Simons, Anglo-French wine merchants, bought Courvoisier. They were the first outsiders to buy into a major Cognac firm, and indeed since then the firm has always been something of an outsider. In 1927 they effectively transformed the brand by introducing the Napoleonic image, boasting that it was "the cognac of Napoleon" – they didn't say which one. The move helped transform the fortunes of the first firm and ensured that since then it has represented a permanent challenge to the domination of Martell and Hennessy.

The Simons were the exception, the only outsiders in a narrow, introverted world which had many parallels with the Chartronnais of
Bordeaux, another largely Protestant merchant oligarchy living surrounded by Catholic peasants in a major centre of Anglo-French trade.
The world of the Cognaçais was recalled by Jean-Frederic Gauthier-
Auriol, sitting in his study in the family house in the rue Saulnier a few
hundred metres from the river.[2] He was talking of the 1920s but could
just as well have been referring to pre-1914 Cognac:

> There were four employees in the office and one very important
> gentleman, the maître du chai. I remember well how the gabares were
> loaded: the workers from the warehouse loaded the cases on big wheel-
> barrows we called "twins". They also loaded cases on to horse-drawn
> carts: they were branded wooden cases – cardboard packaging was a
> revolution . . . My grandmother had a ladies' maid who stayed with
> her for forty years and a manservant she kept for forty-three years. Our
> governess ("la miss") came from England. At lunch we spoke English. If
> you spoke a word of French, they whisked the dessert past your nose . . .
> as I loathed caramel flan, when I saw it in the kitchen before lunch, I
> automatically spoke French! For me English was another native
> language . . . there wasn't a single merchant who hadn't spent a year's
> apprenticeship in England.

The Gauthiers' world was one large family (Gauthier's grandmother was a
Mlle. Delamain), and firmly, exclusively Protestant:

> The Protestants were like a plate of macaroni cheese: if you pulled one
> strand you brought with it the whole plate . . . we adhered to certain prin-
> ciples in our house: we went to the chapel every Sunday . . . my uncle
> Guy remained a bachelor. He had a mistress whom we called "the
> admiral" because she was the daughter of a Breton admiral; my grand-
> mother never allowed him to marry her. For she was Catholic and, what
> is more, she did not come from the same class as us.

Poor uncle Guy (but perhaps he never wanted to marry l'amirale in the
first place) was the very model of the all-round merchant-athlete. In later

---

[2] Reminiscences recorded by Catherine Petit in *Les Charentes: pays du Cognac*, ACE,
Paris, 1984.

life he was described by a British trade magazine as "A sturdy, vigorous, full-statured man, with a toothbrush type of moustache, slightly beetling brows", with "all the alertness, all the sprightliness of the trained athlete" – which he was. He held the French record for the 100 metres, and had been a rugby international. This was natural, for the Cognaçais were the most northerly French supporters of rugby football. Until the economies of the 1990s the major firms were quite prepared to take onto their staff any foreign rugby star imported to beef up the local XV in its efforts to rejoin the first division of the French rugby championship.

Life for a well-established merchant family could be temptingly easy. According to Gerald de Ramefort, who ran Otard for several decades after his family bought the business in 1930, the Otards were "more interested in public and social life than business, living like lords in the beautiful châteaux they bought around Cognac, or in their Paris apartments, and of course, they used to spend a lot of money". The biggest spenders were probably the family of Jules Robin, a firm that was as big as Martell and Hennessy in the late nineteenth century thanks to its virtual monopoly of the trade of cheaper cognacs with France's ever-growing empire. The older generation long remembered their gorgeous equipages and the state they kept.

World War I inevitably resulted in the mass of personal tragedies familiar to anyone who has ever read the endless lists of names of the "*Morts pour la Patrie*" in the tiniest of French hamlets. But apart from the absence of able-bodied men, it did not change the pattern of Cognac's life – although Meukow, one of Cognac's most reputable concerns, was seized because it had been owned by the German Klaebisch family.

By contrast, peace brought an avalanche of problems. The flood of legislation designed to protect the good name of the town did not help financially between 1918 and 1939. In France itself sales were badly affected by a tax on luxuries first imposed in 1917. This started at ten per cent but was raised to thirty per cent in 1924. The locals naturally complained: their drink was taxed, they said, at a higher rate than imported luxuries like furs and diamonds, which paid only ten per cent. Not surprisingly, the French turned increasingly to the mass of newly fashionable, and infinitely cheaper, wine-based apéritifs. Women were increasingly drinking in public, and they too turned to lighter, sweeter drinks.

Abroad the situation was even worse. The only consolation was the article in the Treaty of Versailles that obliged the Germans to recognize the name of cognac. But even this relief was temporary. By the mid-1920s the Germans' financial problems were so severe that they reduced their purchases for a whole generation. Elsewhere the prospects were almost unrelievedly gloomy. The Russian Revolution dealt a severe blow to the firms – especially Camus – which had specialized in sales there. A number of countries, Greece, Spain, Italy, and Portugal among them, protected their local wine and spirits makers with heavy import duties. These were a crucial factor: exceptionally, the Egyptian market remained healthy because duties were low. But the habit of heavy import duties spread to Argentina, whose economy had, in any case, declined dramatically after the war. Indeed the market in much of Latin America suffered from a similar combination of economic misfortune and increased duties, in a pattern that was to recur half a century later. In a few markets such as Holland, a reduction in sales volume did not involve too great a loss in cash terms because imports were increasingly in bottles. As always the cognac community fought an uphill battle against the forces of protectionism, at home and abroad, with James Hennessy launching a petition in favour of free trade in 1927.

Duties had always been a problem. Prohibition was a new terror. It wiped out the American market (although vast quantities were smuggled in through the tiny French-owned islands of St Pierre and Miquelon, south of Newfoundland). The custom spread to Canada and the Scandinavian countries. If sales were not totally forbidden, then they were channelled through state-run liquor boards with little interest in increasing sales. Their baleful influence can be felt to this day, although a small group of merchants – such as Tiffon and Larsen – have specialized successfully in supplying such markets. Even the British market suffered. The Cognaçais were still effectively on a "sterling standard", since many of their costs, like transport and insurance, were payable in pounds. After the war the franc was weak, which vastly increased their costs. And in 1920 the British Government suddenly imposed an additional thirty-three per cent duty on imported spirits. The effect was so severe that revenue from customs' duties dropped by half despite the increased rate of duty. As a result the increase was soon withdrawn. But the damage was done: by 1923 even the Germans were buying more cognac than the

British. In the years after the war British purchases were a mere sixth of the quantity they had taken in the golden days of Napoleon III, and under half of the only marginally less glorious days of Edward VII. Excise duties on all spirits had risen fivefold since 1914 and dashed any hope of a sales rebound after the duty increases were rescinded.

The mood in Cognac was naturally defensive. The most dramatic result was the agreement in 1922 between Martell and Hennessy, effectively to divide up the world between them. They were already used to working together: since the mid-nineteenth century they had set an agreed price for the cognacs they bought from the growers, a lead that was followed by the rest of the trade. The families had, of course, been connected by marriage and friendship ever since Napoleonic times, but fears that one side or the other would be dominant had prevented any formal business links. Maurice Hennessy's father had spent most of his time in Paris, leaving his son alone in Cognac. As a result the Martells became a second family to him: "I spent weekends with them in their house near Royan," he told me. "I had a room in their house. I remember leaving my gambling winnings in a drawer and finding them there untouched the following weekend. It was like home to me." The dramatic drop in the British market altered all that. Maurice himself was in Bogota at the time. He returned post-haste and talked his idea over with his friend, Paul Firino-Martell, who convinced his father and uncle of its soundness.

In a formal agreement designed to last twenty-five years they set up two new companies named Martell and Hennessy, in both of which the two families had shares. Each side took substantial shareholdings in the other; indeed they worked so closely that the post was opened in the same room. They then divided up the world between them. The Martells were allocated the crucial English market, which gave them an immense short-term advantage. The Hennessys retained their traditional Irish connection and in the longer term benefited greatly from the running start they enjoyed after the war in the Far East and the USA – even during Prohibition they could sell some cognac since their agent, Schieffelin, was a pharmaceutical company and so could sell limited quantities of "medicinal" brandy. The partners did not actually prohibit sales in each other's territories. Although Martell was granted a "privileged situation" in Britain, and indeed at one point had eighty per cent of the total market, the Hennessys retained an agent in Britain. In China, traditionally a Hennessy fief, the local agents got together in the 1920s to agree on a common price structure. Between the wars both families had relinquished active management of their businesses. Maurice Fillioux's father, Raymond (who had worked for Jean Monnet for a time), was responsible for a great deal of the Hennessy business, while at Martell distant relations – MM Castaing and Castillon – enjoyed a great deal of power.

The arrangement at least ensured the continuing supremacy of the two houses. In the 1920s, indeed, according to one authority,[3] there were only "two cognac firms of the first rank". Most of the others had suffered from one or other of the region's many problems. The Otards, for instance, had relied too heavily on the Latin American market. They had also got left behind. The last Otard, Marie-Thérèse, had married the Comte de Castellane, and they refused to change. Gerald de Ramefort put it bluntly: when their competitors began to sell their brandies in bottles under their own names, they did not follow the trend. "'We are not grocers,' they said loftily."

Less aristocratic houses also suffered. In the mid-1920s Jean Monnet was called back to Cognac from Geneva, where he had been one of the driving forces behind the fledgling League of Nations. As he wrote in his memoirs, "At Cognac I found a situation which was financially bad and psychologically worse. No sooner had I arrived than I met a friend at the Câfé du Chalet. 'I must talk to you,' he whispered, 'not here, but round the corner.' I had forgotten that side of life in the provinces. 'It seems that you are going into liquidation,' he whispered." Monnet established himself in a delightful little house a few miles outside the town and analyzed the problem. It was simple enough: because Monnet's father believed in quality and loved good cognac, he had accumulated enormous stocks of old cognacs, which he could not sell at a time when the fashion was for young spirits. So sales and working capital were precariously low: "You could go bankrupt in Cognac," he wrote, "despite having a good product and a well-respected brand name; it was enough to believe in what had always been, but was no longer true – the value of rarity and the danger of change. Many other firms were killed by their founders' obstinacy in preserving the practices that had earned them the esteem of a clientele

---

[3] *Lys, Le Commerce du Cognac*, Bordeaux, 1929.

that was both small and sophisticated." Monnet, anxious above all to prevent his father from suffering the same fate, arranged to exchange some of his oldest cognacs for younger, more saleable spirits.

As he himself admitted, Monnet was lucky. His stay coincided with a temporary resurgence in the business, and he left a sound enough enterprise in the hands of his relations before returning to the wider world. But, like almost everyone else in the business, he was on the defensive. They all retreated into their shells or like him, looked elsewhere. Members of the Delamain family had already made names for themselves as scholars, scientists, and amateur archaeologists investigating the region's numerous prehistoric remains. In the 1930s one brother, Jacques, made his name as an orchidologist (many small French orchids carry the family's name), another, Maurice, founded the famous Parisian publishing house of Stock – with his brother-in-law, the writer Jacques Chardonne, as his partner. Robert wrote the classic history of Cognac – a brilliant essay which largely ignores the commercial side of the story in which his family had played such an important role.

The only region where sales were showing signs of life was in the Far East, particularly China and Japan. In his analysis of the exports of cognac, Jean Lys attributed the increase to the fact that the local intelligentsia had returned from their education in France with a taste for the spirit. Hennessy was the market leader (despite problems with local imitations) and enjoyed considerable success with European expatriates as well as the locals. In 1921 Sincore & Co, the Harrods of Shanghai, was selling 500 cases a month, and M. Randon, Hennessy's agent, was adjusting his prices to ensure that Chinese restaurateurs could afford to put two bottles of cognac on a table seating six or eight diners (he also gave regular gifts to the best-known nightclub singers).

But the most significant event of the inter-war years was the arrival on the scene of André Renaud, one of the most fascinating and significant figures in the history of twentieth-century Cognac. In 1924 he took over the then near-bankrupt firm of Rémy Martin. In 1875 Paul Rémy Martin had inherited what appeared to be a flourishing business. Paul was a would-be country gentleman who spent a great deal of his own money in backing efforts to re-establish the vineyard. But he spent much more on the lavish transformation of the family château of Lignières, badly damaged by a fire in 1869. As the cost of Lignières mounted, so did the business decline. It did not help that Paul Rémy Martin distanced himself farther from the business. He moved the offices from Lignières to Cognac, a significant gesture enabling him to live the life of a country gentleman. The banks started to press and new finance was injected, hence Renaud's acquisition of what was by then virtually a bankrupt shell of a company.

Renaud was the classic son-in-law, husband of Pierre Frapin's only daughter, Marie, obviously the single most marriageable girl in the whole region. She is remembered as the classically retiring Catholic provincial lady, content to stay in the background and to devote herself to good works, mostly those organized by the church. But she had found a husband worthy of his father-in-law. He was her first cousin – their mothers were sisters – and had been born at a Frapin château, Barbotin, because it was the tradition for a mother-to-be to return to the maternal family.

By 1919, when he came back after World War I, Renaud had, as the family's official history puts it, "earned the right to marry Marie Frapin". For the forty years after the takeover of Rémy Martin until his death at the age of eighty-two in 1965, Renaud dominated the firm. The only colleague he respected was Maurice Auboin, a highly cultivated man. They shared an office, sat at desks opposite each other, talked long every day, for over twenty years until Auboin retired after World War II. Renaud was a curious mixture, a peasant rooted to the soil, a man who loved to ride through his vines. But first and foremost, he was an intellectual. Throughout his life he read ferociously – it helped that he required very little sleep – thoroughly enjoying an intellectual argument. For he had a doctorate in law, appropriately enough on the subject of how the law could help particular products based in specific localities defend themselves. It was probably of Renaud that Jacques Chardonne was thinking when he wrote "If a Champagnaud invites you to lunch . . . he will lead you to his library, where you will find the latest novel on the table and all the classics on the bookshelves."

Physically Renaud was not an imposing figure, rotund, with a small moustache, invariably wearing a trilby hat, summer and winter, indoors and out. Renaud was not vain, hating to have his photograph taken – yet he engaged the great photographer Robert Doisneau to produce a book for Rémy Martin, with text by another friend, the writer Louise de Vilmorin. One final, curious point about this remarkable man was his fatalism. He insisted that he wanted no memorial, no biography, he didn't want anything written about him after his death, which would, he said, mark the end.

In his business he is portrayed as the classic autocrat who worked his employees hard but looked after them when they were old or sick, the sort of provincial worthy who lunched punctually at midday – and he was impatient, to put it mildly, with any guest, however distinguished, who was a minute late. For quite a time after the takeover it was a small business with only thirty employees, many of whom had worked for the firm's previous owners. He worked them hard. Their day started at 7am – and God help late arrivals – and even when business was slack stopped a full twelve hours later. If orders poured in, then they stayed on, sometimes until 11pm. They worked a six-day week (sometimes extending into the Sabbath) with no thought of holidays. And, as the firm's history has it: "the firm was not well-known for the size of its wages", for Renaud believed that money spent on anything except increasing his stock of brandy was wasted. Outside his business he was never popular. His enemies – who grew in number with his success – saw in him a mere opportunist trying to extract the maximum possible benefit from the estates in the Grande Champagne owned by his wife's family.

In his business life his intellectual capacity was probably best demonstrated by his ability to isolate the crucial elements in a situation. During World War I he was, he said, far too brilliant to be wasted as cannon fodder, and remained a staff officer throughout the war, becoming very close to Raymond Poincaré, who later became Prime Minister and President of France. In addition to his cognac business Renaud was a remarkable stock market operator, while other investments included an interest in the Pathé film company and his support for the publisher Maurice Delamain.

He would clearly have preferred to go into business with his father-in-law – they remained close throughout their lives, would ride together through the vines every day, and the younger man would stop by on his way home from Cognac to seek advice and discuss the day's dealings. But family circumstances dictated otherwise. Pierre Frapin hoped that his son Albert could succeed him even though Albert was tubercular and unable to cope with the strains involved in running the family business. Yet his father never gave up hope that his son would recover sufficiently to take over the business, so would not let his son-in-law near it – although he allowed the younger man to use his stocks.

Renaud's most urgent need was a sales structure, inside and outside France. After Hitler had closed the German market Renaud tried to make the best of a bad job and to distil wine within Germany to make brandy. Renaud's partner in this venture was his German importer, the well-known firm of Sichel, a family which also had branches in London and Bordeaux. It was also the agent for Cointreau. This latter was a family firm which had made a considerable international success of its "triple sec" liqueur, based on a secret formula invented by a chemist in Angers on the Loire, in the mid-nineteenth century, from a secret blend of brandy and orange.

The Sichels naturally introduced Renaud to André Cointreau, head of the family firm, and the two Andrés quickly began to plan joint marketing companies in Europe – a highly original step at the time. But André Cointreau also gave his namesake the idea that to succeed you had to have a unique selling proposition. As Renaud told Cointreau at the time: "you're lucky, you don't have any competition".

It was natural for Renaud to concentrate on selling brandies labelled Fine Champagne, which he combined with the already-established name VSOP, long recognized as the quality immediately above the basic Three-Star level. He thus created "VSOP Fine Champagne", the type of cognac which has formed the base for Rémy Martin's fame and fortune ever since. VSOP Fine Champagne was one of those rare products which transformed a whole market. Indeed Renaud, personally the very anti-thesis of a brand manager, was one of the handful of business minds who pioneered the idea of a premium brand of spirits sold in large quantities. His initiative was typically arrogant, for Rémy was small, poor, and rela-tively unknown. Even in 1939 Rémy Martin was smaller than Frapin. His challenge was fundamental, for major firms have always refused to give exact ages of their brandies and equally refuse to define their place of origin.

To sell his doubly special product Renaud needed salesmen who would put up with his unappealing blend of stinginess, autocracy, and ingratitude ("it's okay" was the highest compliment he allowed himself to give). The key figure was Otto Quien. If Renaud was an archetypal Charentais, Quien was a truly international figure, half Dutch, half-

German, born in Shanghai and educated in Switzerland. He was descended from a family of Huguenots who had fled from France after the Revocation of the Edict of Nantes. Born in Shanghai of a Dutch father he had an unusually wide range of social contacts. Quien's father had set up a wine business in Bordeaux in the 1920s, but he was ruined in the aftermath of the crash of 1929. So in the 1930s, with a wife to keep (and soon a son, Patrick, who worked for Rémy Martin throughout his life), he had to find other work.

As a young man Quien spent six months of every year in Indonesia (then the Dutch East Indies) working for an uncle who owned a major wine and spirits business with substantial sales throughout the Far East. The colony naturally housed a large and thirsty population of Dutchmen, but Quien was the first person to exploit what later became a crucial market for the better cognacs – the generally affluent Chinese living outside their native country. Renaud supplied the family with cognacs, most of which they shipped in cask and sold as "Special Quality" or "St Rémy", and in 1929 Quien went to work for Renaud.

Quien soon started to sell under Rémy's name but to earn a living from the notoriously stingy Renaud, Quien said he would prefer to work on commission. Renaud made a typically ungenerous proposal. Quien accepted what amounted to a bet on his capacity to sell, and he won his bet. But Quien's greatest success, albeit an indirect one, was in the USA. Once Prohibition was repealed Quien found the ideal agent, Joseph Reinfeld. He had left his native Poland just before World War I with a mere fifteen dollars in his pocket and had found his way via Britain, where he sold Champagne to the miners of south Wales, then a veritable aristocracy of labour, to the USA. In 1934 Quien persuaded Renaud to award him the agency.

Within France itself most firms made do with what were called *agents multicartes*, sales representatives who sold a wide variety of alcoholic products and who would naturally concentrate their efforts on best-selling products. But Renaud managed to recruit Pierre Rivière, a charmer and member of the family that owned the Normandin cognac firm. Rivière "had an acute sense of what he could sell to whom" – and how. In Paris Rivière's first points of call were the city's best restaurants, and one by one he converted them to the Rémy cause. Rivière's tactics also ensured that foreign buyers, who would naturally eat in the best restaurants, would be offered Rémy, not by its own representatives, but by the restaurateurs themselves.

With the end of Prohibition and after the slump, there was some improvement, but the recovery was naturally aborted by the defeat of France in 1940. Nevertheless Cognac suffered less from the occupation than most of France. At first the German forces – especially the Navy – confiscated any stocks they could lay their hands on, but order was soon restored with the arrival of a local commandant, Otto Klaebisch. He was a remarkable man who seemingly took neither pleasure nor profit from his powers – he did not even commandeer the family firm of Meukow which his family had lost at the outbreak of World War I. He was also a friend of many of the merchants, for he had been educated in the local lycée when his family had been running Meukow. He was no Nazi and as early as October 1940 foresaw Germany's fate. "The worst thing that can happen to a man," he told Maurice Hennessy, "is to see his country defeated twice within a generation."

The only firm that was in trouble was Courvoisier, liable to confiscation as enemy property, for it had been an English-registered company since the Simon brothers had bought it. Two of the managers, George Hubert and Christian Braastad, calling themselves "Hubert et Cie", bought the stocks and rented the name, using pre-dated documents. Unfortunately, eighteen months later the Germans found out and put in a sequestrator to run the company.

There was little resistance activity in Cognac, although in 1941 the eighty-five-year-old Pierre Frapin resigned as mayor of Segonzac, three years before his death, unwilling to tolerate the whims of the German occupier any longer. By contrast Jacques Chardonne's sentimental attitude towards his own unreal and idealized vision of traditional rural France led him to be a stout supporter of Marshal Pétain during the war.

The key figure of the occupation was Maurice Hennessy. He had only one eye, yet had somehow managed to become a pilot in the French Air Force and could have stayed in Britain after the fall of France. However, he returned home with one simple object: "to try to safeguard our productive capacity, in the form of our vineyards, and our working tool, our stocks of cognac". His basic strategy, as he explained it to his fellow merchants in 1941, was equally simple: "We should think ourselves lucky if after the war we are in a position to start again." He ensured that they all regarded the increasing volume of cognac they were forced to deliver to the Germans as "a tribute imposed by the occupying power on a number of named persons of the occupied country". This definition of "tribute" meant that the merchants were obliged to furnish supplies under a quota system measured as a proportion to their previous volume of business, while no such obligations were imposed on the growers.

The "tribute" was enormous: "In 1940," said one observer, "the Germans took two years' sales in four months." The pace was sustained: over eight million bottles in 1941, 6.5 million in 1942, nearly eight million in 1943, and nearly four million in the few months of 1944 before Cognac was liberated, although the Cognaçais now claim that much of the "tribute" was paid not in true cognac but in alcohol made from beetroots. The French market had soared to nearly thirty million bottles in 1941, a far higher figure than the pre-war record of twenty-two million bottles in 1935. Obviously, ordinary exports, which had been running at just under fifteen million bottles during the pre-war years, dropped to a mere couple of million by 1944. Nevertheless, the region's financial and commercial structure remained intact, as the Germans paid handsomely for their purchases.

Maurice Hennessy had acted, nominally, as president of the town's Chamber of Commerce. He found a partner, Pierre Verneuil, among the growers. Together they used two mechanisms: the *Comités d'Organisation pour Produits Alimentaires*, committees designed to share out scarce foodstuffs; and the *Bureau de Repartition*, established to organize sales to the Germans. As in Champagne and Bordeaux, wartime hardships produced a renewed feeling of communal warmth between growers and merchants, last seen in Cognac in the equally hard times that had followed the phylloxera crisis (Hennessy's partner was the son of the grower who had done so much to re-establish the Cognac vineyards). Although some of the greedier, or more pro-German, merchants wanted to sell more than their quota, the mechanism worked smoothly enough. In Hennessy's words:

Thanks to the prevailing spirit of mutual understanding, if the merchants' stocks suffered considerably, those in the hands of the growers expanded so much that at the end of the war the working capital that the region had at its disposal to take up its place in the world again was bigger, and indeed more usable, than that available in 1939.

9

Thirty Golden years

To the French, the years from 1945 to the first oil crisis are known as *les trente glorieuses* – the thirty glorious years (in fact there were only 28, but let's not quibble) – and the same applied to cognac, with sales reaching a record high of 124 million bottles in 1972, more than in any year since the phylloxera crisis.

Cognac's recovery was helped because, physically, the town was largely untouched by the war. The only air raids were aimed at the airfield at Châteaubernard to the south of the town, which was used by the Luftwaffe's bombers attacking Allied convoys in the Atlantic. Liberation by the French themselves came quickly and quietly in September 1944. It brought with it reprisals against those who were thought to have collaborated, including, most unfairly, André Renaud. In early 1940 his German-Jewish partners the Sichels were forced to flee and spent the following winter as penniless refugees in the Pyrenees. It was André Renaud who sent them regular monthly payments to keep them alive until they managed to procure passports (some of them false) and make their way to Spain and thus to the United States. Typically, Renaud also exploited his friendship with a former friend, Gustav Schneider, one of the *weinfuhrers* (officers put in charge of the wine industry in each wine region), to the full and even enlisted Schneider's help to smuggle what he said were a few hunting rifles to friends in the Unoccupied zone. In the event these turned out to be a dozen superb shotguns and four thousand cartridges. Renaud also worked with the Resistance network commanded by the former sub-prefect of Cognac; but nevertheless was imprisoned for a few months.

More permanent a victim of the immediate postwar years was Jules Robin, which collapsed with the loss of the firm's colonial markets where *fine à l'eau* had been the favourite drink of the hard-drinking colonials. A similar fate befell Chabanneau, which had relied heavily on sales to what were then the Dutch East Indies. The newly independent Indonesia inevitably banned cognac imports. This was a fate which often befell firms that had depended on a single market like Tsarist Russia or Venezuela, a major market in the 1950s. Another venerable firm, Exshaw, was crippled by its former dependence on yet another Imperial market, that of the British in India.

But the day of Germany's surrender, May 8, 1945, was not one of undiluted rejoicing. That night there was a disastrous late frost, which reduced that year's crop to a mere 24,000 hectolitres, a quarter of even the reduced wartime level and one-fifth of the pre-war average of 120,000 hectolitres. But sales immediately soared once the war was over: whereas only nine million bottles had been exported in 1945, twenty-one million bottles were sent abroad in 1946. Of these, 5.5 million went to the USA, nearly four million to Britain and its still extensive empire, and a couple of million to Belgium, leaving only eight million for the French themselves. Inevitably, the merchants had to draw on their stocks: by the end of 1946 they held only 260,000 hectolitres, three-quarters of their pre-war level. But because growers' stocks had doubled the total was virtually the same as in 1939. As a result, and for the first time since the phylloxera period, the growers were able to finance stocks and were not forced to sell their spirit to the merchants as soon as it was distilled. The occupation had provided them with capital and hence confidence. This did not entirely suit Maurice Hennessy. As he wrote after the war: "The risk [and, he implied, the profits] of stocking is one that is inherent in our trade."

The growers' boldest move came in 1947 with the creation of the Prince Hubert de Polignac trademark. The pioneering Coopérative de Cognac had been set up in 1929 to resist the downward pressure on prices, and two years later the growers formed a business they called Unicoop to sell cognacs direct to buyers at home and abroad. In the nineteenth century the growers had relied on the names of their general managers, M. Salignac and then M. Monnet, to sell their cognacs, and inevitably the firms had drifted away from the cooperative ideal. The use of the name of one of France's most distinguished families was a declaration that they were now in the mainstream. Nevertheless the cooperatives have never enjoyed the success of their brothers in Champagne, for the power of the major firms was even greater and the cooperatives have had to rely very largely on the unprofitable business of supplying "buyers' own brands" to French supermarkets.

The change in their fortunes gave the growers the confidence to maintain their wartime cooperation with the merchants, a link symbolized by the foundation of the Bureau National Interprofessionel de Cognac. Like similar bodies in Champagne and Bordeaux, it grew out of the collaboration of an individual merchant working with the growers more systematically, more closely and more personally than ever before. In Champagne Maurice Hennessy's role had been played by Comte Robert-Jean de Vogüé of Moët & Chandon, the initiator of what became the Comité Interprofessionel des Vins de Champagne (CIVC). Fernand Ginestet played a similar role in founding the CIVB in Bordeaux.

Like them, the BNIC could trace its origins back to an earlier, voluntary body without much power or influence – the Union de la Viticulture et du Commerce, founded in 1921. The Bureau National de Repartition had provided a much better model: it included two members each from the growers and the merchants and four nominated by the central government. For eighteen months at the end of the war the fledgling BNIC was directly controlled by the Ministry of Agriculture, but it gained a – relative – independence in July 1946. It is an unusual animal, for, unlike its brethren elsewhere in France, it has official powers normally vested in central government officials.

Nevertheless, it was nearly stillborn. The Cognaçais voted to abolish the Bureau de Repartition, which had been responsible for disciplining the market, but a single voice rose up at the meeting saying simply that this move was ridiculous, that some other body would have to be found to do the same job. Nevertheless the willingness of both sides to cooperate ensured that the BNIC was created, an achievement which owed a great deal to a former civil servant, Henri Coquillaud, then an *Inspecteur Principal des Contributions Indirectes* and therefore responsible for supervising the movement and taxation of cognac. (His predecessor and the first director of the Bureau National, M. Louis-Miron, was originally a civil servant, an *Inspecteur des Fraudes*. It naturally suited the administration to have someone whom they could trust running such an unusual body.)

Coquillaud could rely on the wartime team of Hennessy, Pierre Verneuil and Gaston Briand, two growers with tremendous authority over their thousands of individualistic peasant followers. The final constitution gave growers and merchants the real power: the central government's representatives have acted as observers rather than exercising the behind-the-scenes control usual in France. The Bureau was even endowed with its own source of finance, a one per cent levy on all sales. One maverick merchant mounted a lengthy delaying action over the Bureau's legal status. As result it was only officially confirmed in 1975.

The Bureau shares overall control with the *Administration Fiscale*, which polices the appellation and the quantities of brandy distilled by the *bouilleurs de cru*, and with the *Inspecteurs des Fraudes*, who test the qualities of the cognacs on sale. Many of the home distillers have alembics of a few hectolitres, but if they want to modify their *chaudières*, they have to satisfy not only the BNIC and the *Inspecteur des Fraudes* but also the local representative of the *Institut National des Appellations d'Origine*, the otherwise all-powerful body that supervises all France's *Appellation d'Origine Contrôlées* (AC). For the Bureau involves itself in everything connected with cognac: it supervises the labelling of cognacs, pays for the Station Viticole, and runs excellent statistical and publicity departments.

Because the BNIC represented both growers and merchants it was a natural arbiter between the two in setting the prices to be paid for young cognacs. The long-standing dominance of Martell and Hennessy over the price of wines and brandies ended in 1954, and two years later the Bureau stepped in to try to establish a generally agreed price structure. Years of squabbling ended only in 1960, when the Bureau was given wider powers. The result was a scale of *comptes*. The first two, 0 and 00, are for cognacs that have been made during the current distillation season – although *Compte 00* applies only to the negligible quantity of cognac distilled after March 31 in any given year. These late-distilled cognacs lose a year. The Bureau itself is responsible for guaranteeing the age of the cognacs on offer. Three-Star – now VS – brandies have to be at least thirty months while brandies calling themselves VO, VSOP or "Reserve" have to be at least four years old (technically *Compte 4*) and those labelled "Extra", "Napoléon" or "Vieille Reserve" six years old.

Martell and Hennessy did not like the system but, like much of Cognac's new rule book, it merely confirmed ancient practice, including the price gap of between five and ten per cent between cognacs from the Grande Champagne, the Petite Champagne, and the Borderies (normally priced together) and the different categories of Bois. By 1960 a marked distinction had emerged between the Champagnes and the Borderies, where the *bouilleurs de cru* distilled over half of the total, the Fins Bois, where they represented only a quarter, and the lesser Bois, where the cooperatives were dominant and individual *bouilleurs de cru* accounted for only one-tenth. Overall they were distilling only one-third of the total as against two-fifths at the end of the war. It took the BNIC until 1964 to confirm another usage: that Cognac should not include more than two parts per thousand of colouring matter and two per cent added sugar. With this amount of sugar in it the spirit is reduced to thirty-eight degrees.

Although the age-grading system was extended in 1978 to include a *Compte 6*, it did not cover older cognacs. This enabled the BNIC to quash any pretence that a brand was a specific age; there were to be no more of those "hundred-year-old cognacs" beloved of the unscrupulous. As we shall see the narrow-mindedness of the whole cognac community has slowed further progress in the vital job of matching ages and qualities. But this still does not prevent some merchants from making sometimes exaggerated claims for their pricier brands, often giving the impression that their contents come from casks kept for generations in ancestral vaults.

To the BNIC the same rule implied that cognacs from a single year could not be sold to the public, a decision made in 1962 at the behest of the major companies. This was a logical corollary of the way that throughout Cognac's history the major firms have deliberately concentrated totally on their own brand names and eschewed two planks used by distillers of other spirits: age and origin. In the short term the ban placed cognac at a disadvantage compared with armagnac, which could legally sell single-vintage bottles without any real control over their age claims. It also met with profound objections from those English merchants, and their traditional suppliers (such as Hine and Delamain), who were used to storing single-vintage cognacs for decades and selling them as such.

Martell and Hennessy had split in 1947. The corporate "marriage" had always been personal, based on the mutual trust and affection binding one generation of both families. But Maurice Hennessy's closest friend, Maurice Firino-Martell, had died. Maurice Hennessy was not willing or able to impose his policies on the younger cousins, like Killian Hennessy, waiting to take over, let alone on the even younger nephews, Gerald de Geoffre and Alain de Pracomtal, who were to guide the company through to the 1990s.

Of course, the division of the world between Martell and Hennessy (see previous chapter) had never been absolute: just before the war Maurice Hennessy packed off his cousin, the Honourable Freddie, to England to organize a more aggressive sales stance. Freddie was more English than French. After the death of his grandfather, Richard Hennessy, his grandmother (herself born a Hennessy) had married Lord James Douglas-Hamilton, taking the children, George and Richard, with her to Scotland. George went into politics, became a Member of Parliament, and was ennobled as Lord Windlesham. Freddie proved a worthy scion of the family, shrewd and amiable, and his efforts were part of a process that ended Martell's dominance of what was still cognac's biggest single market. After the war Martell enjoyed an unbelievable eighty per cent share of the British market, much the same percentage as Hennessy enjoys in Ireland, where the name is practically synonymous with cognac.

It is easy to forget how, in Cognac, as in most of the rest of the world, the outlook immediately after the war seemed grey, for no one foresaw the prosperity of the 1950s and 1960s. Even Maurice Hennessy was a prisoner of the past. The 1945 frost, he wrote, had "negated a four-year effort that had succeeded in considerably increasing the reserves of cognac sleeping in our chais". Even when these had been reconstituted the outlook was bleak. He believed that the immediate postwar surge in the demand for cognac came partly from drinkers deprived of Scotch, who would return to their pre-war allegiance as soon as they could. In France itself the retail price, inflated by taxes as well as by an expensive distribution system, was double that paid to the merchants. Hennessy was mortally afraid of such inflation. His dearest wish had always been that cognac should be regarded as an everyday drink of moderate price and not reserved for a few well-heeled connoisseurs. As he wrote: "the cost of cultivating an hectare of vines has risen so high because of the inflation of the past few years that we must fear for the future of our outlets". Hennessy was thinking largely of the USA, once a major market, buying 200,000 cases in 1914. Prohibition killed all that, and the recovery was aborted by the war. And, indeed, in the 1950s it was Scotch, not cognac, that took the fancy of the average American used to whisky. Nevertheless, Hennessy's pessimism proved unfounded. Sales everywhere boomed as Europeans could increasingly allow themselves small luxuries. During the 1950s cognac, like all French luxury goods, was greatly helped by successive devaluations of the French franc. As "father of the Common Market", Jean Monnet helped by ensuring that cognac was not classed as an agricultural product and was not therefore submitted to the disciplines and idiocies of the Common Agricultural Policy.

The first fifteen years after the war were largely devoted to the reconquest of traditional markets. This was truest of Britain where sales trebled within total exports that doubled in the late 1940s and 1950s, but there was clearly scope in non-traditional markets. In 1958–9 Denmark still took more than West Germany, and Ireland more than Italy or the Netherlands.

Within France itself cognac made steady progress. It was still perceived as a luxury drink but the steady reduction in sales of spirits in bars was more than counter-balanced by the natural rise in demand as the country grew more prosperous. The Cognaçais were also helped by the gradual suppression of the rights of the *bouilleurs de cru*. Until the 1950s millions of them had been allowed to distil up to ten hectolitres of alcohol, ostensibly for their own use. In reality half their production – up to forty million bottles annually – trickled out to their families, to friends and to small cafés throughout France, thus competing with the cheaper cognacs.

During the 1950s sales nearly doubled in the USA, which took forty per cent of exports and their value rose at twice that rate. The Cognaçais hired a New York public relations outfit headed by Edward Gottlieb in a pilot effort for the Cognac Bureaux later established in other major markets. Gottlieb's efforts were both imaginative and far-reaching. He lobbied groups of potential buyers like the Physicians' Wine Appreciation Society – those were the days – and he published three books on cooking in which cognac naturally featured prominently. He even produced an embarrassingly titled but indubitably effective promotional film called *Fun at the Chafing Dish* and he ensured that the film was frequently mentioned in the smarter magazines – orthodox enough public relations techniques but markedly more sophisticated than those employed by other French exporters at the time. In the long term the combination of price and his campaigns preserved Cognac's upmarket image.

The biggest beneficiary from the boom was Courvoisier, under the key figure of Christian Braastad. He had been born in Jarnac of Norwegian parents, but his parents had returned home soon after he was born. He naturally learnt the Scandinavian languages so was snapped up by the Simon brothers in the early 1930s to sell to his native markets and, as we saw, during the war was one of the two managers who tried to save the firm from sequestration. By then he had "gone native" by marrying a Mlle. Delamain. But Christian Braastad was not a typical *gendre* – although their son Alain did run the family firm for many years until his retirement in 2001. His father was an even better organizer of salesmen than a salesman himself and in the fifteen years after the war provided Courvoisier with the first example of competent, orthodox, non-family-dominated management the region had ever seen. Braastad continued to promote the firm's connection with Napoleon and introduced the same type of frosted bottle as Rémy had introduced for its VSOP, although Courvoisier's design was more squat and businesslike than Rémy's.

The key to Courvoisier's profitability was that Braastad did not hold much stock. He bought as and when required, often using *courtiers*, the brokers historically so important in Bordeaux but previously largely ignored in Cognac because of the direct links there between growers and merchants. Braastad's strategy worked brilliantly – for a time. Unfortunately the success not only of his firm but also of the region as a whole caught up with him. In 1946 sales had represented six years' sales. By the end of the 1950s they were down to less than four years' requirements. In a 1996 report Jacques Fauré noted that "in the course of the past decades, the region has witnessed years when the trade was profitable while the growers had to tighten their belts. Rarer and above all shorter were periods when the opposite was true." The late 1950s and early 1960s was one of those periods.

In 1956–8 the harvests had been exceptionally low because of disastrous frosts in February 1956, and as a result by the early 1960s Courvoisier was caught with inadequate stocks even of younger brandies and desperately needed a substantial injection of capital to restore them.

André Renaud had anticipated Braastad's difficulties. He had hidden his precious brandy stocks successfully from the Germans and naturally flourished after 1945 when demand, especially for older brandies, was increasing faster than supply. He sold cognacs to a number of firms on generous credit terms for, not surprisingly, he had a hidden agenda. He swooped by demanding immediate payment for all the cognacs he had supplied to an individual house over a long period. He knew that the firm involved would be in deep trouble if it had too small a capital base – and most family firms are at their most vulnerable when sales are growing because of the need to finance ever-increasing stocks.

Two of the most vulnerable of Renaud's customers were Delamain and Courvoisier. The Delamain family managed to find the cash to pay the bill. In around 1960 he presented his bill to Courvoisier in the full expectation that Braastad couldn't pay. He was right. His next step was a proposed takeover on terms which are unknown to this day but were certainly not generous – the locals claim that the bid was made in cash. But he didn't win. For by the early 1960s outsiders from the whole world of spirits were eager to participate in so fast-growing a business in such a healthy field. Within a few months Courvoisier had found what would now be termed a "white knight" in the shape of the Canadian liquor company, Hiram Walker. It bought Courvoisier in 1963, at a time when it was selling more bottles of cognac than any other company.

Hiram Walker's arrival was a signal that cognac was no longer a backwater but was about to become one of the battlegrounds on which the world's liquor giants were fighting. These increasingly felt obliged to establish themselves wherever spirits were produced. The Courvoisier precedent was encouraging, although the extra capital from Hiram Walker enabled the firm to build up excess stocks at the wrong time when the market broke in the early 1970s – a mistake repeated on a much bigger scale after Seagram bought Martell in 1988. Nevertheless, the connection had helped Courvoisier to maintain its sales momentum throughout the 1960s, as did the formation of a distribution company in England owned jointly by two of Britain's biggest brewery groups, Allied Breweries and Whitbread. By the early 1970s Courvoisier was almost as big as Martell in Britain.

Many other firms welcomed outside help. They required more capital or, the classic reason for a takeover in France, there was an *indivision de famille*, a carve-up of the shares. For French inheritance laws ensure that, over the generations, shares in a family property fall into the hands of many heirs, who may be totally uninterested in the business. The bidders came from all over the world. Some of them made quiet, small-scale investments: the English brewer Bass bought Otard and for a time tried to promote its brandies; Jean Monnet's family firm was bought by the German firm Scharlachberg; the apéritif firm Berger bought Gauthier; Benedictine bought Comandon and Denis Mounié (which it subsequently resold); and the Spanish sherry house of Domecq did the same with Lucien-Foucauld. Noticeably, none of these often-hurried investments was successful or lasted any length of time.

But some of the newcomers made a bigger splash. In 1967 the heirs to M. Laporte-Dubouché sold Bisquit to Pernod-Ricard which already owned Renault, producers of superior brandies much appreciated in Sweden. M Ricard, who had built up his fame and fortune selling pastis, confidently indulged in by far the biggest single piece of capital investment since the Martells had constructed their mighty "brandy factory" in the 1880s. He bought the Château de Lignières, an enormous property in the Fins Bois northeast of Rouillac which had belonged to the Rémy Martin family, and turned it into a magnificent sight: hillsides of uniformly regimented vines on a scale unique in the region. At the château he built Cognac's first industrial-sized distillery, with fifty-six stills in gleaming rows. Aiming another blow at tradition, he then transferred Bisquit's stocks from their traditional resting place by the river at Jarnac and lodged them in the newly built warehouses on the same site. He was confident that he could sell the increased production through his firm's incomparable domestic sales force and by aggressive selling abroad. By the early 1970s Bisquit, like Courvoisier, was a major force in the Three-Star market, albeit not for long. Within decades both Renault and Bisquit had virtually faded from the scene.

Sam Bronfman, the former bootlegger who had built Seagram into the world's biggest spirits business, adopted an altogether more subtle approach. In the 1960s he had revolutionized the world's Scotch whisky market. Over a period of several decades he had bought and stored a wide range of excellent Scotches and had then blended them into a new de luxe blend, Chivas Regal. This proved an instant and lasting success. So it was natural for Bronfman to try and repeat the trick with cognac.

Having failed in attempts to buy Martell, Courvoisier or Bisquit, he turned to Augier, basically because it was the oldest firm in Cognac and thus a natural vehicle for launching a new up-market cognac. The partnership was an unlikely one: Jacques de Varenne of Augier was related to the Hennessys (and was one of Maurice Hennessy's closest friends), a descendent of most of the leading names in the town's history, a delightful, wry, aristocratic figure. Bronfman was a brilliant thug. They got on like a house on fire. Bronfman wanted quality; Augier was happy to sell control of his firm and to spend five years buying enough old cognacs to be ready to launch the cognac equivalent to Chivas Regal. This could have had as beneficial an effect on the whole cognac market in the 1970s as Chivas had had on Scotch in the 1960s. But, sadly, "Mr Sam" died in 1971, before the launch, and the idea was abandoned. The stocks were dispersed, and while Seagram kept Augier, it lost interest and, for a time preferred to launch, with no great success, a cognac bearing the name of Mumm, a leading Champagne firm it also owned.

But the fashion was catching, and in 1971 Distillers Company (DCL), the world's largest Scotch distillers, bought the family house of Hine. As so often, there were a growing number of family shareholders and the family took what seemed – indeed proved to be – the most sensible offer. This left the cousins Bernard and Jacques Hine still in place, working for a new chairman, Brian Thomson. He proved invaluable in ensuring the continuing independence of the firm, shielding the Hines from interference from DCL. Unfortunately, because the parent was itself closing distilleries, it was not prepared to invest in Hine.

The takeovers inevitably forced Hennessy and Martell to think about their future. Martell decided it could remain independent. But the shareholdings within the Hennessy family were more dispersed, and Killian Hennessy, who had taken over as chairman from his cousin in 1969 realized the need to merge. A natural partner was Moët & Chandon, another family-owned business in the luxury drinks business, which was already quoted on the Paris Bourse. The merger, a mere two years after Killian had taken over, enabled those members of the Hennessy family who wanted to sell to do so.

Cognac was now largely (though never merely) one aspect of the international spirits business, which itself was increasingly polarized between a handful of international giants and a few highly respected specialists.

This brought some advantages for a company like Hine, which could rely on the agents that distributed brands like Johnny Walker, also owned by Distillers. Courvoisier was less lucky. It found that it was stronger than its parent in many markets. At the time Pernod-Ricard was not big enough to play in the same league. Moët-Hennessy could compete; so could Martell and Rémy Martin, although they had to go it alone, relying on their names, their products, and an increasing ruthlessness with their distribution arrangements. In some countries they had their own subsidiaries; in others they have arrangements hallowed through the years. Rémy Martin was always prepared to be rougher. In Germany, where it was number one, it nevertheless abandoned a long-standing relationship with a local importer and established a wholly-owned subsidiary.

Hiram Walker's timing had been excellent. The reduction of duties that followed the Treaty of Rome had an immediate beneficial effect. By the end of the 1960s the five other countries of the original Common Market accounted for nearly half Cognac's exports, a ten per cent increase in market share during a decade when sales everywhere else were also rising. Sales in Germany, a mere 2.3 million bottles in the late 1950s, had jumped more than threefold in the decade. (These figures did not include half as much again of the young cognacs used to fortify local spirits.) By 1970 Germany had temporarily replaced the USA as cognac's biggest market.

But the biggest surprise came in the East. Sales to Hong Kong rose nearly five times; by 1970 the Chinese there had become by far the biggest consumers of cognac per head in the world. The Japanese government tried hard to keep cognac out by imposing duties of more than 200 per cent to protect its native spirits industry. And when in 1986 it started to yield to pressure to reduce the load it took another eight years to reduce the general preference enjoyed by home-produced spirits. Nevertheless Japan grew into almost as good a market as Hong Kong. But there was a difference between the two markets. The "overseas Chinese" – those in Singapore, Malaysia, and later Taiwan and Thailand, as well as in Hong Kong – were interested only in the best cognacs. They allegedly thought of them as aphrodisiacs (whereas Scotch, it was said, was supposed to induce impotence). They treated cognac as a drink to be taken not in sips after meals but in decent-sized glasses filled with ice with their food. Rémy Martin had a head start because of Otto Quien's pioneering efforts, but other houses were not far behind. By 1970 cognac was France's single biggest export to Singapore.

The Japanese were more cautious: at the time they bought mostly bulk cognac. But this was an exception. Only a few other markets (mainly the Scandinavian state monopolies) retained the habit of buying in bulk. Their purchases had represented one-third of total exports in 1950 but accounted for only one-fifth twenty years later. A vicious price war broke out, in which the cooperatives were largely victorious, so houses such as Hardy and Tiffon, which had relied on selling brandy in bulk, were forced to sell under their own names, sometimes for the first time and inevitably at a major disadvantage compared with better-known rivals.

But there were other opportunities. The Japanese, in particular, were allowed to import three litres of spirits duty-free at a time when foreign spirits were subjected to ferocious duties if bought at home. As a result a substantial proportion of sales in the Far East were made through the duty-free shops. This gave a major opportunity to Camus, "la Grande Marque", an old firm which had nearly gone out of business just after the war, so that its owner, Michel Camus, had to start effectively from scratch. He was, as one friend put it, "a gambler who was both clever and lucky". In 1961, two young American graduates of the hotel school at Cornell University foresaw that duty-free sales, particularly in the Far East, would be a growing market. Their firm, Duty Free Shoppers, acquired the concessions for virtually every airport in the Pacific Basin, their original targets American servicemen returning from tours of duty in the Pacific. The major houses refused them credit, but Michel Camus, anxious to rebuild his firm, agreed to give them extended credit. The result was an enormously successful partnership as the number of Japanese travelling abroad multiplied, and all looked for presents to give their relations and friends.

Michel Camus naturally devised his own brands for the market, notably "Celebration" launched in 1963. This was largely composed of three- to ten-year-old cognacs from the Bois but was promoted as superior to the average Three-Star (he later reinforced the image with a Napoléon). By the 1990s Duty Free accounted for over ten per cent of Cognac's sales worldwide, above all of the better, and more profitable, cognacs. Firms created new brands, like Martell's Cordon Noir and Exshaw's Age d'Or, purely for Hong Kong. Martell even had to produce a

Napoléon for the Oriental duty-free market. These brandies were tailored to the taste of the new drinkers for strong, generally rather dark-coloured brandies which could stand the inevitable dilution with ice, as were the special, usually gimmicky, bottles.

The apparently never-ending increase in sales naturally created pressure from all sides for increased plantings. In France any additional acreage is a matter for prolonged argument, since the *droit de plantation* ("right to plant") in regions covered by the AOC regulations is strictly controlled and thus a valuable asset. Because cognac had been such an unprofitable product for several generations before 1945, the surface planted with vines had remained virtually stationary, at just over 60,000 hectares/148,000 acres, between 1940 and 1959. That year 2,000 additional hectares (5,000 acres) were authorized, another 11,000 (27,000 acres) in 1962, yet another 10,000 (24,700 acres) in 1970, and the same area two years later. By 1971 the area actually under vines had jumped by over one-third to 86,000 hectares/198,000 acres), and much more had been authorized. Production in the 1970s was bound to rise substantially, as the new vines were over three years old and could begin to contribute to the production of cognac.

Production rose even faster than acreage. Better clones of St-Emilion vines, better cultivation, more fertilizer, better insecticides, meant that yields rose from an average of a mere twenty hectolitres of wine per hectare in the late 1940s to fifty hectolitres in the late 1950s and ninety, ten years later, reaching 124 hectolitres per hectare in 1970 and 149 three years later. At that level each hectare was producing enough cognac to fill nearly one thousand bottles. As we shall see (chapter ten) the problem was to get worse and was a major cause of the crisis in the 1990s.

The average quality was also increasing, for growers in the lesser *crus* could transfer their rights to plant. Between 1965 and 1972 the Bons Bois and Bois Ordinaires transferred an extra 1,700 hectares/4,200 acres to the nobler *crus* on top of the new plantings. Despite the apparent generosity of the allocations, the BNIC was under considerable pressure. It had to be seen to be fair to the existing growers, but the average age in the countryside was increasing rapidly, so it naturally wanted to encourage *jeunes agriculteurs*.

The authorities were unable to change the structure of the region. Holdings continued to be tiny – only 3,500 out of 30,000 were larger than five hectares/twelve acres. Even in the late 1970s two-thirds of the cognac vineyard belonged to growers owning between three and fifteen hectares/7.4 and thirty-seven acres of vines. The BNIC also had to allow for the market projections indicating an increased demand for the better cognacs. As a result, the Fin Bois (which received half the new acreage) and the Petite Champagne (which received one-fifth) benefited most. Nevertheless, everyone was left unsatisfied.

Another complication was that by 1970 over three-fifths of the cultivable land within the Grande Champagne and the Borderies was covered with white wine grapes. Inevitably, some of the new plantations were in unsuitable soils. In the Grande Champagne vines were planted in the alluvial flood plain of the Charente, a stretch that peasant wisdom had kept vine-free through the ages. In the Petite Champagne some magnificent chestnut woods growing on stony clays were uprooted to make way for yet more vines. Seeing the spread of vines to unsuitable soils within the Grande Champagne, the growers from the Archiac area, famously the best in the Petite Champagne, appealed to the INAO for reclassification. The INAO was not unwilling to help, but local pressure prevented any revision of boundaries.

The surge in production left a great many growers heavily indebted. They all wanted to continue to distil the vastly increased quantities of wines they were producing – indeed, the capacity of the *chaudières* ("pot stills") owned by the *bouilleurs de cru* jumped by a half between 1966 and 1973, although only to thirteen hectolitres, half the permitted maximum. An ambitious grower (and there were many) could spend 80,000 francs on an alembic holding fifteen hectolitres; a tractor and its attachments cost 70,000 francs; and vats and equipment cost another 80,000 francs. At the same time many of the growers were converting their alembics to gas, another heavy capital expenditure. At the time the investments seemed profitable enough, for incomes were rising as never before. The cash yield per hectare of vines tripled to nearly 23,000 francs between 1959 and 1973, with the Fins Bois doing almost as well as the nobler *crus*.

With prosperity came greed. In the words of Gerald de Geoffre, who succeeded his uncle, Maurice Hennessy, as the merchants' chief representative on the BNIC, "inevitably, between 1965 and 1973 the growers got into the habit of assuming that everything they produced would go for distillation at steadily rising prices. Although production in those years never actually fell below consumption, prices were rising more than they were paying in interest to the Crédit Agricole, so they were naturally unwilling to sell to us." The Bureau National reckoned that prices rose only ten per cent annually through the late 1960s, but, as a study by the Banque de France showed, cognacs kept during the crucial years from 1967 to 1973 could double or triple in value.

Nevertheless, the stock level had stabilized. Courvoisier's crisis marked the low point. In 1961–2 stocks represented less than three and a half years' sales. During the rest of the decade they struggled upward to stay at a little over four years'. The *bouilleurs de cru* managed to hang on to the advantage they had gained during the war. Together with the cooperatives (whose stocks attained prominence only in the late 1960s), they still held over one-third of the total in 1970, a fall of only three per cent since 1946 and a rise of 300,000 hectolitres to 473,000 hectolitres, enough to fill sixty-seven million bottles. But stocks were dangerously concentrated on younger spirits. Stocks of cognacs more than five years old increased by less than one-fifth between 1948, when they represented nearly half the total, and 1972, when they constituted a mere one-sixth. These figures further increased the pressure for even more acreage to be planted, for even the BNIC's apparently sober forecasts showed no real improvement in stock levels through most of the 1970s.

The situation was complicated by the arrival at Rémy Martin of André Hériard-Dubreuil, who had taken over Rémy Martin after André Renaud's death in 1965. Renaud had three children, a son, who was killed in a riding accident while still in his teens, and two daughters. There were, however, not one but two sons-in-law ready to take over the business. One was Max Cointreau, the son of Renaud's friend André. It had been assumed that he would marry Renaud's elder daughter, Anne-Marie. But he preferred her younger sister, Geneviève, a choice which thirty years later was to lead to the most extraordinary family drama in the history of the Cognac region. For during the war Renaud had been forced by new company legislation to reorganize the shareholdings in Rémy, leaving a majority to Anne-Marie who, at the time, was the only daughter old enough to be legally entitled to own shares. The legacy thus gave her the right to control the company when her parents died.

Nevertheless, Max Cointreau was clearly the favourite son-in-law, as opposed to Hériard-Dubreuil, who had married Anne-Marie in 1941. Renaud dismissed him as "just an engineer". Yet the burly, self-confident Hériard-Dubreuil proved to be a better, and above all even more far-sighted, businessman than his disapproving father-in-law. Moreover he was no outsider. His great-uncle, Elie Hériard, had been a partner of the last Rémy Martin. His father (yet another son-in-law) had married a Mlle. Gautier, whose family owned a merchant firm in Aigre, in the Fins Bois west of Cognac. After his parents died he was sent away to school as a boarder at a famous college run by the Jesuits in Sarlat, 160 kilometres east of Cognac. He was one of the select band who were bright and hard-working enough to attend the Ecole Polytechnique and then an even more elite academic establishment, the Ecole des Eaux et Forêts, and was thus the first graduate from one of France's top institutes of higher education to run a major cognac company. His first stay in Cognac was brief since he soon had to flee to Paris and find protection with Pierre Rivière to avoid being sent to forced labour in Germany, but when he returned in 1944 he started to make his mark. He always claimed that if he hadn't met his future wife he would have embarked on a totally differ-ent career: "anything except be a cognac merchant like my father", he would say.

Once Hériard-Dubreuil had succeeded his father-in-law in 1965 he moved swiftly. Over the following thirty-five years he transformed what was still a relatively modest firm into one of the giants of French – indeed world – drinks industry, a unique achievement in the long his-tory of cognac. By the time of his death in early 2002 at the age of eighty-four, Hériard-Dubreuil had elevated Rémy into second position in Cognac and had transformed sales of VSOP. Even in 1945 only five per cent of all the cognac sold in the world was above Three-Star level. Thanks largely to Rémy Martin (although the Oriental taste for the classier brandies also played an important part) the proportion is now up to a third. And despite an ever-increasing number of competitors, the firm is still responsible for two out of every five bottles of VSOP sold in the world.

Throughout his reign – there really is no other word for his time – Hériard-Dubreuil was always looking to the long term, always eager to expand his empire away from cognac – perhaps a reaction from the nec-essarily frustrating decades he had spent working for his father-in-law.

Financially his most successful takeover was of the famous Paris wine firm of Nicolas, making an enormous profit by transferring the (extremely valuable) stock from its old premises in Bercy on the eastern edge of Paris and selling the land freed by the move. In the 1970s he had bought De Luze, a major Bordeaux merchant, and used it as the base for an even bigger unit, Grand Vins du Gironde. In the mid-1980s he bought two leading brands of Champagne, Piper Heidsieck and Charles Heidsieck, to add to Krug, which he had bought back in 1973 and subsequently sold at a handsome profit. He then allowed a winemaking genius, the late Daniel Thibault, cellar-master of Charles Heidsieck, the finances – and the seven or more years – required to transform it into a model Champagne. Outside France his record was less successful. He set up an – unsuccessful – vineyard, Château Rémy, in Australia, where Otto Quien had protected the firm's interests during World War II. In California he launched an ambitious, but in the end pointless, joint venture making double-distilled "alembic brandy" mostly from the Colombard grape, in conjunction with Schramsberg, makers of California's best sparkling wines.

For all his worldwide ambitions he combined far-sightedness with the same inherent earthiness as his father-in-law, and he lived and died in Cognac where he regularly entertained locals with whom he loved to discuss everything under the sun. Despite his dominance of the firm until the day he died, he allowed executives their say. His major problems were with his bankers, whose patience he stretched as a result of his expansionary ambitions, and, more publicly, with his family.

In the 1960s Hériard-Dubreuil had naturally pressed the case for the growers in the Champagnes to be allocated a greater share of the new plantings. He had also paid substantially more for their cognacs than had Martell or Hennessy, always worried by any shift in the balance of power towards the growers. But that was not enough. He realized that the links between merchants and growers had to be formalized, could no longer be left to handshakes over successive generations. Hence the creation of Champeco, a new type of cooperative involving both Rémy and the growers, led by Paul Hosteing, together with formal three-year contracts. The whole business represented a revolution in the region, the first time in its history of a systematic, institutionalized partnership between the two sides. The agreement also enabled Rémy to expand more quickly because the cost of holding the stocks – by far the biggest capital requirement in the business – was shouldered by the growers and Champeco. That, combined with his insistence on quality – "you have to sell cognac expensively, you have to sell it well", he would say – enabled the firm to triple its sales in the fifteen years after his father-in-law's death. In 1973 he even appointed a technical director, whereas other firms relied exclusively on their blenders, their chefs de caves. For the job he chose a science teacher Robert Leauté, his role being "to translate the ideas of the marketing people and tell them which were impossible". For marketing people, not understanding the nature and creation of cognac, are always liable to come up with ridiculous notions.

In the 1960s Rémy became a cult both in traditional markets and in the Far East, thanks to the pioneering efforts of Otto Quien and a later, equally legendary, salesman, Nik Schuman, a Dutchman who was as lean and weather-beaten as a first mate out of Conrad. Not surprisingly, within a few years of Hériard-Dubreuil's efforts, Rémy was presenting an increasing threat to Martell and Hennessy. They hated Rémy – and not just because Renaud had been considered rather a shady operator. There was a genuine hatred at work, and the Hériard-Dubreuils were simply not received by the Martells and Hennessys. Throughout the 1970s Martell and Hennessy were almost transfixed, obsessed by Rémy's success. Old-timers remember how salesmen would come back to base paralyzed by the success of Rémy's VSOP Fine Champagne and unable to mount any sort of counterattack. All they could do was hope that the company's increasing indebtedness would cause its downfall.

The Rémy threat was the more profound for two reasons. Martell and Hennessy had founded their fame and fortune on two rather distinct types of cognac, the basic Three-Star, and superior brandies like Hennessy's XO and the Cordon Bleu that Martell introduced between the wars and which was for a long time the best-selling upmarket cognac in the world. To them the whole idea of VSOP was inevitably an unhappy compromise. More crucially, because they relied so heavily on brandies from the Bois – and from the Borderies, a major constituent of Cordon Bleu – they were extremely reluctant to sell any cognac (apart from the very oldest) as coming purely from the Champagnes and labelled as such. So in late 1970 Martell, Hennessy, and Courvoisier took the offensive: they decided to omit the words "Fine Champagne" from their labels, claiming that the quality of cognacs from the Champagnes had greatly deteriorated. It was an open and direct challenge to Hériard-Dubreuil and provided him with an immediate and unrivalled opportunity to emphasize the superiority of the name.

He resigned as president of the Syndicat des Exportateurs which included the eleven most important firms in Cognac, and immediately set up a rival grouping, which he called "Tradition and Quality". Helpfully, he was followed by Otard and two lesser houses, Boulestin and Gaston de Lagrange, a brand created by Martini. His act, he explained, was "to protest against the efforts of the Big Three to disgrace and to standardize their unique product. Cognac's policy ought to be to increase cognac's value in order to reward the growers." It was a superb public relations exercise, emphasizing his firm's unique links with the growers, the community from which he (or rather his father-in-law) had sprung. The ensuing "Cognac war" as the papers called it, was splendid publicity for Rémy, until it fizzled out, as such affairs do in France. It was also music to the ears of the growers in the Champagnes, afraid of domination by the permanent majority enjoyed within the growers' "college" by the lesser breeds from the Bois. It may have been a farcical conflict but it was one with extensive repercussions within the cognac community.

The newspapers naturally seized on the *guerre de cognac* with great glee. Poor Coquillaud, the director of the BNIC who had tacitly encouraged the reformers, made matters worse with a bland declaration: "There is no cognac war and one is inconceivable . . . What they are trying to say is that there is only one good cognac, Fine Champagne. That's ridiculous and could even become dangerous." The mayors of the canton of Segonzac, the heart of the Grande Champagne, immediately protested, and the 3,750 growers from the Champagnes walked out of the Growers' Federation. Individual growers went even further; they assumed the whole thing was a plot, with the BNIC in league with Martell, Hennessy, and Courvoisier.

The three major firms counter-attacked, writing to the papers to refute suspiciously similar articles that all represented Rémy's point of view. Their only weapons, they claimed, were facts: that the words "Fine Champagne" provided absolutely no guarantee of quality; that Rémy represented under five per cent of the total sales of cognac; and that the "Big Three", far from despising or neglecting Champagne cognacs, had the first choice among them and regularly bought seventy per cent of the total. Their protest was in vain: even the normally level-headed magazine *L'Express* painted the contrast as "on one side industry, on the other craftsmanship, art indeed". The association with the art form of cognac was even more useful for Otard, which did not enjoy the same worldwide reputation for quality as Rémy Martin. It seized the opportunity to launch its own Fine Champagne, Baron Otard. Rémy Martin and Otard, said its export director loftily in an interview with a Canadian paper, "refuse to degrade their cognacs. We believe in a certain code of quality and honour. The good name of France itself is at stake, and the house of Otard, which honours this name in fifty-four countries, will not lower its flag of high quality."

The war was clear evidence of a breakdown in the consensus that had governed cognac since the war. It was partly a matter of generations. Hennessy and Verneuil had retired without leaving successors who enjoyed the same moral authority. The only local political figure with enough stature to act as mediator, Felix Gaillard, a former Prime Minister, had died in the mid-1960s. The gap remained unfilled, and relations between different classes of growers (and between them and the merchants, themselves now divided into three groups) were strained even before the crisis of the 1970s. But there was also a vital sub-text to the "war". Rémy in particular was emphasizing the importance of individual appellations, most obviously the Champagnes. By contrast Martell and Hennessy continued to refuse to admit the role of terroir, putting their faith in blending and the overwhelming importance of the brand. "Doubtless," Maurice Hennessy had said, "some terroirs contribute their own special taste to well-made products but quality can be found anywhere if you look for it. And [quality] is the result of man's work," and thus, implicitly, could be guaranteed only if you bought the right brand.

In the short term the war was clearly too damaging to the image of cognac to be allowed to continue – in public anyway. Within a few months a truce was declared. Both sides promised to keep quiet, and "Fine Champagne" soon appeared on other companies' labels, a tribute to Rémy's success. Since sales were rising at about twenty per cent annually at the time, no one felt that the episode had done any permanent harm. But it had: greed had weakened the unity forged in slump and war. As Claude Belot, a radical local professor, wrote in 1973: "It is undeniable that in the last few years something has changed in this region of ours, which was so cautious for so long."[1]

For Hériard-Dubreuil, wittingly or not, had created two gulfs. Helped by the animosity shown by Martell and Hennessy, the merchant community was divided as never before. Worse was the ever-deepening gulf between the growers in the Champagnes and the rest of Cognac. Effectively Hériard had set off a conflict between the growers in the Charentes, mostly from the Champagnes, and those from the Charentes-Maritimes – known by their departmental numbers as sixteen and seventeen. It was the end of the "cognac community" so far as the growers were concerned, with two syndicats and even two magazines representing them. It was *coexistence armé*; a sort of cold war. Both divisions were to prove highly damaging in the troubled decades that followed the traumatically sudden end of the *trente glorieuses* in 1973.

[1] *Norois* magazine, 1973.

10

The Suicidal Decades

Returning after twenty years in which I had not visited Cognac nearly enough I felt like the wine writer Edmund Penning-Rowsell on his return to Bordeaux after the crisis of the early 1970s. He found it "rather like revisiting a friend's family that has been afflicted by an accident, to a degree unknown to the visitor. Who, one asks cautiously, has died, how many are alive and well, and how are the convalescents?" As in Bordeaux, so in Cognac many of the wounds were self-inflicted, and all were accompanied by unprecedented splits within the community.

The story of the last couple of decades in Cognac can be told from three points of view: the commercial, reflecting the roller-coaster ride in sales; the social, with particular concentration on the growers and the distillers who felt the shocks involved; and, perhaps most important, the psychological. For it was in the last two decades of the twentieth century that, for the first time, Cognac ceased to be a self-contained, largely independent world and was transformed into a series of production units for the four major international groups. "For centuries," wrote Michel Coste,[1] "cognac the drink and Cognac the town had been synonymous to a degree unmatched elsewhere." But over the past twenty years "the world has evolved so that, insensibly the destiny of the town and the drink that made it famous have separated. This inimitable spirit lives its life elsewhere . . . and the town becomes an ordinary sub-prefecture." And because of the forces let loose in the previous years, the Cognaçais could not face their new problems with the same solidarity they had shown when invaded by the phylloxera a century earlier. Moreover, and notably unlike the situation in Champagne, the other region of France where

[1] Michel Coste, *Cognac: les clés de la fortune*, Librairie du Château, 2001.

brands and blends are dominant, the major companies were not prepared to work together for the common good.

The stark reality was spelled out in a remarkably frank document "what future for the economy of Cognac" written in 1996 by Jacques Fauré, then the director of the BNIC (not surprisingly, his contract was not renewed). He asked the basic question, "will cognac continue to be sold, has it got a future?" and went on to ask the corollaries: the appropriate size for the vineyard and the number of growers it could support. He came up with the figure which has been the gospel ever since, that of 55–60,000 hectares/136–148,000 acres, which would provide a living for the growers and satisfy the requirements of the merchants.

Looked at from outside, cognac has not suffered too badly since 1973, after which so much of the world's disposable income was diverted to tee-total Muslims. But somehow cognac translated the stagnation since 1976 into the biggest crisis since phylloxera. In fact exports rose by a quarter in the eight years after the first oil shock. For the effects of the relatively unhappy years since the collapse have been exacerbated by the way the Cognaçais had assumed, arrogantly, that demand would be limitless. They had forgotten a fundamental lesson first enunciated by Jean Martell. He was, he said, "less ambitious to do things on a large scale than to do them little and well". His words remain to this day a suitable motto for the town.

Financially the Cognaçais suffered worse than their rivals in the luxury goods business because the cost of storing maturing cognac had resulted in ever-increasing interest charges, which more than doubled between 1973 and 1982 to account for over eleven per cent of sales. Moreover, they had taken two steps in the wrong direction. One was to haunt the region for thirty years: the panic that there wasn't going to be enough cognac led to gross overplanting, with the vineyard reaching a peak of 110,000 hectares/272,000 acres in 1976, nearly double the figure at the end of the war. The major firms were so frightened of lack of supply that they'd even bought firms in Armagnac to provide a second string to their spirituous bow. They had ignored, not only the failure of sales to rise inexorably, but, even more importantly, the extent to which vinous productivity had grown by leaps and bounds.

During the 1970s cognac was saved from collapse largely by the steady growth in the American market, which nearly trebled to over seventy million bottles. Until the 1970s the cognac habit had been largely confined to the East Coast. It steadily "went national" during the decade. A major, and still unexplained, boost came with vastly increased consumption by the black community – in 1980 the depressed, but largely black city of Detroit, one-quarter the size of New York, drank two-thirds as much cognac. This ethnic predisposition to brandy attracted all sorts of explanations. The most vivid, libellous, and unreliable vignette is of black – not white – drug dealers carrying half-bottles in their hip-pockets to make "black-smack", cognac and cocaine.

Inevitably, marketing efforts were concentrated on the USA. Rémy Martin even introduced a VS quality both in Britain and in the USA (by this time the star system had become so devalued – Salignac even had a Five-Star – that the Cognaçais substituted the VS label to try to associate their cheaper brandies with the VSOP quality). Rémy spent lavishly, up to US$2 a bottle, on advertising. Martell was originally reluctant to lay out the vast sums required but was eventually persuaded to do so by its importers, Brown-Forman, famous for Jack Daniel's.

The figures[2] tell the story of cognac's bumpy ride during the last decades of the twentieth century. In 1985 world sales were just under nine million cases, by 1990 they had risen to nearly 12.5 million and by 2001 were down to 9.5 million. Of course it did not help that sales in Europe steadily declined – from five million cases in 1985 to 3.6 million in 2001. In France the situation was, if anything, rather worse. In 1983 François Mitterrand, the first French President born in the region, greatly increased the duty on cognac and by the end of the century the state was taking well over half of the price of a bottle of cognac. The government take consists not only of direct taxes and duties, but also national insurance and other levies, so that cognac was paying nearly sixty times as much tax per bottle as wine. Between 1985 and 2001 sales declined by nearly two-fifths.

Even though sales are above those in the late 1970s profit margins are far lower, a direct result of the increased costs and collapse of sales in the Far East, where they were predominantly of cognacs of VSOP quality and above. For virtually none of the cognacs sold there was VS, and when the

[2] Unless otherwise indicated these come from the *International Wine & Spirit Record*, London, an authoritative source.

drinkers did move downmarket it was only from XO to VSOP. Again the figures tell the story clearly enough. Sales of brandies of above VSOP level nearly trebled in the last five years of the 1980s during a period when the Far East accounted for thirty-seven per cent of sales in volume terms and forty-five per cent of the cash paid. Indeed in the four years from 1989 sales of VS were lower than those of superior qualities. In the early 1990s VS was responsible for 47.5 per cent of sales, by the turn of the century it was fifty-seven per cent.

The roller-coaster ride in overall sales was largely due to events in the Far East. Between 1985 and 1990 sales to Japan more than doubled from 570,000 to 1,250,000 cases and in 1990 the BNIC stated confidently that they were bound to increase, since cognac accounted for a mere one per cent of the money spent on hard liquor. Nevertheless, by 2001 they had fallen back to under 500,000 cases. The decline was largely due to the steady darkening of the economic outlook during the decade. This had as a side effect the degradation of the image of cognac as a luxury drink. This was partly because of reductions in taxation but mostly because the firms panicked and tried to counter the reduction in sales by discounting, thus transforming cognac from a luxury product to just one among many competing spirits.

The ride was even bumpier among the overseas Chinese where sales nearly trebled in the last five years of the 1980s, from 636,000 cases to just over 1.7 million cases by 1990, only to slump to 450,000 by 2001. By contrast, mainland China looked more hopeful. The rise was later – culminating in sales of nearly a million cases in 1995 – but even in 2001 was 440,000 cases, two-and-a-half times the figure fifteen years earlier. This impressive rise came despite the crackdown on excessive expenditure by government officials – notably on luxuries like cognac – that had marked the mid-1990s. Throughout the Far East cognac suffered temporarily from the Asian crash of 1997 but its longer-term problems are largely due to a generation change, since in general no one drinks the same drinks as their parents. This tendency has been particularly apparent among the Chinese diaspora where the younger generation, often educated in the USA, have revolted against their parents' habits of dining with a bottle of cognac on the table.

Cognac has also been caught up as an innocent sufferer in trade disputes between the European Union and the USA, based on American hostility to the Common Agricultural Policy. The first row in the 1970s – the so-called "chicken war" – led to increased American tariffs on cognac while the "soya war" in the early 1990s led to a dramatic fall in shipments to the USA in 1991 and 1993. And the Cognaçais have had to cope with the fluctuations inevitable from floating exchange rates since the dollar floated in 1971. Since 2002 they have at least been spared the problems within the "eurozone" but can do very little when – as happened in early 2003 – the euro strengthened by nearly a fifth against the dollar.

The whole cognac community had hoped that theirs would no longer be considered a luxury product. Maurice Hennessy had always worried that in previous slumps cognac had proved only too dispensable, hence the hope he expressed, just after the war, that cognac would be regarded as a normal article of consumption for ordinary people. But in Britain particularly this slice of the market was taken by "French brandy" made of neutral spirit blended with very strong "esprit de vin" often from Champagne. In his report Jacques Fauré noted the confusion between Cognac and brandy which was perhaps not "necessarily a disadvantage for the biggest producers of brandy" – which in effect meant some of the biggest firms. But obviously it harmed the image – and the consumption – of cognac.

Cognac is bound to be pricier than its competitors, even spirits expensively matured in oak casks, if only because the raw material costs five times as much as the barley used for Scotch whisky. The Scots also had the sense to provide the ignorant majority of drinkers with a double support, the brand and its exact age, while the Cognaçais in their arrogance relied on their brand with meaningless terms like VS, VSOP, and XO. For cognac was inescapably a product, as Fauré put it, "whose production, stocking, maturation are all expensive and thus can only be sold in a luxury niche" which, by definition, has only a limited place in the market for spirits. For Hériard-Dubreuil cognac "represents a mere drop of water in the ocean of spirits. In price terms it can never compete with whisky. By devaluating its production, you do the same with the product itself." Roland de Farcy of Hennessy agrees with his analysis. Whisky, he says "will always win in the volume game because their costs – above all of raw materials – are so much lower, for even the basic VS cognac is still a premium product". Not surprisingly it was firms like Rémy and notably Hennessy – which actually increased its prices during a downturn in the

1990s – which retained their image and prospered during the past thirty difficult years.

But the Cognaçais are attacking a target which is moving rapidly upmarket. Not only are premium blends of whisky taking an increasing share of the market, but single malts, which in the 1960s had represented a mere one per cent of total sales, were taking one bottle in seven by the turn of the millennium. To make matters worse, until the last years of the twentieth century the Cognaçais were carrying a ball and chain around with them by refusing to copy the Scots and not promoting cognac's historic mixability.

For the Cognaçais still have a long way to go, especially in France. A study by the BNIC in 1999 showed that the number of regular cognac drinkers had fallen from 9.3 per cent to a mere 5.4 per cent of adults in the previous five years and that the fall was even steeper among the under-thirty-fives, who were looking for lighter, less obviously strong drinks like rum and vodka. It was also unfashionable: cognac was not perceived as a "modern" drink. As a result the regulars were largely older males, drinking at home, for cognac was still overwhelmingly perceived as a digestif, to be drunk neat at the end of a good meal. Worse for cognac's image was that more cognac was used in cooking than was drunk, and that in most cases the same cognac was used in cooking as for drinking. By contrast whisky was perceived as more modern, more fashionable, and preferred by heavier drinkers.

One obvious result of stagnant sales, increased pressure, and the switch to cheaper cognacs was the increasing concentration of the business. As Fauré pointed out, by the mid-1990s the number of firms had fallen by three-quarters since 1900 and by a half since 1945, and the Big Four accounted for four-fifths of the total, as against only a half fifty years earlier. This does not leave much for the 250 or so other "merchants" the region's ten cooperatives. The worst effect was the disappearance of many of the medium-size family firms which had brought considerable stability in a business which demanded continuity, if only to allow time for the precious stocks of cognac to mature. In Coste's words, the "globalization" of cognac persuaded the owners of family firms that "only such multi-national firms could cope with all the changes". It was in the late 1970s, said one jaundiced cognac lover, that professional managers took over. In Alain Braastad's words, the disappearance of so many family firms led to "the disappearance of almost all the services, the decision-making centres, which left cognac and its region, for the multinationals left at Cognac only their production facilities". When sales, accounts, and management moved away from Cognac, this not only reduced the number of managerial-level jobs, but also greatly reduced the morale of a town that was used to being a capital and had become merely a series of "branch plants".

The dominance of the Big Four was reinforced because they, and they alone, could afford to form their own subsidiaries outside France to cut out the middlemen. It was Sir Anthony Tennant of IDV who remarked that he was sick of allowing so many of his foreign agents to become millionaires. The general attitude was that "we don't want to entrust our product to anybody. We need to accompany it right down the chain". In doing so they often formed alliances with other giants. Fauré had noted the biggest single change: that cognac was now in the hands of multi-national firms for which it was not necessarily the first priority unless a specialized sales force was set up for it. Otherwise it could easily get lost in the vast portfolio carried by every salesman – a problem which did more than anything to prevent Pernod-Ricard from selling Bisquit and Renault cognacs, lost as they were in a sea of very profitable Pernod.

Of course there were exceptions. The most significant was probably Michel Coste, the very archetype of the mood of gritty realism that seized the region after 1973. He realized that there was no hope of creating a new major brand. "Rémy Martin caught the last train," he once said, and he has always looked for niche markets. An accountant by training, he was drawn to cognac primarily because his beloved yacht was moored at Arcachon. For a decade or more he worked at Otard, rising to become managing director. Then in the mid-1970s he made his bid for independence with the help of a loan from the Société Générale and took the opportunity of buying up many of the firms stranded by the slump. His CCG – Compagnie Commerciale de Guyenne – took over Meukow with its stocks of old cognac, and he bought Lucien-Foucauld from Allied Domecq with spacious premises in the centre of Cognac, while Richard Frères contributed a well-equipped warehouse and bottling complex at Saint Jean d'Angely. In Nik Schumann from Rémy Martin he found the Otto Quien of the 1970s, to sell his Meukow VRXO in the Far East. By the turn of the century he – and his managing director and son-in-law,

Claude Burgerolle, whose family firm Coste had acquired – was concentrating almost entirely on Meukow. This was typical of the way many family brands, absorbed by larger groups, were simply dropped as surplus to requirements over the years. Denis Mounié, Augier, and Jules Robin are only three well-known names no longer available. For groups are concentrating on single brands, using others for specific purposes – like selling to supermarkets and individual countries rather than trying to sell a sprawling, often undifferentiated range of products.

Camus, number five in the pecking order, albeit far behind the Big Four – and thus by far the biggest family-controlled company – has survived despite two major blows. It was heavily dependent on the duty-free business in the Far East, where its sales collapsed by four-fifths, more completely than those of any other company anywhere. It was also at risk when LVMH made one of its rare errors and bought Duty Free Shoppers in the mid-1990s at the top of the market. Fortunately LVMH, while virtually eliminating its other rivals from the shelves, retained Camus, because, one suspects, its products had been such an integral part of DFS's range.

Of other well-known brands Otard was lucky. It had been floating for some years, since Martini – which had bought the brand from Bass – showed no great interest in it. Today it is benefiting greatly from sharing distribution with its parent company, Bacardi-Martini. Nevertheless, it still depends for a large proportion of its sales on the thousands of visitors to the château itself, where the magnificent banqueting halls are still used for major events. Marie Brizard, the parent of Gautier and Pascal Combeau, itself nearly went under, but has recovered and is now selling only the brandies from Gautier.

But some old-established firms were less lucky. Hardy, owned by the Hardy family and the French bank Crédit Commercial de France, had depended acutely on the French market and it went bankrupt after its sales in France dropped by nearly nine-tenths from a peak of 87,000 cases – a fall echoed by Martell, the former number two.

Indeed the French market has proved a graveyard for all the brands, like Courvoisier and Bisquit, which had previously held major positions. Today sales are overwhelmingly made in supermarkets which rely on anonymous, and by no means distinguished, cognacs, often from the Distillerie des Moisans which until recently sold exclusively on price. By contrast the major British supermarket chains have selected their cognacs so carefully that they have won a number of medals at the International Spirits Challenge.

The dramatic events of the last decades showed most dramatically in the very varying fortunes of the Big Four. The big winner was Hennessy, whose sales virtually doubled in the period, increasing its market share from seventeen per cent to well over thirty per cent, a percentage unapproached in the history of cognac. Yet it remains terribly dependent on the USA, which accounts for about half its sales – in a market where over ninety per cent of sales are of VS. Nevertheless, until well into the 1990s Hennessy remained staunchly traditional in its management, even though it was part of the ever-expanding LVMH-Moët-Hennessy empire, which took in an incomparable range of luxury products from Dom Pérignon to Tag Heuer watches and from Christian Dior to Louis Vuitton.

At Hennessy itself, the leading figures for twenty years after the merger, Gerald de Geoffre and Alain de Pracomtal, were both nephews of Killian Hennessy. Nevertheless, during much of the 1980s and 1990s the company was effectively run by Maurice Fillioux and his nephew Yann, who produced the brandies, and by Colin Campbell. This remarkable character had abandoned his studies at Oxford after only a year and soon found a job working as a guide at Hennessy. For the next forty years he rose steadily through the ranks before he retired at the end of 2002 as commercial director of Moët-Hennessy. He spent much of the time building up Hennessy's business in its two biggest markets, the USA and the Far East. He also proved the crucial link between Moët-Hennessy and its British partners, once called DCL and now called Diageo. For Hennessy owes its present dominance largely to the unprecedentedly deep relationships he developed with importers and agents – notably that in the Far East with Jardine Mathieson, the giant trading firm – and the subsidiaries Hennessy acquired through him, most obviously Schieffelin, its agents for nearly 200 years.

Hennessy's success owed a lot to the many mistakes made by its competitors, though, inevitably, the firm made its fair share. An outside managing director, Christophe Navarre, recruited from Hoegaarden the beer people, in the late 1990s transformed the management. "He brought the firm from the nineteenth to the twenty-first century in one fell swoop," says one of his colleagues. But the 1990s also saw the introduction of two unsuccessful cognacs named after two of the firm's distilleries, Le Peu and Camp Romain, as well as Pure White, a technical triumph but an unlikely prospect in the black-dominated American market. Even more damaging was the introduction of a Hennessy whisky in Japan.

By the end of the millennium Hennessy's only real rival was Rémy Martin. In fourth place as late as 1985, it increased its sales by a half, and its market share from less than nine per cent to sixteen per cent in the following fifteen years. This was a remarkable achievement given that the vast bulk of its sales remained in the VSOP sector rather than VS. In doing so it effectively transformed the Big Four into the Big Two. Until the early 1980s Rémy had comfortably bucked the general trend; exports multiplied over four times between 1974 and 1982 to reach 646 million francs, ninety-five per cent of total turnover. So Rémy Martin had continued to increase purchases of wines or brandies by up to twenty per cent every year. The inevitable slow-down was made more abrupt because of the family problem. The minority shareholders, M. and Mme. Cointreau, were clearly not going to subscribe to a capital increase while they were denied any say in the running of the company. So Rémy, like the growers, had to rely increasingly on expensive bank borrowings. The financial limits first showed up in late 1976, when the French government was desperate to find a French buyer for Château Margaux. Hériard-Dubreuil could not find the seven million francs involved.

Later in the decade his golden years seemed to come to an end with two problems. First he put his elder son Michel at the head of the firm. This was almost fatal, since Michel's managerial inadequacies led to the departure of his key sales director, Yves Blanchard, and the demotivation of the rest of the management team. A few years later, but after the damage had been done, Michel was deposed – he was later ordained as a priest in the Orthodox church – and his father, still only in his late fifties, took back control. His second, and far more serious problem was with M. et Mme. Cointreau.

Hériard-Dubreuil's increasing emphasis on links with the growers had another purpose: they enabled him to contemplate a break with his in-laws, for Max Cointreau's wife, Geneviève, had inherited just under half the capital in Rémy Martin, a minority holding which, under French law, gave her substantial rights. Hériard-Dubreuil was not going to accept the situation indefinitely and indeed did not allow his in-laws any say in the running of the company. The family battle began in 1973 when Max Cointreau presented himself as a candidate for mayor of Segonzac. He was opposed – unsuccessfully – by Roger Plassard, Rémy's chief buyer and thus the executive closest to the growers. The feud worsened after the death of Madame Albert Frapin, "*tantine*", the beloved aunt of both Anne-Marie and Geneviève, in 1978, shortly after she had rewritten her will. In it she left control of Frapin to her younger niece, Geneviève Cointreau, partly because Anne-Marie's husband controlled Rémy. Hériard-Dubreuil promptly stopped buying any cognac from Frapin, which virtually disappeared from the market until the late 1980s. There ensued an inconceivably bitter and complicated legal battle that lasted for over a decade, which Hériard-Dubreuil, in particular, tried to keep secret. Basically the battle concerned two points: was "*tantine*" capable, mentally and physically – she was crippled by rheumatism – of altering her will; and the high-handed way the minority had been treated. The battle went to the *Cour de Cassation*, France's highest legal tribunal, seven times, until the Cointreaus eventually allowed themselves to be bought out of Rémy at a handsome profit. A few years later Hériard-Dubreuil rounded off his empire by buying Cointreau. which was no longer run by Max's branch of the Cointreau family.

By the time the legal battles were over Hériard-Dubreuil had, nominally at least, handed over to his two sons, Marc and François. But he found them much less able than his daughter, Dominique, and in the mid-1990s he was realistic and open-minded enough to install her instead of his sons. Since then she has combined running the group to general applause with a number of high-profile roles, most obviously as chairman of the Comité Colbert, which brings together thirty of France's proudest purveyors of luxury products.

Today the group remains independent, a powerful force in the world liquor scene. Even the supposedly excessive debts incurred in his expansion have been greatly reduced. Even the family battle has a happy ending. Following Hériard-Dubreuil's death in early 2002 the two sisters were reconciled, as their daughters had already been, and both have been successful, for Beatrice Cointreau, guided by her father Max, not only restored Frapin to a prosperity and reputation even greater than it had enjoyed under her great grandfather, Pierre Frapin, but also bought and resurrected Gosset, the oldest firm in Champagne.

In the four-horse race the back marker was Courvoisier, with sales down by fifteen per cent in the late 1980s and 1990s – although, ironically, the firm suffered less from the slump because it had so feeble a position in the Far Eastern market. The problem was managerial, due in part to successive takeovers. In 1981 Allied Breweries merged with Hiram Walker. For some years the management was preoccupied by the merger – and by the subsequent takeover which created Allied Domecq in the early 1990s. Then came several years of inadequate management and it was not until 2000 that a new, and infinitely more effective, chief executive took over. The better people, structures, and policies – including a proper emphasis on mixability – he put in place took two years to produce their first results.

But the real disaster was Martell. It had been number one as late as 1985 with nearly a fifth of the market. It was already starting to slip – Hennessy had overtaken it – when in 1988 after a long bidding war with Grand Met it was sold to Seagram at a ludicrously inflated price. Such was the inflamed state of the market at the time that the underbidder was so keen to own a cognac firm that it immediately bought the – much smaller – Godet, but resold it six years later. Seagram made every mistake in the book, indeed people now talk of a "ten-year no-man's-land". The group as a whole was drifting because the young chairman, Edgar Bronfman Jnr, was far more interested in the music and show business group he was building up. Dozens of new products were introduced without any real planning but they were never backed by adequate promotional expenditure, and in key markets like the Far East Martell was grossly neglected in favour of Chivas Regal Scotch whisky, whose profits and profile both suffered from heavy discounting.

At the same time Martell was accumulating ever-increasing stocks to avoid being too dependent on the grower/distillers, who of course had done well out of the – temporary – boom of the late 1980s. In cold figures, sales in the 1990s fell by nearly forty per cent and Martell fell to number three in the pecking order, a relegation unheard of since it first came to prominence in the middle of the eighteenth century. As sales declined stocks rose to reach an extraordinary eleven years of sales, partly because of the perpetual optimism required of its sales force. Martell had to cut its purchases by a half. This threw the Borderies, in particular, into confusion and enabled other firms – most obviously Hennessy – to make farther inroads into a region which had been largely Martell's fiefdom for 200 years. In 2001 the break-up of Seagram led to the takeover of Martell by Pernod-Ricard. The changeover was delayed by interminable regulatory problems, which made the loss of momentum even worse.

Pernod soon realized that Martell was in a parlous state and Pernod had to cut purchases by half. The new management admitted that it had "missed the train" in the USA but it hoped to catch the next one, and was basing its hopes on Cordon Bleu, once the world's leading premium cognac – emphasizing the particular qualities of brandies from the Borderies. On the production side the new management found that Martell had been operating out of no fewer than nine premises, which Pernod decided to reduce to three. This involved exploiting the Martells' family estate at Chanteloup in the Borderies (best known for the superb single-estate cognac it used to produce) as a tourist attraction. More fundamentally Pernod proposed to transfer the bottling line at Martell's fortress in the centre of Cognac to Rouillac, thirty-two kilometres/twenty miles to the northwest where Bisquit already had a modern plant. This latter had proved far too big because of Pernod's failure to expand sales of the brand. In doing so Pernod was following the example of the other major houses, which had already moved their bottling lines away from the centre of town to the suburbs. Inevitably the move involved 140 redundancies on top of hundreds of others which the workers had suffered a full decade of mismanagement by Seagram. They promptly went on strike, with three of them going on hunger strike. The management stood firm, and after one of the hunger strikers had been taken to hospital they gave up.

Perhaps the most interesting aspect of this debacle was the total failure of the growers to support their fellow proles. The growers' attitude was simple: "They didn't do anything to support us," one of them told me, "when we made our major protest a few years ago." She was referring to the three-day demonstration launched by the growers in 1998 which had demonstrated clearly the gulf between the industry's workers and the growers and distillers.

Martell's troubles threw a spotlight onto the perpetual problem of how the cognac growers could cope with the boom-and-bust mentality which had afflicted the region over the ages. In the late twentieth century the problem had been exacerbated by the increased size of production, of the vineyard and the increasingly abrupt swings in sales, as well as the new toughness shown by the Big Four which, apart possibly from the case of Rémy, contained not a shred of the historic paternalism. Only cold-blooded managerial calculations now decided the livelihoods not only of 6,000 direct employees but of 29,000 growers and their families as well.

But if the firms continued to go their very different – and sometime disastrous – ways, the same applied in spades to the growers and distillers. As stocks rose and interest rates remained high they were caught in a web of increasing financial commitments, and in any case the "cognac war" had divided them.

In the early 1970s stocks had dropped to a dangerously low figure of four-and-one-third years' sales, but had reached seven years' sales a few years later. Between 1973 and 1982 total stocks rose by just over one-third to over 2.75 million hectolitres. Basically the growers and *bouilleurs de cru* were helpless. All the merchants had to retrench, and the easiest way was to reduce their commitments to the *bouilleurs de cru*, although the handful of major independent distillers, like Boigneau, survived relatively unscathed. Hennessy and Martell merely cut down the amounts they took from "their" growers, but other firms (notably Bisquit) had to cancel some of their contracts. The trade also managed to shift the financial burden to the growers (who enjoyed relatively cheap loans through the Crédit Agricole). As a result in the late 1970s, for the first time in half a century, the growers had more cognac in stock than the trade. Moreover – a problem that was to recur on a larger scale in the 1990s – of the extra one million hectolitres accumulated between 1973 and 1982, 700,000 hectolitres were over five years old. Many of the growers were merely holding on to thousands of casks of mediocre spirit that was never very saleable and was never going to improve greatly. (Stocks of older brandies have often been greatly exaggerated. As recently as 1968 the vast majority even of Hennessy's stocks was less than six years old.)

As the reduction in acreage and yields kicked in, stocks gradually dropped to reach just over five years' sales in 1988–9, triggering one of those false alarms of lack of grapes so characteristic of cognac's history. Then came the crunch: in 1990 – 1,800,000 hectolitres were distilled, but a mere 350,000 were needed as the Japanese crisis took hold – yet the growers had been tempted to break their contracts because of the short-lived boom in the Far East. Ten years later stocks were back up to an average of eight years' worth, later subsiding to a steady seven or so years' worth by the millennium.

But it is the age structure, rather than the size of the stockpile, that is the most worrying. In the early 1990s only a fifth of the total was of *Compte 6*, but as the many – usually inferior – young cognacs rejected by the major firms were supplemented by the reduction in sales of older brandies by the turn of the millennium, by the new century more than a quarter of all stocks were over nine years old, many of them from the Bois and thus surely past their sell-by date.

In the late 1990s at least two of the Big Four reduced their stocks, Rémy from ten to under seven years' of sales, nearly half of which is owned by cooperatives, and Courvoisier from six-and-a-half years to five-and-a-half between 1995 and 2001. This was easier because three of the big four houses depend so greatly on their sales of the younger VS; Hennessy for seventy-five per cent of sales by value, eighty per cent for Courvoisier, and eighty-two per cent in VSOP or VS for Rémy. And, with the obvious exception of Martell, the Big Four have managed to limit the number of contracts they have broken. For instance Courvoisier had to cut purchases by a third, but managed to abide by three-year contracts.

The Cognac vineyard had reached a post-phylloxera peak of 110,000 hectares/270,000 acres in 1976, and production of brandy was running at ten hectolitres for every hectare. Thanks to the notorious Common Agricultural Policy, over the next five years more than half the region's production – not only of spirit, but also of wine – was destined to go for distillation into industrial alcohol. New plantations were forbidden until at least the end of 1986 and a programme of *arrachages* ("uprooting") inaugurated which did indeed reduce the total under vines by nearly a quarter to 78,000 hectares/193,000 acres. Nevertheless, the problem was so serious, as average production rose so sharply, that the normal mechanism devised by the EC to siphon off excess production became inadequate. For Cognac remained one of the largest wine regions in France and probably the largest in the world devoted virtually exclusively to white grapes. Moreover *arrachages* were always slow because growers took a long time to decide to abandon their traditional means of livelihood and their precious plots. Fauré would have preferred a system by which they still enjoyed the theoretical right to plant, with *arrachages temporaires* ("temporary uprooting").

Again it was the taxpayers of Europe who had to foot the bill. European Community premiums were being given to growers prepared to dig up their vines, although they could replant within eight years if conditions permitted. Production on the reduced area was severely restricted. Only a certain amount of alcohol could be distilled as cognac from wines whose production was itself limited; the surplus was carted off to be distilled as industrial alcohol, again with the help of Community funds. Growers were allowed to load only a proportion of even their limited crop on the market. By 1982–3 they could sell immediately only about half their production, 4.5 hectolitres for every hectare of vines; the rest had to be stocked at their expense.

They received some help from ORECO, Coquillaud's idea of a cooperative organisation to stock surplus brandies. He had founded it while still director of the BNIC, but no funds were available. However, it now stores 28,000 hectolitres, bought from 12,000 growers. These stocks are financed at special rates through the Banque de France and stored in buildings all over. Coquillaud also launched SIDECO, which provides finance for buying and selling cognacs on extended terms. The merchants did not escape the burden: they now have to buy ten per cent more stock than they sell in the course of a year – an obligation that obviously weighs particularly heavy on the smaller concerns. The same sort of pressure was being felt by the *bouilleurs de profession,* subject to a squeeze by the bigger firms. As Jacques Fauré put it in 1996: "Today's stock level will weigh for a long time to come on the economy of the region and on the buying capacity of the merchants and the growers."

It had taken some time for the depth – and length – of the crisis to sink in. In the beginning the growers refused to face reality, claiming that it was up to the industry to get the quota increased. For their underlying assumption, common to all producers under the AC system, was that if the growers produced a wine or brandy it is up to someone else to sell it. To make matters worse the great majority of the growers had been almost completely sheltered from market reality for so long by the major firms. The situation was much worse than in the Gironde because Cognac was a single-product region, whereas there was lots of work outside the wine business in and around Bordeaux. The problem was also greater in the Charentes than in the Midi, which suffered even more badly because of over-production. At over 30,000 francs a hectare the cost of production in Charentes was fifty per cent higher than in the Midi.

The growers did not show much, if any, social cohesion when they were faced with the basic problem: that even after the start of attempts to reduce the size of the vineyard in the late 1970s. there were too many grapes. This was understandable because they were in such different circumstances. There were many growers who could rely solely on producing grapes and wines for transforming into cognac and could still make a decent living – at least until artificial limits on yields of alcohol were imposed in the 1990s. By contrast growers from the outer regions needed help, not just to uproot their vines but also to find other outlets for their grapes – for table wine, table grapes, for transformation into fortified or sparkling wines. The double requirement was summed up in the catchphrase: "for each market its [appropriate] production and for each parcel of vines its outlet", together with the need to find "an alternative product which will exploit the know-how of our growers". The unlucky growers were naturally concentrated largely in the lesser appellations, often in the Charente-Maritime. Indeed the shorthand description of the battle was that it was between sixteen and seventeen. In theory the steady reduction in the number of holdings – and the consequent increase in their average size – should have helped, but in the last decades of the twentieth century the growers seemed to be running up a down escalator. Fifty years ago, according to one observer, it was thought that you needed at least four hectares/ten acres of vines to support a family. By 2000 the figure had risen to fifteen hectares/thirty-seven acres and the average exploitation was less than ten hectares/twenty-five acres – though of course expectations of lifestyle had risen dramatically.

Not surprisingly the over-production of the early 1990s created a new crisis which has proved increasingly difficult to surmount, because all the "easy" *arrachages* had been by growers who were either retired or nearing retirement. By the late 1990s people were being asked not, as before, to pull out their vines when they retired but during their working life. Moreover the alternative uses are growing steadily less profitable. There was very little, if any, profit to be made from table grapes, or from those used for cheap sparkling wine.

Given the reduction of the size of the vineyard since 1976 the final shrinkage involved, between 5,000 and 7,000 hectares/12,000 and

17,000 acres, a tenth of the total, is not enormous and the BNIC believes it would be possible to reduce the vineyard by up to 1,000 hectares a year. Nevertheless, says one insider, "people are frightened, the problems are both financial and psychological" – especially as nearly three-quarters of the problem is in the Charente-Maritime. To make matters worse the alternative uses for grapes were proving difficult – a far cry from the situation in the late 1940s when the price for table wine grapes had been the same as those destined for distillation. At the same time the crops which growers had planted instead of vines – most obviously the sunflowers which increasingly dotted the landscape of the Cognac region – were becoming less profitable as the restrictions on the CAP gradually increased – and the EU's support for *arrachage* stopped in 1996. It was only partially replaced by a levy of 110 francs per hectolitre to help finance farther *arrachages*.

In the late 1990s the government weighed in with mixed results. In 2000 Jean Glavany, the Minister of Agriculture in the Socialist government of Lionel Jospin, had visited the region together with a senior civil servant, Jacques Bertomeau, who was later to issue a rather discursive report on the state of the French wine industry. Unfortunately they both descended on the Charentes with their ideas already formed. One, as we shall see in the next chapter, was extremely useful: to allow the BNIC to have a local President. The other, for the region to have a single union (*syndicat*) representing the growers, was more dubious since the visitors from Paris seemed to have no idea of the ever-increasing divide between the two classes of growers. The first viticultural elections in 1998 had a major beneficial result, because the Communist-led *syndicat*, refused to participate, claiming that the elections were fraudulent, but in reality because they had no real support, although they had previously managed to create a great deal of trouble – one chairman of the BNIC had to resign after his house was besieged.

By the millennium the argument centred on the amount of alcohol a distiller could extract from his wine, an apparently technical argument which in fact defined two very different approaches to a grower's holdings. The "democrats" in the outer regions wanted the misery to be shared equally by limiting the yield of spirit. On the other side Hennessy is typical in wanting a higher production quota from fewer hectares for stable prices. To placate the outer regions the BNIC reduced the yield that could be distilled as cognac to a mere six hectolitres for every hectare, this at a time when potential productivity for wine had risen from 120 hectolitres of wine to 180 for every hectare – a potential of triple that amount. On the other side there was a growing revolt among the more professional distillers. They were wanting only to make cognac, again naturally concentrated in the better regions, and claiming, rightly, that the limit was far too low to allow them a decent living, let alone profitability and in 2003 the legal yield was raised to seven hectolitres.

It was a well-known grower and merchant, Jean-Louis Brillet, as chairman of a new syndicat SVBC, who spelt out the situation in much the same way as Fauré, to reduce the area under vines by fifteen per cent, or 12,000 hectares/30,000 acres. This would leave between 6,000 and 7,000 to be pulled out, 5,000 devoted to vin de pays and 10,000 to wines used as the base for mousseux and *vins vinés* ("fortified wines"). That would allow the remaining hectares to produce eight hectolitres of spirit per hectare, giving a production of 460,000 hectolitres, which just about equals the region's annual requirements. The opposite point of view, as expressed by Didier Braud of the Charente-Maritime, is simply that any *arrachage* of fifteen per cent would separate the region into two, one devoted entirely to cognac and the other abandoned to "other outlets". He, of course, was dreaming of a universal solution, which refuses to recognize the distinction between the quality – and thus the demand – in the different sub-regions. Unfortunately he, like so many other people in the region, seemed to be unaware that the world had no need for cognac, and that for no one was it a basic necessity. Fortunately a wide spread of the Cognac community had started to fight back, with increasing effectiveness.

11

Fight Back

In the last decade of the twentieth century the Cognaçais started to fight back – patchily yes, belatedly certainly, but with increasing effectiveness. The most important element in the renaissance was a recognition that they could not stand loftily above the fray, and would have to behave like the producers of lesser spirits, above all Scotch whisky. But this is not the only factor: by the turn of the millennium cognac was enjoying better, and above all more solid prospects than at any time since the 1970s. Sales in most major markets were growing and new ones were opening up. Korea is now as promising as was the Far East as a whole thirty years ago – moreover the Koreans, who started with VSOP, are now moving up to XO. Even more promising is Russia, where the new elite loves strong drink and conspicuous consumption. Indeed Moscow houses the merchant with the single largest collection of cognacs in the world. At first these brandies were largely destined to be drunk in mafia-run and -frequented night clubs in Moscow where expensive blondes are popularly supposed to drink them with Coca-Cola. But "when a country opens up," says one leading merchant, "it is a handful of rich men – or in Russia the former *nomenklatura* – who buy the top qualities". But Russia is now moving out of that position with a democratization of brandy in a country which is used, perhaps more than any other, to the appreciation of spirits.

The unsung hero of this renewal is the BNIC. In 1996 a new director was appointed from outside the region, Alain Philippe, with a long and successful career in the construction business behind him. The President had always been a bureaucrat *parachuté* from Paris, but in 1998 Cognac was liberated by the Minister of Agriculture Jean Glavany. "It was emancipated," says one insider; henceforth Cognac was to enjoy a new independence. The region was lucky in its first local president, Bernard Guionnet, "the only grower with a broader vision of the future" as one of his colleagues puts it. He's not your typical peasant, for he had studied at the top agro-engineering schools in Montpellier and Toulouse, and had been President of one of the major growers' groups. Quiet, fiftyish, decisive, he had been running an eighty-hectare/200-acre family estate in the Grande Champagne and the Borderies and was open-minded enough to understand the problems faced by the region. In principle, as in other regions like Champagne and Bordeaux, the BNIC hope that a grower will alternate with a merchant – and indeed in 2003 Jean-Pierre Lacarrièm, a director of Rémy Martin, duly took over the presidency.

The BNIC also stepped up its promotional efforts. Since the early 1980s it had been organizing a film festival devoted exclusively to detective films. The festival was the idea of the late Colonel Gerard Sturm, for a long time the BNIC's public relations director. It is characteristic of the narrow-mindedness of the Cognaçais that the major firms have been reluctant to support the initiative, while to the growers it was no accident that the BNIC had once awarded a prize to a detective thriller in which the author used the word "*alcool*" to describe cognac as though it was an ordinary spirit. The festival has now become a small, exclusive but widely recognized event in the festival calendar. In 2002 it cost a mere 460,000 euros but, according to the BNIC, attracted over two million euros' worth of cognac-related advertising and fulfilled the BNIC's role of promoting cognac in the home market, almost totally neglected by the Big Four.

The BNIC was one of the pioneers of promoting cognac in France as a long drink, although, regrettably, it has nailed its colours to the mast of mixing it with tonic, one of the few soft drinks with which it clashes – in my view, anyway. In November 1996 it even trumpeted "the month of cognac". More recently it has avoided the severe restrictions imposed on drinks advertising in France – amounting to an effective ban in some cases – with a poster campaign asking the question, "what sort of cognac are you?" featuring cognac neat, on the rocks, and with a mixer – inevitably tonic. Unfortunately, this, like so many of the Bureau's initiatives, is largely confined to France, where the Big Four are not very active. Outside the domestic market their influence ensured that for some years it even had to cut its – by no means expensive – representation. But throughout the world it has had considerable, if largely unpublicized, success in defending the name of cognac – a task which, as we have seen, requires eternal vigilance. Above all it has set up stronger defences against fakes, working with the WTO (World Trade Organisation) in Brazil, Russia, and Central Europe – and succeeding in being the first AC recognized in Vietnam.

It helps the Cognaçais' efforts that overall quality is improving. Exports in cask now account for only a twelfth of sales, half the percentage of only ten years ago. Moreover, as the map on p. 2 shows, production is now concentrated in a rectangle roughly corresponding to the terroirs most suitable for cognac. In other words, by and large the market, and pressure to uproot vines, has succeeded in carrying through the reforms I suggested twenty years ago in the first edition of my book. My programme was echoed by Patrick Daniou, a leading geographer. In 1983 he wrote that: "it seems eminently desirable, in order to defend the quality of cognac's brandies, to take greater account of terroir in a new definition of the cognac appellation, which should be based on scientific criteria and on boundaries that should not necessarily be administrative ones."[1]

The concentration on the best terroirs has been backed by lots of initiatives, which include more attention to design. Most firms are getting away from the frosted glass bottle, first made famous by Rémy Martin's VSOP, which had become ubiquitous but had lost its status over the decades as it was increasingly used for the infamous "French brandies". But even a simple rethink can help. Otard, for instance, found that sales of its XO leaped when an elegant, light new bottle replaced its rather forbidding darker predecessor – "it changed people's perception of the brandy" says Otard; it also helped that the cognac is smoother. Camus has helped itself in Duty Free by its policy of regularly introducing new cognacs. It has enjoyed lasting success with Josephine, a light, floral cognac designed to appeal to Japanese "office ladies", which is sold in a slim, elegant 50cl bottle with a label imitating the great Art Nouveau artist Mucha. Other novelties are put on sale for only a season or two. "Every time a Japanese goes abroad," says Cyril Camus, "they have to bring back a new product" – hence the firm's fifty-strong range of "collectibles", often in the shape of porcelain books. For Duty Free is by

[1] Patrick Daniou, *Annales GREH,* 1983.

no means dead. Its abolition within the EU has not hurt sales, indeed on the contrary, for travellers within Europe are buying more than ever.

Probably the biggest challenge faced by the Cognaçais has been the fight against Scotch. This has taken three forms, all of them recognizing the colossal gaps which previously had allowed single malt whiskies to triumph: increased control over quality and age statements; allowing single vintage cognacs, thus filling a major gap in the market for the better cognacs; and, above all, promoting cognac as a long drink. The Big Four have imitated the Scots by despatching their *chefs de caves*, and even specially trained experts, as brand ambassadors throughout the world to spread the gospel of cognac, a policy initiated by Rémy with Robert Leauté.

Unfortunately they are not allowed to compete with the Scots when it comes to giving the precise age of their offerings – apart from single-vintage cognacs – while most premium Scotch whiskies, blends as well as single malts, feature the age of the youngest spirit in their whisky,[2] an invaluable weapon. I first realized the importance of exact ages when touring Japan in 1988 to launch the first edition of this book. I was over-whelmed with questions from local sommeliers asking for the precise ages of the cognacs I was discussing, but of course I could provide only vague indications. For, historically, the Cognaçais have depended too much on their mystique, refusing to give not only the age but also – apart from Rémy – the precise provenance of all but their most expensive offerings.

Some progress has been made, above all in extending the official definition of age of maturing cognacs beyond *Compte 6*. During the 1990s the BNIC gained clearance for up to *Compte 8* which came into force in 1999, and *Comptes 9* and *10* have belatedly received for official blessing – changes like this are dogged by the need for official approval of texts from the EU as well as the French government. In fact, given the – excessive – stocks of older brandies there is no reason not to extend age definitions even further. Most firms agree with the BNIC in wanting XOs to be a minimum of ten years, but some of the smaller firms in one of the three merchants' unions are complaining that such a regulation would favour

[2] According to EU rules you can only promote a drink according to the age of its youngest constituent.

the big ones. Of course this is rubbish, since the real winners would be small producers and firms relying on quality rather than price.

Ideally the Cognaçais should copy the port wine community which simply grades tawny port by its taste – if it tastes like a ten-year-old it can be labelled as such. Most firms prefer to attach names to different ages – a ridiculous idea given the need to compete with the Scots, who combine brand and age so successfully. As it is, Ragnaud-Sabourin, one of the most reputable of all growers, was prosecuted for putting an age statement on some of its cognacs. Nevertheless many companies get round the ban on providing an exact age by giving hints in their promotional literature or even on their labels. The most blatant instance is the Tesseron family, famous for its incomparable stocks of old brandies, which numbers its cognacs by the date they were distilled (90 for the 1990) – Ragnaud-Sabourin does much the same. For its part Moyet, another firm famous for its stocks, gets round the ban by attaching a separate label to each bottle giving the approximate age of the cognacs.

Belatedly the Cognaçais have, however, responded to the challenge presented by the Scots – and the Armagnaçais – with their single-vintage brandies. This does go against tradition. Typically, Camus' brochure states firmly that vintages "are not representative of the quality of cognac" which should be "highly complex blends". The path to avoidance of the 1962 ban on single-vintage cognacs – apart from those matured in England – was opened by the Royer law of 1975, named after the then Mayor of Tours. This involved a formula that allowed distillers to describe cognacs as coming from a single vintage, provided that they could produce documents showing their origin, and unless someone objected – previously producers were assumed to be guilty. The law was national, overriding local regulations as long as firms could prove the age of the brandy. As a result a number of reputable firms, notably Hine, Delamain, and Croizet, were able to sell single-vintage cognacs because they had stocks under a double lock and key which had been supervized by the French authorities. Nevertheless only one of the Big Four, Rémy, is taking advantage of the relaxation and launching a single vintage – in its case a superb 1965.

The local restrictions were lifted in 1987 (carbon dating should have been able to help, although the ban on atomic explosions in the atmo-sphere as a result of the 1963 test ban treaty greatly reduced the ease with which brandies could be dated precisely after that date). From 1987 on firms could stock cognacs designed to be sold as single vintages – so that the first of the "new" single-vintage cognacs will be the 1988. Many firms, like Hine and Rémy Martin, reckon that these brandies will need at least fifteen years, although Ragnaud-Sabourin started to sell its 1988 vintage after only twelve years in bottle.

The return of single-vintage cognacs is proving a great success, especially with sommeliers bored with standard products. Even more helpful is the rise – or return – of upmarket brands. For the Big Four are too big to have room in their portfolio for smaller, niche products, a tendency similar to that in other industries where the rule is "the bigger the groups, the bigger the gaps in the market".

The most obvious case of trials and tribulations with a happy ending is Hine. When Guinness took over Distillers in 1986 the new "marketing-led" management concentrated on FOV, the relatively undistinguished cognac made by Hine which accounted for the majority of the firm's sales and was sold exclusively in the Far East. It also imposed ridiculous accounting requirements and looked for sales volume at the expense of the quality image that had served Hine so well for the previous 200 years. The nightmare came to an end after a mere fifteen months when Guinness transferred the firm to a – rather reluctant – LVMH-Moët-Hennessy as part of a world wide deal linking the two groups. For a further fourteen years Hine muddled along under a number of chief executives who sometimes wanted to offer a full range of cognacs, not a sensible ambition for so small a firm.

Fortunately for the firm – and for Bernard Hine who had survived the traumas, and had ensured that the underlying quality remained superb – in 2001 Moët appointed Mark Cornell, a former British army officer, to simplify and modernize the firm. With the help of the veteran marketing genius Tom Jago – whose credits included Baileys Irish Cream and Classic Malts – Cornell improved the packaging and slimmed down the line. The result was a range of a mere three brandies plus a few single vintage cognacs, some offered in what might be called "sampling packs" of three 20cl bottles. This policy is being enthusiastically pursued by International Brands a spirits group which bought Hine in 2003. As a result Hine looks to be one of the handful of upmarket firms to be able to compete with the Big Four.

There have also been a number of initiatives by enthusiasts who are helping to diversify cognac's image. The biggest success story started, improbably, with Pierre Voisin, the agent in the Cognac region for Fiat and Volvo, who had a passion for cognac. He started to mature some from the Premiers Fins Bois and in the early 1980s launched Leopold Gourmel, a brand named after his wife's maiden name. Since then the firm has suffered a number of vicissitudes, but in the late 1990s under Olivier Blanc, M. Voisin's son-in-law, its range of brandies – all from the same source – has enjoyed great success. This is not only because of their underlying quality but also because the buyer has the choice of different ages, and therefore different stages in the development of the cognacs, from the fruitier ("Age des Fruits") to the spicier ("Age des Epices").

M. Voisin was not the only outsider to have bright ideas. A Swedish industrialist, Otto Kelt, had the inspiration of copying the old idea of maturing cognac by shipping it round the world. The result, in his case, is cognac which is naturally richer and rounder than the competition. Others – like two businessmen, Marc Georges and Pierre Dubarry of Moyet, and Ferry de Bakker, a former advertising executive – are searching out cognacs from individual regions, a policy also pursued with great success (from a quality point of view anyway) by the Japanese-owned Louis Royer. Other major newcomers are the Swedish V & S liquor monopoly and the giant US Gallo company, both of which have gained medals at the International Spirits Challenge. Gallo's arrival is particularly significant since it already dominates the US brandy scene with its E & J offering, and clearly sees enough of a future for cognac in the USA to justify the major investment required to launch its own brand.

In a smaller, but still significant move, Rémy has taken control of another original firm, de Fussigny, founded twenty years ago by Alain Royer, of the family that formerly owned Louis Royer, to offer single "lots" – batches or even single casks – of cognac, and is now expanding its range. In other words there is increasing room for specialists, and not only amongst the producers. In France specialist grocers, the *epiceries fines*, are good clients, as are the better restaurants and, in Britain, a handful of specialist importers like Brandy Classics, Cognac & Company, and Eaux de Vie[3] are providing outlets for even the smallest specialists.

---

[3] Their addresses can be found in the Directory.

Specialist producers now include an increasing number of growers, not only in the Grande Champagne, but also in the Petite Champagne, the Fins Bois, and even the Bon Bois. The biggest is of course Frapin, while its neighbours, Raymond Ragnaud and Ragnaud-Sabourin, have also been selling their splendid cognacs directly for several generations. But the increasing unreliability of the contracts with the Big Four since 1973 has greatly increased the number of direct sellers. Moreover a younger, well-educated generation is taking over, far more prepared than their parents to launch themselves into direct selling. Unfortunately these growers suffer from a major disadvantage as against their equivalents in other wine-making regions. Most private clients – the base of any direct sales network – are simply not going to buy cognac in the quantity that they do in the case of, say, Champagne. Moreover, growers simply do not have enough stock to produce reliable blends. They usually have to rely on brandies from a single vintage, and because they are still mostly in the Grande Champagne their VSs and even their VSOPs are not as good as those on offer from the best merchants.

More helpful for growers in lesser terroirs is the increasing success of Pineau des Charentes. Technically this is a *mistel*, a type of drink familiar all over rural France, in which the fermentation of fruit juice (not just grape juice; in Normandy they use apples to make their Pommeau) is stopped by the addition of brandy. To be legally entitled to the name Pineau des Charentes, the drink must contain between sixteen and twenty-two degrees of alcohol and has to be matured in wood for a year before it is sold. But it can happily age for up to ten years in cask, at which point the red – in fact it's pink – variety in particular has far greater depth and subtlety than virtually any other apéritif I know. Pineau had been a pretty marginal item in the region until the first crisis of the early 1970s, when growers started to get interested. The result is that sales have risen five times to absorb around 100,000 hectolitres of grape juice. Nevertheless, it remains largely a cottage industry as it can be produced only by *bouilleurs de cru, bouilleurs de profession* – who can use only their own grapes – and cooperatives, although some firms make a point of offering it. Even so it forms an additional tool for growers to sell to the hundreds of thousands of tourists attracted largely by the region's many fine beaches.

Other outlets vary widely as growers weigh the difference in price between selling their wine for compulsory distillation, as *vin de table*, or as a base for low-grade sparkling or fortified wines (*vins vinés*), all of them increasingly unprofitable outlets. But the same is not true of one of the success stories of the past few years, the growth in the production of *vins de pays*, officially authorized in 1981. The idea is not at all absurd – for years the Sauvignon Blanc used by Messrs Dourthe to make their fine Dourthe No 1 has come from a cooperative in the very north of the Gironde, a few kilometres south of the Cognac region. Some varieties – notably Merlot, Colombard, and Sauvignon Blanc – can produce wines that are excellent value for money, and production trebled in the 1990s.

Not surprisingly it was the far-sighted André Hériard-Dubreuil who did the most to help. Five years before his death he set up the first proper wine business by planting 350 hectares/860 acres round the family's former country house at St Même, where the gravel banks round the Charente were far better suited to Merlot, a Bordeaux variety, than to Ugni Blanc. Today there is even a cooperative devoted to the production of table wines. Although these wines have found a ready market they have been something of a disappointment. The BNIC had hoped that table wines would account for 5,000 hectares/12,000 acres, but are unlikely to cover more than 3,000 hectares/7,400 acres within the foreseeable future. But this is already over three times the size of small appellations like Pomerol, a fact which highlights the task facing the "diversifiers" simply because of the sheer size of the cognac appellation.

All these initiatives, however successful, are simply on too small a scale to affect overall sales, although they undoubtedly help spread the "gospel of cognac" within a context which is favourable for the drink. For cognac is a social statement, and as such terribly vulnerable, like all alcoholic drinks, to the whims of fashion. Today it is benefiting from a change of generations throughout the world. There is a general rule that children tend to avoid the drinks preferred by their parents, and today, youngsters find it quite fashionable and are prepared to try cognac, or cognac-based drinks, rarely touched by their parents. But the producers have to accept the existence of two very separate markets, superior and basic, and should promote most of their precious spirit as one that could be mixed. The division is natural enough, for when it comes to Bourbon the Americans have always made a distinction between "sippin' whiskeys" and those destined for diluting or mixing as long drinks. Of course some

Cognaçais don't like the idea, fearing what might be described as "brand dilution", that it will be all too easy to replace cognac with some other, less expensive spirit and thus devalue its name.

The idea of selling cognac-based mixed drinks was not of course new; just think of Cointreau and Grand Marnier. The quantities of cognac absorbed by these historic outlets doubled in the last decade of the twentieth century to account for over a tenth of total sales. More of them are steadily being launched on what appears to be a receptive market. An early and substantial success, above all in the USA, has been Alizé, a blend of cognac and passionfruit juice, launched by the Lafragette family, which also sells some very decent cognacs, proving that there is no incompatibility between the two markets. Thanks largely to excellent promotion by its importers, Alizé is now one of the biggest sellers of cognac-based drinks, and now number two in the USA behind Hennessy, by a long way the market leader. More recently Rémy Red, a blend weighing in at seventeen degrees of alcohol and designed to get drinkers used to "the real stuff" sold a million bottles in its first year, while Merlem, a grower, launched Hypnotic, a similar blend which sold the same amount.

Whisky was always welcome because it was sold and appreciated as an apéritif, a long drink. And indeed even before the latest marketing efforts a great deal of cognac was already being drunk with Coca-Cola (or coke), or lemonade. Moreover the enquiry into the French market conducted by the BNIC in 1999 revealed that a quarter of cognac drinkers took their cognac with ice and the same proportion in cocktails, although the idea of it as a long drink had not yet caught on – even though Gilles Hennessy had launched Hennessy glacé on the French market as early as 1988. But the lag in promotion was the fault of an industry which, until relatively recently, refused to face the fact that its future lay in promoting the mixability of its precious product. Now that it has, in most markets, the idea of promoting cognac-based long drinks has many fathers. These include the BNIC, which was certainly early on the scene, and the small firm of Godet, which promoted its "Sélection Spéciale" as a base for many of them (the firm is now blending cognac with tea for the Taiwanese market). But probably the biggest influence has been Hennessy. Until the early 1990s cognac had suffered badly from the elitist image so systematically pursued in the USA. It was Hennessy that first broke the taboo of cognac as a long drink or as a base for cocktails. Now every firm is promoting the idea – and Rémy has performed a miracle with its Grand Cru Petite Champagne VS, to my palate the first successful attempt to produce a young cognac from the Champagnes – its previous VS, a Fine Champagne, was a markedly less successful product.

But the most surprising element in the new fashionability of cognac is its affiliation with Afro-American rock, rap, and hip-hop artists. Hennessy has understood the potential and now has two levels of sponsorship. In Britain it has sponsored the Hennessy Gold Cup, a leading steeplechase, for over fifty years but now also sponsors parties for rapsters and their fans, and promotes the MOBO music awards in the USA. Hennessy may have been the first to latch on to the market but the competition is hard on its heels. Indeed de Fussigny has even launched a brandy called NYAK, after the way the rap community pronounces Cognac. Courvoisier – which is doing well in the USA with its VSOP as well as its VS – has been more systematic. The firm has also been exceedingly lucky in that its cognac featured in a hit by Busta Rhymes that reached the top five of the American rap charts last year called simply "pass the Courvoisier":

Give me the Henny, you can give me the Cris
You can pass me the Remi, but pass the Courvoisier

And yes, he is equating the cognac he drinks – from Hennessy, Rémy Martin, and Courvoisier – with Louis Roederer's Cristal, most upmarket of Champagnes.

He was not alone. Puff Daddy and Snoop Doggy Dogg have also serenaded the charms of "gnac", while Devino Fortunato, a popular Californian rapper, first achieved success with a little number called "Cognac Loungin". But perhaps the rap atmosphere is best conveyed in a number entitled "So Much Pain (featuring 2Pac)" by Ja Rule:

Feel the rage this world has bestowed upon me
And I don't give a fuck 'cause they don't give a fuck 'bout me
So I keep – drinkin Hennessy, bustin at my enemies
Will I live to see twenty-three? There's so much pain

Stars like these simply cannot be bought. Even if they were willing, their fee would simply break any promotional budget. To build on the brand's new-found trendiness, Sandy Mayo, Courvoisier's new young Australian-born marketing director, has set up the grandiosely named House of Courvoisier, designed to add "style, glamour and luxury" to the brand's traditional values of "heritage, tradition and artisanship". Building on this heady mix came ads for new products created by legendary hip-hop impresario Russell Simmon, founder of Def Jam Records, featuring luxury items like boots and fancy underwear plugging Courvoisier – in an echo of Louis Vuitton's famous intertwined LV logo. Martell's come-back in the USA is now headed by an advertising campaign featuring more respectable, upwardly mobile, black professionals. Even when these initiatives – and the rap habit on which they are based – have become merely examples of the ephemeral nature of popular cultural fads, cognac will again have taken its place as a major element in the world spirits business, a place which fashion, and the arrogance of the Cognaçais, had deprived it of for so long. And since cognac represents a mere one per cent of the world market in spirits there will always be room for it in the many guises I discuss in the next chapter.

part III

The Enjoyment of Cognac

The enjoyment of cognac, like everything else about this miraculous drink, is a complicated matter. As I've suggested throughout this book, you can drink cognac neat, or diluted with ice, or with soda water or other sparkling waters, or exploit its unique complexities by combining it with any compatible mixer.

But of course the purest pleasure associated with cognac comes through sipping the best brandies, essentially the XOs and above, though including some of the best VSOPs. It's not a simple business. Jacques Chardonne provides a wonderful and – for him – precise description of one M. Pommerel. This master taster "poured a drop of cognac into a crystal glass shaped like a half-opened tulip . . . he took the glass and then delicately, between two fingers, he lifted it up without agitating it, breathing the fumes gently as if, through slow and silent exhalations, he was absorbing all its flavours".

In the past, and in many circles even today, the enjoyment of fine cognac has been bedevilled by the image. In a famous scene in *Brideshead Revisited* Evelyn Waugh uses brandy in one example of the insufferable snobbishness which permeates the whole book. The hero, Charles Ryder, is dining with the upstart Rex Mottram in a restaurant clearly identifiable as the Tour d'Argent. The cognac offered to them is "clear and pale and it came to us in a bottle free from grime and Napoleonic cyphers. It was only a year or two older than Rex and lately bottled. They gave it to us in very thin tulip-shaped glasses of modest size." Predictably, Rex does not like it: he "pronounced it the sort of stuff he put soda in at home". So "shamefacedly, they wheeled out of its hiding place the vast and mouldy bottle they kept for people of Rex's sort . . . a treacly concoction", which left "dark rings round the side of his glass . . . a balloon the size of his head", (still often seen in pretentious surroundings the world over, but never in Cognac itself). Waugh was being deliberately, outrageously snobbish. But he had clearly separated the two markets which developed amid the cigar smoke and lush living of Edwardian England: the older, "purer" tradition, of aristocratic sips of light, intense, delicate cognacs shipped early and bottled late, and the newer and more vulgar novelties symbolized by "vast grimy bottles" and "Napoleonic cyphers".

Mottram was not alone in his attitude, one which still deters younger drinkers. Above all the glasses used, the vast balloons still offered to diners – and not only those as ignorant as Rex Mottram – not only lend an air of absurdity and snobbery to the drinking of fine brandy, their very size precludes proper appreciation of their aromas. In the words of Georg Riedel, the glassmaker, "with large glasses you have large surfaces and lots of evaporation and this means that the fruit disappears, so all you have left is the alcohol".

Basically you need a glass with a top that is narrower than the bottom, but, unlike balloons of whatever size, not too large to allow the flavours to be lost. I've even used a Champagne flute, but the best is that employed by professional tasters, the bulbous "tulip" glass described by Chardonne, which has a small chimney on top of the bulb. This has the desired quality of combining small quantities of spirits with the maximum capacity to entrap and concentrate the bouquet.

Riedel, ever the perfectionist, offers two types of glass – and, possibly rather shame facedly, a balloon for old-timers. His VSOP glass is taller than the usual tulip glass and is designed to play up the fruitiness of the brandy and minimize the harshness, the burning sensation so evident in most VSOPs. The idea works: a VSOP nosed in this glass is warmer and less fiery than when tasted in the tulip-shaped glass used for older brandies. Because these should have lost their youthful harshness, the glass can be designed to maximize the power of the complex aromas of rich, chocolatey fruitiness and nuttiness typical of the best cognacs. (Of course Riedel is not alone in offering well-designed cognac glasses; Baccarat, for instance, now has a good one.)

Tasters obviously have to rely very largely on their sense of smell, for even the strongest stomach cannot survive the small sips ingested when sampling fifty or more cognacs in a row, especially freshly distilled or immature ones. They, like the rest of us, are judging on three criteria: age, *cru*, and the general style resulting from the combination of the age, the *cru*, and the oak. They will instantly reject the harsh oiliness imparted to both nose and palate by the raw spirit used in even the best grape brandies. The *cru* is more difficult to distinguish. Most cheap cognacs are relatively anonymous; the better will, however, have a certain character. With less routine cognacs it is immensely enjoyable to look for the nuttiness provided by cognacs from the Borderies, and to try and detect the age of the cognac employed in different "Champagne" cognacs.

Of course the brandy should be at the right temperature. The ideal is about 18°C, since too warm a brandy evaporates too quickly and thus tastes too alcoholic. Better to start with a relatively cold glass than the warmed ones traditionally used – and if the brandy is already the right temperature, it's obviously sensible to hold it by the foot or stem to avoid over heating.

Compared with wine, the colour of the brandy is of little importance, since most cognacs are coloured with caramel to provide the element of standardization important in maintaining the brandy's vital brand image. Indeed in Cognac itself the tasters use blue-coloured glasses to eliminate the colour factor entirely. Nevertheless it is pretty safe to assume that brandies which are too deep in colour are overly viscous, because they contain too much caramel. Personally I've not come across many dark cognacs which offer any elegance, while all the best older brandies have a golden streak. You can also judge – roughly – the age of a brandy by the traces, the "tears" as the professionals call them, that trickle down the inside of the glass; for the older the cognac the slower they fall.

Cognacs are far more difficult to taste than wines – not surprisingly many wine writers simply refuse to taste brandies, basically because they are so strong. Inevitably amateurs can cope with a far smaller number than professionals. Personally I will taste five or six in a flight, accompanied by large doses of water – which I spit because swallowing would include some of the brandy. I try not to do more than twenty in a morning (my greatest achievement, which I hope never to repeat, was to taste thirty-two South African brandies – a few of which were excellent – in a morning). But I was younger then.

Tasting for enjoyment should be done in two stages to separate the more volatile constituents from the heavier ones. So the first impression should be gained by lifting, not swirling the glass, and with the nose slowly approaching the rim of the glass, which can then be rotated rather slowly to capture the depth and variety of aromas which should be emanating from the spirit. This first "nosing" should not be too near the glass or it will be overwhelmed by the strength of the flavours. You then pause to catch your breath and put your nose in the glass to capture the less volatile, more alcoholic components. Only then do you actually taste. Now the glass has to be twirled, just like with a wine, to check for the individual taste components – the fruit, the balance, the length, the finish – which should be far longer than with wine.

Whatever the sensations, the drinker can generally be guided by the style of the house which blended the cognac. Most are commercial, for few blenders can afford the attitude of Alain Braastad, the former chairman of Delamain, who says simply: "I blend what I like." These house styles are a strange mixture of the taste for which customers developed a fondness in ages past, of the personal favourites of the blenders, sometimes of a deliberate, almost perverse complexity, and now, increasingly, a pandering to the tastes of particular groups of buyers, be they Chinese or cigar smokers. "The more you simplify cognac, the easier it is to imitate," says Robert Leauté of Rémy Martin. For once you rise above the VSOP level, the choice is almost infinite. As might be expected, Martell and Hennessy have very different house styles: Martell, as we have seen, is almost obsessively dry and clear on the palate; Hennessy goes for a much richer, almost voluptuous, taste in its blends. The theme of "richness", of a desire to extract as much of the grapiness as possible from the fruit, is also common to Rémy's distillation policy. (House styles are discussed individually in Part V.)

Old cognacs, those that have absorbed all they can from the wood, are a class apart. But the most satisfying can often be as young – in brandy terms – as thirty-five years old when they have already developed the vital *rancio* described in Part I, Chapter 3. The best "expand inside the mouth". Once they are fifty years old, the best of them have acquired an inimitable, golden-bronze colour and a harmony achievable only with age. Age can also bring with it a kind of anonymity, blurring the original distinctions between different styles, so some of the real golden oldies, like Rémy Martin's Louis XIII and Hennessy's Paradis, resemble each other more than they do their makers' more ordinary blends.

Style applies more to younger, mid-range blends. The contrast between two widely respected cognacs, Frapin's Château de Fontpinot and Delamain's Pale and Dry, is particularly striking. The Frapin is infinitely more woody; the oak, though dissolved and matured, is still emphatically present. In pre-feminist language, it is a "masculine" cognac, where the infinitely more delicate Delamain is "feminine", all lightness and elegance. To my palate, the best balance is achieved by a single-vineyard cognac, from Raymond Ragnaud, Frapin, or Ragnaud-Sabourin, which combines both sets of qualities. But cognacs like these are rare enough to prove the rule that the only way to establish a reliable house style is to blend the products of many stills.

Beware, above all, of the oldest cognacs. Some have been left far too long in cask and so are far too woody. Even the cognacs from the Grande Champagne will not age for more than about seventy to eighty years, and must be taken out of the cask much earlier to stop them deteriorating. Others will have been in a sort of "solera system", diluted over the years with younger brandies, while others were never very good in the first place, their faults merely emphasized by their decades in wood. The older the cognac the truer these reservations. Virtually no cognac distilled before 1800 is either drinkable or available, as storage was suspect. Cognacs bottled before 1857 had to be blended and sold without a producer's name and much was poorly aged. Corks will also taint the cognac and need to be changed at least every twenty years.

Moreover there has always been a well-founded suspicion as to the accuracy of the ages given to cognac. Charles Tovey put it bluntly: "We place but little reliance," he wrote, "upon the cognac shippers' declarations with regard to vintages; and the only security the merchant has is to get his vintage brandy over to England into his own bonded stores as soon after the vintage as is convenient." Maurice Healy described an early example of a "solera" system: "Bisquit Dubouché offered to supply apparently unlimited quantities of their 1865, their 1834 and even their 1811. If a cask of 1811 brandy had got down to its last tenth, and was then refilled with brandy of a younger but sympathetic vintage, say 1834, the cask became within a few days a full cask of 1811, the older vintage having endowed the younger with its quality, while receiving the strength and virility of the other."

And my own personal tastes? Like the locals – a long-lived bunch – I drink relatively little of it neat, though much more as a long drink. For me a good or great cognac is more than the sum of its parts. I am looking for length on the palate and the length of the finish. In the end what matters most is the impact from the fruit from which the cognac was made. This can be richer or leaner, for it is no more ridiculous to talk of the "backbone" of a good Martell, the "elegance" of a Delamain, the "fruitiness" of a Hennessy cognac than it is to attribute the same qualities to clarets from Pauillac or St-Emilion. For the best cognacs have one advantage denied even to the finest wines: they are longer, because the sheer strength of the drink means that its qualities linger longer. You can taste for hours and still keep finding new depths, new flavours – even next morning when the glass has been empty the whole night long. But no one has put the experience better than the Abbé Talleyrand. At the end of a sumptuous supper, one of the guests tossed down his glass of Fine Champagne in one gulp in the Russian manner. Talleyrand took the liberty of advising his friend quite quietly:

> *That is not how you should drink cognac. You take your glass in the hollow of the hand, you warm it, you rotate it with a circular movement so that the spirit gives off its aroma. Then you carry it to your nostrils and inhale . . . and then, my dear sir, you put down your glass and talk about it.*

In the past drinkers made a clear distinction between "sippin'" brandies and those suitable for what the Americans call "Bourbon and branch water" – ice, soda-water or water. Charles de Gaulle himself liked a *fine a l'eau*, brandy and water, which was a favourite of Parisians and the Frenchmen sent out to rule the country's then-extensive empire. For such a drink you need stronger cognacs – VSOPs made from brandies from the Champagnes are ideal for long drinks because they will be tough enough. There are those who claim that by far the best way of drinking cognacs from the Grande Champagne which are less than ten years' old is with ice. But the ice should be made with pure, bottled water to avoid the chlorine taste inevitable with so many waters from taps around the world. Fizz need not necessarily be simply soda water even though B&S, brandy and soda, was a standby of late-night, night-cap drinking in Britain in the past. Personally I prefer Perrier as a mixer, finding its slight saltiness an agreeable counterpoint to the richness of the brandy, but other brandy bores find it too salty and prefer Badoit or other sparkling waters.

Other key mixers are based on ginger. The British pub used to sell masses of brandy and Stone's Ginger Wine. I find this a bit, how shall I put it, in your face. I prefer a dry ginger mixer – dry like Canada Dry, and not the sweeter American Ginger Ale, for the brandy is quite sweet enough.

Cognac lovers may have noted one absentee in my list of suitable mixers: tonic. The BNIC deliberately chose tonic as its mixer of choice. I am not alone in thinking that the tartness, the aggression of the tonic does not form an agreeable contrast with cognac. It does not blend, it clashes; the qualities of the two are incompatible.

Shorter drinks, especially cocktails, offer a far wider range and are increasing in number by the day as London's bartenders get to work on what is for them a new spirit. Because it is made from grapes, cognac is eminently suitable for cocktails that will not react too violently with the wine drunk later in the evening. The old wives told the right tale: grain and grape really do not mix. This warning rings hideously true to this writer the next morning if he has taken even the smallest tincture of whisky before drinking wine in any quantity. Cognac-based cocktails really are healthier.

Fortunately for cognac, its virtues as the spirit of choice for cocktail makers has come at a time when Britain – more particularly London – is emerging as the cocktail centre of the world, replacing the rather smug, unadventurous, long-time capital, New York. The reasons are many: "They don't make bad cognacs," says Dick Bradsell, London's acknowledged cocktail king, aware that there is less quality control in the making of competing spirits. He and his fellows are discovering that cognac is mellower and softer and has the necessary smoothness and balance. It helps that you don't need relatively expensive VSOP: VS does fine for cocktails. Moreover, cognac was due for a revival because it had been out of fashion for so long. As a result, in Bradsell's words, cognac had "missed out on all the funny drinks of the 1970s and so doesn't have any gimmicky connotations". It also helps that, in the USA anyway, drinkers believe that cognac is stronger than competing spirits, possibly because it has more character and far greater complexity.

The basic formula for most of these drinks is relatively simple: something sour with something sweet to exploit the flavour and strength of the cognac, together with a touch of character from bitters or the like. The flexibility of cognac is also important point. "Any mix is fine," says Dave Steward, a cocktail expert, "provided you can taste the cognac" – a direct contrast to the distillers' attempts to make a competitor like vodka as anonymous as possible. As he points out, "we hope that these mixes will lead us back to the better cognacs – drunk neat". Also in its favour is its capacity to provide more interesting variants of the classic whisky-based cocktails – barmen sometimes admit that they're often doing the equivalent of merely re-inventing the alcoholic wheel. But then some of these – notably the julep – were originally based on cognac, only to be usurped by Bourbon.

Citrus fruits – orange, lime, and lemon, though not, to my knowledge, grapefruit – are superb partners to cognac. This truism has been exploited for up to two centuries by the producers of ready-made liqueurs like Grand Marnier and Cointreau, which combine orange and brandy, but you can make your own brandy lemon juice and Mandarine Napoléon. Though obviously you want a richer style of cognac – say Courvoisier or Hennessy – to compensate for the bitterness of the citrus fruit.

There are obvious mixers apart from fruit, like cream, chocolate and coffee. Just think of the Brandy Alexander favoured by Anthony Blanche, another character in *Brideshead Revisited* – though Waugh is clearly painting him as a bounder. The Alexander normally uses dark crème de cacao and grated nutmeg, though Blanche obviously wanted cream with his. Either way it's fine because although it's inevitably sweet, you're not overly conscious of the individual constituents but only of the blend. But then brandy and cream (or butter) have been culinary stand-bys for centuries. No self-respecting mince pie is complete without brandy butter, and brandy cream is a feature of most traditional dessert trollies.

In 1999 Rémy Martin did the first experiments in matching cognac with food and came up with some surprising successes. "Our cognacs," it declares proudly, "have enough concentration to cope with any food." Its pilot restaurant, La Ribaudière, a deservedly Michelin-starred establishment on the banks of the Charente, now sells fifty special *menus gastronomiques* a month which find accompaniments for the brandy in such unlikely dishes as red mullet. Among the successes: a rich, firm shellfish dish with as little sauce as possible to go with a full-flavoured VSOP, and *tartare de saumon* or langoustines for the Grand Cru VS. XO goes really well with *ris de veau* and *morilles* – you need something strong to cut through the richness of the dish, and the same applies to foie gras where the cognac provides the dish with some structure. The 1738 is excellent with vieux mimolette cheese which – like old Gouda – goes so well with claret.

As is inevitable with any suggestions by a French company some of the suggestions, like foie gras with Szechuan pepper, are, shall we say, slightly off the wall, but others are calculated to make you think. These include dishes such as sushi and blue cheeses, which need the strength and tartness of the cognac, as well as lobsters or serious game dishes. But what Rémy is really doing is not suggesting specific marriages so much as insinuating in the mind the general proposition that it is not inconceivable to associate food and cognac. The best parallel is with Champagne firms like Krug which encouraged the association of their beverage not with mindless enjoyment and a seductive atmosphere but with serious appreciation of a serious wine such as Krug.

part IV

Cognac – the Law and the Figures

The Cognaçais are governed by three authorities: the Direction Générale des Impôts, which regulates the quantity distilled; the Direction de la Consommation et de la Répression des Fraudes, which polices the quality of the spirit; and the BNIC, which, among its other duties, issues the *certificats d'age* stating the age of the cognac being sold.

The basic legislation[1] covering the use of the word "cognac" is the Decree of May 15, 1936, which further refined the definitions of *terroirs délimitées* ("sub-zones": terroirs or *crus*) first set out in the Decree of May 1, 1909 and the law of May 6, 1919. All three provided that the term "cognac" (and also the terms "eau-de-vie de Cognac" and "eau-de-vie des Charentes") could be used only for spirits produced and distilled in the region illustrated on the map on p. 2.

The sous-appellations, Grande Champagne, Petite Champagne, Borderies, Fins Bois, and Bons Bois, on the same map were defined in a series of decrees, the first issued on January 13, 1938, the latest dated February 16, 1978.

The word "Fine" can be attached to any *sous-appellation* (sub-Appellation), as in "Fine Borderies". But "Fine Champagne cognacs" have to contain at least fifty per cent spirit from the Grande Champagne, with the rest coming from the Petite Champagne. The word "Grande" is reserved for cognacs from the Grande Champagne. There is some confusion concerning the use of words such as *cru*, *clos*, *château*, etc. In theory they can be used only when all the spirits involved come from a specific plot of land, but merchants have been allowed to use the term for

---

[1] Sources BNIC and Marguerite Landrau, *Le Cognac devant la loi*, L'Ile d'Or, Cognac, 1981.

châteaux that do not produce all the spirit in the bottle. Nevertheless, the BNIC exercises strict control over labels, ensuring, among other things, that the addresses given on labels are those of the merchants' or growers' actual establishments and not merely post boxes.

Permitted grape varieties are divided into two categories. The "principal" varieties are the Folle Blanche, the Ugni Blanc (also called St-Emilion-des-Charentes), and the Colombard. In addition Sémillon, Blanc Ramé, Jurançon Blanc, Montils, and Select can be used in up to ten per cent of the total.

Winemaking must be conducted according to local custom. The use of continuous "Archimedes" presses is specifically forbidden. In the Charente itself no sugar can be added to the must. In the Charente-Maritime sugar can, in theory, be added but only to musts destined to provide table or sparkling wines. Growers have to declare the area of vines and quantities of wine produced (including wines set aside for home consumption). Growers also have to declare the quantities of each variety. These declarations must be completed before any *titre de mouvement* is issued, and this alone allows the cognac to be transported on a public highway.

Article 443 of the Tax Code (Code Général des Impôts) forbids the movement of any wines or spirits without the appropriate documentation. Each certificate must include details of the quantity, the type and the appellation demanded. All cognac carried on the public highway has to be accompanied by an *acquit jaune d'or*, the famous golden-coloured permit used by no other drink and first authorized in 1929.

DISTILLATION

To call itself cognac the spirit has to be double-distilled, to a strength not exceeding seventy-two degrees of alcohol. Continuous distillation is expressly forbidden. The *alembic charentais* ("pot still") consists essentially of a still heated by a naked flame, with a *chapiteau* ("head") with or without a *chauffe-vin* ("wine-heater") and a cooling coil. The alembic used for the second distillation must not hold more than thirty hectolitres, nor be loaded with more than twenty-five hectolitres. Bigger alembics holding up to 140 hectolitres are allowed for the *première chauffe*. The cognac should be aged in casks made of oak from either the Tronçais or the Limousin type.

There are three classes of distillers: the cooperatives, the *bouilleurs de profession* (including the cognac merchants), who buy the wine from the growers, and the *bouilleurs de cru*, who can distil only their own wines and must produce more than fifty hectolitres of pure alcohol. The use, purchase, sale or repair of the alembics is subject to supervision by the local tax office, whom the *bouilleur de cru* has to inform when he wants to start distillation. Manufacturers and salesmen of alembics have to maintain a register providing details of all alembics bought, manufactured, repaired or sold.

Before sale cognac has to be reduced to between forty and forty-five degrees of alcohol through the addition of distilled water or weaker spirit (which must also come from the Cognac region). Additives are restricted to caramel, oak chippings and sugar. Sugar, limited to two per cent of the total volume, can be in the form of either syrup or sugar soaked in spirit of a strength of between twenty and thirty degrees. Such additions may reduce the strength of the cognac to thirty-eight degrees. Colouring matter is limited to two parts in 1,000.

AGEING

All cognacs are registered by age, and the certificates giving the age of any parcel of cognac are an indispensable adjunct to the *acquit jaune d'or*. The age classification is as follows – ageing starts officially only on March 31 each year:

00 is for cognacs distilled between the harvest and the following March 31, at which point they turn into 0 cognacs. Brandies distilled after April 1 retain their 00 designation until the following March 31.

1 is for cognacs more than one year old on April 1 of any given year. 2, 3, 4 and 5 cover cognacs from two to five years old on April 1. A *Compte 6* was introduced in 1979, 7 in 1994, 8 in 1995 and 9 in 2000.

Compte 10 is now official.

The youngest cognac that can be sold must be at least thirty months old (i.e. *Compte 2*). It can be called only VS or Three-Star.

To be called Reserve, VO or VSOP, the youngest cognac in the blend must be at least four and a half years old (i.e. *Compte 4*).

To be labelled Extra, XO, Napoléon, Vieux, Vieille Reserve and the like, the youngest eau-de-vie in the blend must be at least *Compte 6*.

There are no official regulations covering cognacs older than *Compte 10*.

In addition, many countries have special requirements, and may demand a certificate of age.

ALLIED PRODUCTS

Esprit de cognac is a tripled-distilled cognac, of between eighty degrees and eighty-five degrees of alcohol, used when making fortified wines. Pineau des Charentes consists only of wine from the Cognac region fortified during fermentation, once only, with cognac, to give a beverage of between sixteen and twenty-two degrees.

In *fruits au cognac* only cognac can be used. If it is *à base de cognac*, then at least fifty-one per cent of the total liquid content must be cognac.

For a *liqueur au cognac* the minimum cognac content is thirty per cent.

Vins vinés of up to twenty-four degrees of alcohol, mostly for export to Germany, are also covered by German law, which now corresponds to French regulations.

LE BUREAU NATIONAL INTERPROFESSIONEL DU COGNAC (BNIC)

The BNIC is a quasi-administrative joint board, with specific legal rights and financial autonomy. The functions of the BNIC are to study and prepare all the regulations covering the buying, distillation, stockage and sale of wines and eaux-de-vie produced in the Cognac area; to supervise the preservation of the historic methods of making cognac; to control the quantity of cognac produced or allowed to be sold; and to promote any measures likely to improve the production or sale of cognac.

The General Assembly of the BNIC controls its policies. The decisions at which it arrives are submitted to the Commissioner representing the Government. In certain cases the decisions are confirmed by official decree. The BNIC is financed by a quasi-fiscal levy that covers its administration and promotional activities.

RECENT RESTRICTIONS

Over the past decades a number of restrictions have been introduced to reduce the growing surplus of cognac.

Since 1975 there have been limitations on the alcoholic yield of a hectare of vines and separate quotas covering the quantity that can be distilled and (a lower amount still) the quantity that can be sold. As a result of EC regulations, in 1982–3 only 100 hectolitres of wine could be produced per hectare under Cognac's own restrictions; only 4.5 hectolitres of spirit could be sold freely; one hectolitre could be stored; a further three hectolitres could be kept or sold under certain conditions; and any surplus spirit could not be kept or sold as cognac. In 1980 further plantings of vines were forbidden until November 30, 1986, a ban which has continued since that date, and a bonus of 13,500 francs per hectare was provided for growers who pulled up their vines.

part V
A Directory of Cognac

Because of the prevalence of wholly unremarkable cognacs I have chosen only to list or highlight those which have some distinguishing features or a noticeable house style, at whatever level. Unfortunately I have not been able to taste all the cognacs on the market.

* – indicates what the *Guide Hachette* calls a *coup de coeur*, in other words a personal favourite.

Maca – indicates notes from the book *Cognac* by the late Mac A Andrew, one of the few writers whose opinions I really respect.

ISC – indicates winners at the International Spirits Challenge.

Only a few British merchants specialise in cognacs. Three of the best:

BC – indicates cognacs imported by Brandyclassics, 87 Trowbridge Road, Bradford-on-Avon, Wiltshire BA15 1EG, Tel: 01225 863988, brandyclassics.com.

C&C – indicates cognacs distributed in Britain by Cognac & Company, South View, Orchard Lane, Upper Heyford, Oxon OX25 5LD, Tel: 01869 232465, e-mail info@cognac-co.com.

Edevie – indicates cognacs distributed in Britain by Eaux de Vie, 3 Harcourt Street, London W1H 4EY, Tel: 020 7724 5009.

Figures representing the ages of the cognacs are supplied by the producers. Inevitably they are approximate averages because the cognacs involved are blends.

All cognacs are forty degrees of alcohol unless otherwise stated.

Visitors are generally welcome in even the smallest firms and producers provided they telephone to give due warning and show real interest in the producer's cognacs. The Big Four all welcome visitors to their distilleries.

LES ANTIQUAIRES DU COGNAC

Lartige, 16200 Jarnac, Tel: 33 5 45 36 55 78

Unique set-up. The Pinard family, distillers, offers a range of single *cru*, single vintage cognacs as well as a range of blends.

Grande Champagne (GC): Long, flowery, dry with a hint of spice (Maca).

Fins Bois: Very long, complex, fruity (Maca).

AUDRY

H Boisson & Cie, 12 Rue St-Vivien, 17103 Saintes, Tel: 33 5 46 74 11 72

Family business founded back in 1878. It stopped selling any of its – inevitably growing – stock of cognacs for half a century until Bernard Boisson took over in the mid-1980s.

Reserve Speciale 15

Memorial 35+

Tres Ancien

Both of the last are excellent, traditional, round and yet elegant brandies.

JEAN BALLUET

1 Rue des Ardillères, 17489 Neuvicq le Château, Tel: 33 5 46 16 64 74, jean.balluet@wanadoo.fr

Distinguished family – including Hippolyte, a resistance hero – which has been distilling cognac from its 35–ha estate in the Fins Bois since 1845. Has been selling its own brandies to outside buyers for fifty years since a major customer reduced its order.

VSOP 8

Tres Vieille Reserve 26

MICHEL BARLAAM

Les Landes, Rioux Martin, 16120 Chalais, Tel: 33 5 45 98 17 75

One of the few growers in the Bons Bois selling brandies from his 7 ha of vines to private clients.

Michel Barlaam 10+

Michel Barlaam VSOP 12+

PAUL BEAU

Rue Millardet, 16130 Segonzac, Tel: 33 5 45 83 40 18

C&C

Housed in Segonzac itself, Beau is one of the most distinguished distillers in the Grande Champagne. Unfortunately the family has sold its vineyard in the Borderies which produced some of the finest brandies in the region.

Hors d'Age Vieille GC: Complex brandy with overtones of eucalyptus, exotic fruits, and spice.

Old Borderies: The real McCoy, rich fruit and nut chocolate, very dense and long. C&C has a few bottles, otherwise unavailable.

JAN BERTELSEN

Brand created by Leopold Gourmel (q.v.) and named after its Norwegian agent.

VSOP Prelude 8: Young, fresh floral nose, a little short.

XO Symphonie 13: Rich, some *rancio*.

Extra Orchestra 23: forty-two degrees, rich, floral, long.

BISQUIT

Renault Bisquit, Domaine de Lignières, 16170 Rouillac, Tel: 33 5 45 21 88 88

Founded in 1819 by an enterprising local, Alexandre Bisquit. His daughter married a M. Dubouché, who added his name to the firm. Their daughter married a local notable, Maurice Laporte, who promoted sales in the Far East. In 1965 the family sold the business to Paul Ricard of Pernod-Ricard, who also bought Château Lignières, the largest estate in the region with 200 ha of vines. He built a vast distillery and an ultra-modern *chai*. Unfortunately the brandies, though rich and excellent, proved unsuccessful and are now being phased out.

DANIEL BOUJU

Chez Lafont, 16130 Segonzac, Tel: 33 5 45 83 41 27,

cognac.daniel.bouju@wanadoo.fr

Goes his own way in a lovely valley in the Grande Champagne which he claims has a very special microclimate. Declared his independence from the big boys, to whom he had previously sold his brandy, in 1974, and now has 25 ha of vines. Distils hot on lees "a Grande Champagne without lees is not a real Grande Champagne", he says, and immediately reduces to fifty-five degrees to conserve the richness. New casks so some find his brandies rather woody and lacking elegance.

* Selection Speciale: Lovely round, fruity nose, round and rich, some wood behind, but one of the best VSs from the Champagnes.

VSOP: Rather spirity nose, less fruity, lots of wood.

Napoleon: Wood well absorbed, rich, some *rancio*.

XO 25: Very rich chestnut colour, rich *rancio*, no apparent wood.

Extra 35: Round, complex, *rancio*, good example of a GC.

Brut de fut 40: fifty degrees, characteristic rich woodiness hides the strength.

Royal: At sixty degrees one of the strongest cognacs on the market, but very rich and concentrated so appears to be only fifty degrees.

LOUIS BOURON
Château de La Grange, BP 80, 17416, Tel: 33 5 46 332 00 12

Family business housed in a 14th-century castle, blending fine cognacs from 90 ha of vines, 40 ha each in the Borderies and Petite Champagne and 10 ha in the Fins Bois.

XO: Surprisingly light but plentiful aromas, round, long (Maca).

Tres Vieille Reserve: Long, complex, touch of natural sweetness (Maca).

BERNARD BOUTINET
Le Brissoneau, Breville, 16370 Cherves de Cognac, Tel: 33 5 45 80 86 63, cognac.boutinet@wanadoo.fr

Brandies of quality exclusively from a family-owned 26-ha estate north of Cognac in the best Fins Bois.

* Fine (VSOP) 6: supple but firm in the mouth, long, with some power on the finish.

Vieille Fine/Napoleon 12–14

Tres Vieille Fine/XO

Coeur de Fins Bois 50 degrees 6: deliberately aged in very old casks. As a result the brandy is very fresh with overtones of dried fruits and suitable for long drinks.

Extra: Complex, long, rich.

BRILLET

Les Aireaux, 16120 Graves/Cognac, Tel: 33 5 45 97 05 06

In theory a merchant, but in practice Jean-Louis Brillet relies mostly on grapes from the family's 60 ha of vineyards in the Petite and Grande Champagne. Distils on the lees in the family's four stills in his delightful, albeit rather ramshackle, property.

Reserve PC: Good floral richness, long, the burn disappears leaving pear fruit.

Tres Vieille Reserve XO GC: Candied fruit, nutty nose, seriously elegant, long plum fruit.

Tres Rare Heritage GC: Serious *rancio* on nose but fresher and fruity on the palate. Again very long.

DOMAINE DES BRISSONS DE LARGE

SARL Bertrand & Fils, Reaux, 17500 Jonzac, Tel: 33 5 46 48 09 03

The owner, Jean-François Bertrand, comes from a long line of growers and merchants. All the brandies come from an 80-ha estate in the heart of the Petite Champagne owned by the family since 1731. The style is dark and intense because the cognacs are kept longer than usual in very old cognac casks.

BRUGEROLLE

Business established in the early nineteenth century and now part of CCG, which uses the name only for a few unremarkable cognacs sold in European markets.

CAMUS

Camus La Grande Marque, 29 Rue Marguerite de Navarre, BP19, 16101 Cognac, Tel: 33 5 45 32 28 28, f.bernard@camus.fr

See also Chabanneau and Planat

The fifth largest firm in Cognac, and the biggest still owned by the founding family. The founder, Jean-Baptiste, started the business as La Grande Marque, a consortium of growers, and later added his own name to the firm. Camus relied largely on sales to Tsarist Russia and thus suffered very badly from the Russian Revolution. By the 1960s it was virtually bankrupt but was saved by a deal struck by Michel Camus with the two young Americans who founded Duty Free Shoppers. Still has the knack of finding new cognacs to please the ever-choosier Duty Free market. For its better cognacs the family relies greatly on the family's 125-ha estate in the Borderies.

Borderies XO: Nutty, rather woody, reminiscent of almond kernels.

* Chateau de Plessis: Beautiful rounded cognac from the family's own estate in the Borderies, distils all the region's qualities. "We make it for our own pleasure," they say – and it's mine as well.

Josephine: introduced in 1995 for sale in Duty Free to young Japanese office ladies, light and floral.

CASTEL SABLONS
Le Bourg Saint Maigrin, 17520 Archiac, Tel: 33 5 46 70 00 30

The Roux family owns 26 ha of vines in an excellent part of the Fins Bois just south of the Petite Champagne. Recently has specialized in enterprising new products.

Crystal Dry 3: Deliberately young and virtually colourless, designed as a base for cocktails.

Brulot Charentais 58 degrees: Designed to be used in the traditional drink of the same name, when the spirit is ignited over a cup of coffee to make a fine pick-me-up.

CHABANNEAU
Historic firm founded in 1830 by a Dutch cognac trader selling to the Dutch East Indies, and M. Pierre Chabanneau, manager of the wine cellar of the Grand Hotel in Paris. Flourished until Indonesia was formed in 1954. Now a subsidiary of Camus (q.v.) and used as a second label for cheap cognacs.

DENIS CHARPENTIER
59 Avenue Theophile Gautier, 75016 Paris, Tel: 01 45 27 86 07

CHÂTEAU DE BEAULON
Château de Beaulon, 17240 St Dizant-du-Goa, Tel: 33 5 46 49 96 13
BC

The most remarkable – and beautiful – estate in the whole region, indeed virtually the only one which corresponds to the idea of a château as the term is employed in Bordeaux. The château itself is an historic monument dating back to 1480, and in the 17th century was owned and managed by the Bishops of Bordeaux who introduced Bordeaux varieties. The present owner, Christian Thomas, continues the tradition.

Significantly, the estate is within sight of the Gironde Estuary opposite the Médoc. The quality of the brandies – and the Pineaus, among the finest in the region – made by the Thomas family provides proof that the sub-region is capable of producing brandies comparable with the Champagnes, especially when, as here, they include Montils, Colombard, and Folle Blanche as well as Ugni Blanc.

Fins Bois: Seven years, so young but very long with a delightful floral finish.

Fins Bois: Ten years old. Rich, fruity nose, some plumminess, long, dense, concentrated, ends a little woody.

Napoleon: 20 years, all four major appellations. Round, rich – one American taster compared it with a Renoir.

* Extra: Around 50 years old. All the complexity of a great Fins Bois, long, fruity, raisiny. Because of the number of varieties involved (which include Sémillon) it is far more complex than brandies made purely from Ugni Blanc, and proof that brandies from this sub-region can age as well as those from the Champagnes.

CHÂTEAU DE MONTIFAUD
17520 Jarnac, Tel: 33 5 46 49 50 77, vallet@chateau-montifaud.com
BC
Estate of 50 ha in the Petites Champagnes d'Archiac owned by the Vallet family for a century and a half. Looking for a light, unwoody style, they distil on the lees and include 10 per cent of Colombard in the blend.

* VSOP 10: Lovely floral feel like a good FB de Jarnac, but richer.

CHÂTEAU PAULET
Domaine de la Couronne, Route de Segonzac, BP24, 16101 Cognac, Tel: 33 5 45 32 07 00
Owned by the Cointreau family (see Frapin) and now not seen much.

CHÂTEAU ST-SORLIN
Saint-Sorlin de Cognac, 17150 Mirambeau, Tel: 33 5 46 86 01 27
Madame Castelnau-Gros is the great granddaughter of one of the

nurserymen who provided the vines for replanting the region after the phylloxera. Likes the cognacs she makes from her 20-ha estate on a chalky patch opposite the upper Médoc. Slightly sweetened with syrup.

CHOLLET
16100 Boutier-St Trojan, Tel: 33 5 45 32 12 93
In 1977, after Salignac stopped buying Jacques Chollet's cognacs, he started selling them himself. He likes his cognacs soft.

PASCAL COMBEAU
Owned by Marie Brizard (q.v.).

COMPAGNIE COMMERCIALE DE GUYENNE
26 Rue Pascal Combeau, 16100 Cognac, Tel: 33 5 45 82 32 10
Founded as late as 1976 by Michel Coste (q.v.), one of the most remarkable figures in the recent history of Cognac, who bought up a number of firms like Brugerolle, Lucien Fourcauld, and Meukow (q.v.), now its principal brand.

COGNAC DE COLLECTIONS
See La Gabare.

ANDRÉ COUPRIE
La Roumade, 16300 Ambleville, Tel: 33 5 45 80 54 69, couprie@club-internet.fr
Michel Couprie's family has been settled on the same 22-ha estate in the heart of the Grande Champagne for over two centuries, and continues to sell only its own cognacs.

Like so many grower's cognacs from the GC, the VS, and VSOP have simply not had the time to lose their rough edges, though the VSOP has a nice floral nose.

Napoleon 12+: Good *rancio* and elegance.

Tres Vieille reserve XO 20+: Good florality on nose, nice light, elegant cognac.

* Hors d'Age: 41.5 degrees, forty years. Some Folle Blanche and it shows in the florality and elegance of a fine cognac.

1936: All the qualities of a rich, *rancio*, fully mature cognac.

1903: Like so many old old cognacs this is too woody for comfort.

COURVOISIER

Place du Château, 16200 Jarnac, Tel: 33 5 45 35 55 55,
catherine.mattei@adsweu.com

Most untypical of the Big Four. Has never owned its own vines but has always relied on outside distillers, a dependence which cost the firm its independence in the early 1960s. Its brandies have always been rich and round and have gone through periods of inferior quality, though not recently.

* VS: Rich, typical of the firm throughout the ages. Excellent for mixing because of richness. ISC Bronze 2000.

VSOP Fine Champagne: made from 6–8-year-old brandies, long, elegant but some burn on finish.

VSOP Fine Champagne: For Japan, 8–10-years, much richer and more Courvoisier in style.

VSOP Premier: 10–15 years, very nearly a Napoleon. All four *crus*, very elegant on the nose, nice touch of floral Fins Bois.

* Exclusif VSOP: The most expensive of its VSOPs. Brandies from 4 to 12 years old, rich enough to show candied fruits, truffles, Borderies nuttiness.

XO: GC and PC and some old Borderies. Deliberately richer for the Far East market.

Initiale Extra: GC and Borderies. Although only half Borderies they dominate the blend, especially on the nose. A very natural richness with a feel of *sous bois* – the fresh, wet earth, mushroomy feel. ISC Gold 2000.

CROIZET-EYMARD

BP3, 16720 St-Même-les-Carrières, Tel: 33 5 45 81 90 11

The Croizet family have been growing grapes in the region since the seventeenth century and founded their firm in 1805. In the late nineteenth century Leon Croizet was awarded the Legion d'Honneur for his work replanting the vineyard with grafted vines. The firm is still run by the Eymard family – descendants of a Mlle. Croizet who married a M. Eymard in 1892. Sells a lot of ordinary brandies but its pride and joy are those from its 150 ha of vines in the Grande Champagne. Also has a substantial stock of old brandies. In 2003 was selling the 1963 and 1973 vintages.

VSOP: Light, floral, delicious.

Some splendid vintages including 1963, 1973, and 1977.

DAVIDOFF

One of the first cognacs designed to accompany cigars. Blended by Hennessy for the cigar company of the same name. The cognac is too rich for a non-smoker.

DELAMAIN

Rue J & R Delamain, PO Box 16, 16200 Jarnac, Tel: 33 5 45 81 08 24, delamain@delamain-cognac.com

The firm and its brandies are both unique. The brandies have always been the favourites of the English aristocracy, the first class to appreciate the finer brandies from the region. Many of them were Early-Landed, Late Bottled, i.e. shipped to cool, damp cellars in London or Bristol immediately after they were distilled and then sold as individual vintages. Their quality has been unquestioned since the early 18th century, and the firm is still run by the family – a Mlle. Delamain married a M. Braastad, grandfather of one of the present directors. The firm still buys only from the Grande Champagne and then only brandies of at least ten years of age, matured in old casks, thus giving all the firms brandies their unique elegance.

Pale & Dry: Floral, delicate, long.

Vesper: Deliberately completely different from Pale & Dry, with a natural richness comparable to a Hine.

Très Venerable: combines the delicacy and richness of the two lesser offerings.

* Très Vieille Reserve de la Famille: Classic GC with flowery overtones. Long, complex.

AE DOR

4 Bis Rue Jacques Moreau, 16200 Jarnac, Tel: 33 5 45 81 03 26, AE.Dor@wanadoo.fr

Family firm best known for its fabled but alas inevitably now diminishing stock of historic brandies, many bought by M. Dor soon after he had founded the firm in 1858.

DUBOIGALANT

Former name of brandies always made by the Trijol family (q.v.).

FAMILLE ESTÈVE
Les Corbinauds, 17520 Celles-sur-la Né, Tel: 33 5 46 49 51 20
C&C
Serious family growers in the Petite Champagne but very near the boundary with the Grande Champagne, so produces excellent brandies of great delicacy.

Jacques Estève Tres Vieux Cognac de la propriété XO: 35 years. Very rich and *rancio* on the palate, but still a bit woody throughout.

Jacques Estève Hors d'Age: Excellent balance of fruity and flowery aromas, nutty and trace of wood, round and very long (Maca).

* Jacques Estève Reserve Ancestrale 50: An excellent example of an old PC, lighter, more elegant, less *rancio* than an old brandy from the GC, about as good as you can get from the PC.

EXSHAW
An old-established firm, once famous in Britain – and India. Post-war decline led to sale to Otard (q.v.) in 1975. Now used as upmarket brand.

VSOP: Brand for Hong Kong, rich, ideal for drinking with ice cubes.

* No 1: GC. Lovely floral concentration on nose and palate. Excellent chocolate fruitiness on the finish.

PIERRE FERRAND
Gabriel & Andreu, Château de Bonbonnet, 16130 Arces, Tel: 33 5 13 83 22 44
Two businessmen bought the rights to use the name of old-established producer Pierre Ferrand (who has set up as Pierre de Segonzac q.v.).

GC Ambre 10 years old casks

* Reserve 20: Delicious, crisp, baked-appley.

Borderies: Light manzanilla colour; light style but unmistakable Borderies nuttiness.

Selection des Anges 30 years

Abel 45 years

Cigare blend

Also sells cognac from four small estates: Château de Clam FB 8 years; Domaine Varennes Borderies 15 years, Domaine Fleuret PC 25 years, 42 degrees, and Domaine de Communion GC 35 years, 43 degrees.

JEAN FILLIOUX

La Pouyade, 16130 Juillac-le Coq, Tel: 33 5 45 83 04 09,
cognac.jeanfillioux@wanadoo.fr
Founded in 1880 by a renegade member of the Fillioux family, distillers
for Hennessy for a century and a half. Since then it's been selling cognacs
from its own 22-ha estate in the Grande Champagne as well as those from
two other estates.

* VSOP 8: Nice baked apple nose, very classy for its age.

Réserve Familiale: Fruity aromas dominate; dry, round, long (Maca).

MICHEL FORGERON

Chez Richon, 16130 Segonzac, Tel: 33 5 45 83 43 05,
cognacforgeron@wanadoo.fr
BC
Classic GC producer, established a few miles east of Segonzac in the mid-
nineteenth century. In the 1960s the independent-minded Michel started
turning what had been a largely agricultural estate into a vineyard. He
built his own still in 1965 and started selling direct in 1977, largely
through his dynamic wife, Françoise.

VS Standard: Surprisingly fruity for a young GC, nevertheless rather
spirity.

VS Plus: Very woody.

* VSOP 43 per cent Nice, rich, well-balanced at 12 years. Any other
producer would have called it a Napoléon.

XO: 45 degrees, over 20 years. Rich but still some burn on the finish,
probably due to the strength.

Hors d'Age: A truly serious 50-year-old, exceptionally concentrated
and so well-balanced that you don't notice that it's fifty degrees

LUCIEN FOUCAULD

Old-established firm now part of Compagnie Commerciale de Guyenne
(q.v.). Name used only for brandies sold to German supermarket group
Metro.

PIERRE FRAPIN

BP1, Rue Pierre Frapin, 16130 Segonzac, Tel: 33 5 45 83 40 03,
info@cognac-frapin.com

Frapin, based around a rose-haunted courtyard, is the only major firm to be based in Segonzac. It is based on the biggest single estate in the rolling chalky heartland of the Grande Champagne, and a key element in the history of Rémy Martin (q.v.). Since 1984 when Beatrice Cointreau took over what was then a forgotten brand, it has been selling increasing quantities of brandies which have been kept in new wood for longer than their competitors, so confident is it of the quality of its brandies and the size of its stocks, which represent 18 years of sales.

VS 5–6: Light colour, delicious florality on the nose.

* VSOP 10–12: Nice colour, feels even older than it is – I would have guessed a 15-year cognac, i.e. between Napoléon and XO, because of the number of older cognacs in the blend.

XO: Light and flowery with good florality, some nuttiness and good *rancio*.

* Château de Fontpinot: A veritable festival of fruity, floral aromas and tastes; long, the perfect 35-year-old. ISC Trophy in 1998.

Extra Reserve: A model of an older cognac. ISC Trophy in 2002.

Also a number of excellent single vintages – the 1979 and 1982 both won gold medals at the ISC 2003.

A DE FUSSIGNY

23 Place Jean Monnet, 16100 Cognac, Tel: 33 5 45 81 62 59,

cognaca@a-de-fussigny.com

Founded by Alain Royer, of the Louis Royer family, to sell small lots of fine cognacs. Now controlled by the Hériard-Dubreuil family of Rémy.

NYAK: The way the rap world pronounces cognac. Not your average VS. Rich, lots of brandies from the Champagnes.

The Connoisseurs' Collection: Three cognacs presented like Classic Malts.

Extra: GC, 45ish. Successor to Royer's individual lots. Light chocolate colour, powerful wood, good *rancio*.

Ebony Blend VSOP: Rich, almost porty feel about this superior VSOP.

XO Fine Champagne: Nose slightly aggressively young, but otherwise an agreeably civilized cognac.

* Tres Vieille Grande Champagne: 42 degrees. Flowers, fruits fresh and candied, decent *rancio*, in fact all things nice.

Cigar Blend: Has the requisite chocolate richness to cope with a good cigar.

COGNACS DE COLLECTION LA GABARE
16370 Cherves de Cognac, Tel: 04 93 99 72 52, fdebakker@wanadoo.fr

The result of a happy partnership between Ferdinand de Bakker, a retired PR executive, and Jean Grosperrin, an experienced Cognac broker. He selects small lots of fine and often old cognacs, which de Bakker sells. Their best offerings, which obviously change from time to time, include:

1972 Fins Bois: fine and floral.

1944 Bons Bois: A remarkable brandy. Very pure nose and like a fine bourbon whisky on the palate.

E & J GALLO
Gallo, the giant of the Californian wine – and brandy – business, has teamed up with Louis Royer (q.v.) to produce a Gallo cognac to go with its best-selling E & J brandy. Still being test-matured, but could be a winner.

E & J VS: ISC Silver 2002.

Cognac: ISC Bronze 2003.

GASTON DE LA GRANGE
Brand invented by Martini, and now part of Otard (q.v.).

VSOP: Rather sharp.

XO Rouge: Nice round, fruity nose, good commercial cognac.

* XO Black: GC. Rich fruitcake nose, candied fruit.

GAUTIER
28 Rue des Ponts, 16140 Aiger, Tel: 33 5 45 21 10 02

Now part of the Marie Brizard empire. Housed in a picturesque eighteenth-century water mill in Aigre, in the heart of the Fins Bois.

VS: Nice floral feel on nose and palate. ISC Bronze 2003.

Myriade: FC, crisp and round, not very long, but easy drinking, an excellent introductory cognac.

XO Gold & Blue 15+: Again easy drinking, round, unremarkable.

Pinar del Rio: Hard and rich, named after the leading cigar-making appellation in Cuba.

JULES GAUTRET

Brand from Unicognac (q.v.).

Rois des Roi XO: Rich, fruity, 20+, a little caramelised.

Extra: Very old, virtually no reduction, traditional style, very long, concentrated but a bit woody.

GODET

1 Rue du Duc, 17003 La Rochelle, Tel: 33 5 46 41 10 66

The only survivor of the numerous families of Dutch origin who settled in La Rochelle in the sixteenth century when it was the leading port for exports from the region. Originally, like its competitors, it exported cognac only in cask, but now sells in bottle. Bought by the British giant, Grand Met, in 1989, then bought back by Jean-Jacques Godet, an enthusiast for Folle Blanche, six years later.

VS de Luxe: As the name implies it is indeed a superior VS with lots of Borderies.

Selection Speciale 10: A superior VSOP; nice refreshing floral nose, good length, no burn.

* Folle Blanche 12: Floral roundness, very deep, but light, exceptionally elegant.

Gastronome: FC, especially bracing, refreshing, tonic cognac; unripe gooseberry on the nose, no apparent wood.

Excellence: One-third Borderies and it shows, nutty but not heavy, refreshing. ISC Gold 2000.

Borderies 50: A single lot, deep, characteristically nutty.

XO 35: Classic light *rancio* nose and palate.

Réserve and Grande Réserve de la Famille GC Ambleville

Vintages: 1965 GC, 1970 PC, 1971 FB, 1972 FB, 1975 FB, 1979 GC

LEOPOLD GOURMEL

BP 194, 16016 Cognac, Tel: 33 5 45 82 07 29, Leopold-Gourmel@leopold-gourmel.com

One of the happiest new ventures in the region, and one of the handful of firms exploiting the very special qualities of the best brandies from the Fins Bois. It was founded by M. Voisin, who owned the franchise for Volvo and Fiat in the region. He was passionately interested in cognac and discovered a couple of suppliers of fine brandies in the Premiers Fins

Bois de Jarnac. He stored casks of their cognacs and then started to sell them under his wife's maiden name. Today the business, run by his son-in-law Olivier Blanc, exploits the very different qualities of the brandies as they mature, starting off floral, then fruity, and then getting more complex and spicy as they age – well, and for far longer than most brandies from the Fins Bois.

Petit Gourmel 8: No malolactic fermentation, orangey, nutty-peary nose.

Age des Fruits 13: Relatively rich and round with strong overtones of almond kernels.

* Age des Fleurs 16: Vanilla, floral, delicate, long, rich.

* Age des Epices 22: Oily, grapey, peppery, with a lovely roundness and complexity.

Quintessence 30+: Changing this to younger casks after a decade in older wood gives a delicious lightness and freshness as well as complexity – but no *rancio*.

GOURRY DE CHADEVILLE
Domaine de Chadeville, 16130 Segonzac, Tel: 33 5 45 83 40 54
One of the oldest estates in the Grande Champagne. Not afraid to give precise age of its brandies.

GRONSTEDTS
House brand of the Swedish alcohol monopoly. Excellent basic quality cognacs.

VS: ISC Bronze 2003.

VSOP Monopole: ISC Bronze 2003.

HARDY
Old-established firm which went bankrupt in the late 1990s and has now been absorbed by Unicognac (q.v.).

HENNESSY
1 Rue de la Richonne, 16101 Cognac, Tel: 33 5 45 82 52 22
One of the two dominant forces in the cognac trade since the French Revolution and today the unquestioned world leader – its VS alone accounts for over one bottle in four of all the cognacs sold in the world.

Family-owned until 1971 when merged with Moët & Chandon, it is now part of the giant LVMH-Louis Vuitton combine. Its cognacs are still blended by a member of the Fillioux family which has been responsible for blending for over 150 years. They generally combine richness with a certain structure and are rarely labelled as coming from the Champagnes, although it has a major distillery in the region.

VS: Nice, warm, round, grapey nose and palate, relatively mature, typical traditional Hennessy.

Pure White: A technical, if not a commercial triumph. Lighter and more floral and fruity than the usual run of the firm's brandies.

Fine de Cognac VSOP: Light, elegant, but a bit short, not very Hennessy.

Privilège VSOP: Traditional rich, warm, grapey nose; good concentration and depth, but still clean. Strong enough to drink with an ice cube.

XO: Very rich but not too heavy, long thanks to brandies from the Grande Champagne, lots of new wood.

* Private Reserve: As the name indicates it was indeed originally blended for the Hennessy family. Very elegant and long, made from 20–30-year-old brandies, though Hennessy never talks about the age of its cognacs.

* Paradis Extra: A superb brandy, long with some *rancio*, more elegant than normal house style.

Richard: The incredibly expensive *summum* of their brandies, richer but less elegant than the Paradis.

HINE
16 Quai de l'Orangerie, 16200 Jarnac, Tel: 33 5 45 35 59 59

Founded in 1782 by an immigrant from Dorset who married a Mlle. Delamain. For nearly two centuries the firm's brandies, like those of Delamain, were British favourites, many of them Early-Landed, Late-Bottled. The family sold to the British Distillers Company which itself was taken over by Guinness in 1986. Sold to Moët-Hennessy, it languished until 2001 when it was restored. It now offers a few beautifully balanced, rich but elegant brandies which had been distilled and blended under the watchful eye of Bernard Hine, the last member of the family to be involved in the firm. Early in 2003 the firm was sold to the CL group which specializes in rums.

Rare & Delicate: An upmarket VSOP – the average age of the brandies, at around ten years, is far above that of the usual offering – and the combination of age and the usual Hine elegance makes it one of the few serious challengers to Rémy Martin. ISC Silver 2000 & 2001.

* Antique: Combines balance with a touch of *rancio*, that almost indefinable quality which brandies acquire after their twentieth year in cask and resembles the mix of nuts and candied fruit found in a rich fruitcake. Normally it would be classed as an XO. ISC Trophy 2001.

Also offers a couple of single vintages, an Early-Landed and an older one matured in Cognac, as well as a vintage pack with three 20cl bottles from the 1957, 1975, and 1981 vintages.

KELT

Château de St Aubin, Reans, 32800 Eauze, Tel: 33 5 62 09 98 18

After his retirement, a Swedish businessman, Otto Kelt, a former maker of crisp diet rolls, had an apparently mad, but splendidly successful idea: to copy the eighteenth-century habit of selling cognacs only after they have been round the world in casks in the hold of a ship. The result is a speedier maturation and a well-integrated cognacs.

VSOP Tour du Monde: One of the rare VSOPs from the GC, and it shows.

* XO GC Tour du Monde: Rich and powerful, but not cloying or blowsy.

LAFRAGETTE

L & L Cognac Sa, 17 Rue des Gabariers, 16100 Cognac, Tel: 33 5 45 36 61 36, organic.lafragette@wanadoo.fr

One of the rare organic producers. Cognacs are made in an organic distillery from organic growers' wines from the Champagnes.

Fin and Bons Bois: Lovely pure floral nose combined with excellent bite.

LARSEN

66 Boulevard de Paris, BP 41, 16100 Cognac, Tel: 33 5 45 82 05 88, frederic.larsen@wanadoo.fr

Viking firm still run by the family of former immigrants from Norway and

specializing in ceramic containers, including Viking ships. Very enterprizing, one of the first firms on the net, and has a shop in Jarnac.
Arctic XO: balanced aromas, on the dry side, long (Maca).

GUY LHERAUD

Domaine de Lasdoux, Angeac-Charente, 16120 Châteauneuf, Tel: 33 5 45 97 12 33

A typically long-established – in its case since 1639 – family which now
owns 62 ha on some of the best chalky slopes in the Petite Champagne.
The handful of casks of Colombard and Folle Blanche help enrich the
family's best brandies. Uses new oak but no caramel, boisé or syrup, so all
its brandies are clean and true to their origins.

20 PC: Warm and rich, yet not caramelly. Excellent fruit.

* Paradis Antique: Distilled in 1942. Lovely light, well-balanced nose,
everything well-absorbed. You forget it's 45 degrees.

LOGIS DE MONTIFAUD

16130 Salle d'Angles, Tel: 33 5 45 83 67 45

Christian Landreau, and now his daughter Diane, are famous for their
pineaus and their wines, as well as their cognacs from their estates in
Grande and Petite Champagne.

Vieille Reserve: Full bouquet of flowery aromas, dry and smooth, long
(Maca).

XO: A single-vintage XO with pronounced aromas, hint of dark chocolate and spice, round and very long.

Hors d'Age: A magical mix of fruity and flowery aromas, dry, round
and extremely long. Maca gives it his rare 10/10.

LOGIS DE LA MOTHE

16300 Criteuil, Barbezieux, Tel: 33 5 45 80 54 02

Since 1865 the Jullien family has owned 61 ha of vines in the Grande
Champagne centred round a beautiful logis – fortified farmhouse.

* VSOP: Lovely round, plummy nose and palate with the depth of a
Napoléon.

Trois Ecussons VSOP

XO: Serious rancio nose but younger and less full than the VSOP.

MARTELL

Place Edouard Martell, 16101 Cognac, Tel: 33 5 45 82 44 44

For two centuries one of the two family companies which, with Hennessy, dominated the world of cognac. Unfortunately in 1988 the family sold the company to the US group Seagram, which promptly proceeded to wreck it and introduced hordes of new cognacs without much success. Now being revived by its new owners, the Pernod-Ricard group.

Throughout its history Martell has gone its own way in the style of its cognacs. For over a century they were blended by the Chapeau family who fulfilled the same role as hereditary *chef de caves* as the Fillioux at Hennessy. Martell has always relied on a relatively neutral style of brandy, made from wines from the Fins Bois and the Borderies which provided their unique qualities. The brandies' dry character was largely formed by maturation in casks made from oak from the Tronçais.

* Cordon Bleu: The first mass-selling upmarket cognac. Has always relied on the Borderies and continues to offer the deep nuttiness typical of the region.

Reserve: ISC Silver 2001. Intense, good nuttiness.

XO Supreme: The distillation of all the nutty violet best of the Borderies.

VS: Decent floral nose, some depth and concentration.

VSOP: Good concentration, warmth and depth.

JP MENARD ET FILS

16720 St-Même-les-Carrières, Tel: 33 5 45 81 90 26,
menard@cognac-menard.com

C&C

Family property of 80 ha where the family has been producing brandy since 1815.

VSOP: Called Grande Fine but in fact pure GC. Rich grapey nose but a trifle harsh because only 8 years old.

* XO 35: Very clean and fruity nose and pure, classic *rancio*.

Ancestrale GC 50: 45 degrees. Rich nose, slightly woody, classic stuff but not that exciting or complex.

MENUET

16720 Saint-Même-les-Carrières, Tel: 33 5 45 81 99 78

BC

Family established since the 1680s with 20 ha in the Grande Champagne. David, the sixth generation since the business was founded, says that "I offer what I like", and very fine cognacs they are too, even though he leaves them for 20 months in new oak.

XO: Dry roses, vanilla, and wood well balanced by the nose; fruity, hint of spice, round, touch of chocolate, and long (Maca).

Extra: Very floral, touch of chocolate but lots of fruit (oranges, apricots) on the palate, round complex, very long (Maca).

Hors d'Age: Smoky, dry fruits, hint of old port, touch of tobacco, lots of body, dry, and long (Maca).

MEUKOW

Old-established firm now part of, and flagship brand of Compagnie Commerciale de Guyenne (q.v.).

VSOP: Good warm nose, a little caramelly, nice commercial cognac.

XO: Specially blended for the Russian market, crisp, floral, appley feel.

Extra: Half PC, half FB. Light, delicate brandy.

Rarissime: 41.3 degrees. Seriously well-balanced floral/fruity cognac.

H. MOUNIER

See Unicoop.

MOYET

62 Rue de l'Industrie, BP 106, 16104 Cognac, Tel: 33 5 45 82 04 53

An old firm rescued by two businessmen, Marc Georges and Pierre Dubarry. When they took over in 1984 Moyet was truly a sleeping beauty, home to splendid casks of old cognacs cherished by a cellarmaster, Honoré Piquepaille, for 70 years. The cognacs' qualities were discovered in 1984 by some leading Paris restaurateurs and since then Pierre Dubarry has built up a deserved reputation for providing fine cognacs.

Cognac des Fins Bois: Nice floral nose, elegant, spring flowers on the palate though some *brulé*.

FC VSOP: Delightful cognac, well above the average VSOP, chocolatey with a little *rancio* – unusual in a VSOP and due to some age.

Cognac de Petite Champagne: Agreeable florality.

Cognac Fine Champagne: rather heavy, not as delicate or elegant as the firm's other offerings.

* Cognac des Borderies: 43 degrees, the real nutty stuff, tastes over 20 years old.

Cognac Fine Champagne XO: 35ish. Round, fat, oily nose with real chocolatey *rancio*.

It also always has a number of special lots on offer that are well worth tasting.

NORMANDIN-MERCIER

Château de la Peraudière, 17139 Dompierre, Tel: 33 5 46 68 00 65,
Cognac.normandin-mercier@wanadoo.fr
C&C

Family firm founded in 1872 by a broker, M. Normandin, who worked with his mother-in-law, Mme. Mercier, and soon bought the château just north of La Rochelle where the firm is still based. For 25 years after 1945 the firm specialized in selling old cognacs to major firms but since the 1970s has specialized in selling fine old brandies, for Jean-Marie Normandin buys only from the Champagnes and matures them in his own cellars. Because these are damp, due to the proximity to the sea, the cognacs are not aggressive.

Fine Petite Champagne 6: Very elegant nose, slight burn on end, but very persistent, light fruit.

Tres Vieille Grande Champagne: Elegant, round, long; aromas of flowers and hints of fruits develop with time, magic palate of considerable length (10/10 from Maca).

Petite Champagne Vieille: Rich aromas, dry, finesse, touch of spice, pleasant *rancio*, hints of curry, tobacco, and jams and jellies, very long (another 10/10 from Maca).

OTARD

Château de Cognac, 127 Boulevard Denfert-Rochereau, 16101 Cognac, Tel: 33 5 45 82 40 00

Historic firm founded in the late eighteenth century by M. Dupuy, a local grower, and M. Otard, who, rather unconvincingly, claimed descent from a distinguished Scottish family loyal to the Stuart pretenders. It flourished during the Revolutionary period, buying the magnificent château at the head of the bridge over the Charente cheaply, and in the early nineteenth century was on a par with Martell and Hennessy. The firm is is now part of the Martini-Bacardi empire. Its sales, especially of the Otard VSOP, are greatly boosted by direct sales from the château, the biggest tourist attraction in Cognac.

Napoleon: Not well-balanced.

XO: Excellent, round, commercial cognac.

XO: 55 degrees. Excellent concentration and while naturally rather hard does not taste nearly as hard as its strength would imply; could be 47–48 degrees.

PAYRAULT
See Château de Montifaud

PIERRE DE SEGONZAC
La Nerolle, 16130 Segonzac, Tel: 33 5 45 83 41 82

Soon after he had sold his name to Gabriel & Andreu (q.v.) Pierre Ferrand set up under a new name to sell brandies from his estate in the heart of the Grande Champagne, owned by his family since 1702. He's the archetypal peasant, complete with beret, and his farm buildings are equally typically Charentais.

Selection des Anges: Well-balanced on the nose, a touch of spice, round, very long (Maca).

PLANAT
Subsidiary of Camus (q.v.) which bought it from M. Pionneau, who had his own ideas about cognacs: he liked old-fashioned brandies. The new owners use the brand for some fine cognacs, including a number of single-vintage brandies.

XO: Nicely floral and fruity.

Extra Vieille XO: Classic 30-year-old with good *rancio*, long.

FB 1967: Heavy floral nose, baked apple feel on palate.

PRINCE HUBERT DE POLIGNAC
In 1947 the Polignac family, who then owned Lanson and Pommery Champagnes, licensed the Unicoop cooperative (q.v.) to use the name of Prince Hubert de Polignac.

VS Nice round nose, fruity, albeit a bit sugary; ideal for mixing with ice, etc.

VSOP: Run-of-the-mill, not concentrated enough for mixing.

Dynasty: Good *rancio*, complex aromas, round, long.

PRUNIER

Maison Prunier, 7 Avenue Leclerc, 16102 Cognac, Tel: 33 5 45 35 00 14,
prunier@gofornet.com

BC

Small but highly regarded family firm whose members have been distilling since 1700. Now run by the Burnez family which was called in by a
M. Prunier in 1918.

Fins Bois: 20 years old, delicious.

XO: As delicate and profound as a Delamain.

20-Year-Old: ISC bronze 2000 and 10/10 from Maca who describes it
as, "a perfect cognac; awesome".

RAYMOND RAGNAUD

Le Château, Ambleville, 16300 Barbezieux, Tel: 33 5 45 80 54 57,
Raymond_ragnaud@le-cognac.com

BC

C&C

Classic GC estate of 44 ha at Ambleville. Already in 1860 the family
owned a small estate in the GC. Paul Ragnaud installed himself at the
château – in reality a small manor house – and in 1974 the family, as it
put it, "declared its independence" by selling direct. It doesn't filter so the
cognacs are rich.

Selection Four Year Old: Lovely fruity nose, round and rich, but burns
a little, suffers from not being blended.

Reserve: Tastes like a seven-year-old, very elegant and pure, fruity,
rather over-woody, slightly spirity on the nose.

Napoléon: Chestnut colour, wood well-absorbed, long, complex, rich
nose of candied fruit, some *rancio*.

Grande Reserve: 15 years old, no new wood.

Réserve Rare: 18-year-old taste.

XO 25: rich chestnut colour, full, *rancio*, very little wood, fresh.

Extra Vieux: 42 degrees. Around 25 years old, and it shows, in this
truly classic GC with all the balance and notes of candied and dried fruits
appropriate to the age and *cru*.

Tres Vieux 40: Fat, buttery, concentrated.

* Hors d'Age: 43 degrees, 35 year old. The full complexity of a great GC: rich, immensely satisfying brandy.

Tres Vieille: 50 degrees. Single vintage – it won't state which one, merely that it has aged for 50 years in wood. The sheer age and concentration prevents this great brandy from appearing too alcoholic.

Heritage 45 degrees.

1988: Very refreshing, full-bodied and intense concentration; floral nose.

1906 vintage

RAGNAUD SABOURIN

Domaine de la Voute, Ambleville, 16300 Barbezieux, Tel: 33 5 45 80 54 61, Ragnaud-sabourin@swfrance.com

Edevie

Gaston Briand, whose estate, la Voute, was just south of Fontpinot on the same sacred slopes, was a well-known figure who helped to found the *Institut National des Origines Contrôlées*, which applies the law to France's hundreds of thousands of highly individualist winemakers. But throughout his long life (he died in his eighties as recently as 1957) he steadfastly refused to market his brandies, preferring to sell them to his friends, the Hennessys. In the 1930s he was persuaded by the great French wine writer Raymond Baudoin to sell his brandies to a few select restaurants, but right up to his death the label on each bottle was laboriously hand-written – usually after Sunday lunch – by Briand and his son-in-law Marcel Ragnaud. (I suspect that most of the handwriting on lesser bottles sold by other growers to give the impression that they are of the highest quality is an imitation of Briand's fair round hand.) Since Briand's death, his daughter, son-in-law, and now his granddaughter Patricia Ragnaud-Sabourin have continued the tradition: to sell their own cognac, yes, but only their own. Like Pierre Frapin and, his successors, they were not prepared to reinforce their stocks by buying brandies from other producers.

Reserve Speciale: Buttery, rich, 20 years old.

XO: Rather routine compared with the family's other cognacs.

*Fontvieille 35: Superbly balanced, elegant, long, *rancio* but not heavy.

* Florilege 45: 46 degrees. Some of the purest *rancio* I have ever come across; lovely fruit cake feel at the end.

RÉMY MARTIN

20 Rue de la Société Viticole, 16100 Cognac, Tel: 33 5 45 35 16 15

The most extraordinary success story in Cognac during the 20th century. All the firm's brandies still come from the Champagnes and are still distilled on their lees to provide greater richness.

Grand Cru: Originally made in 1970s as a VS FC, now purely Petite Champagne from the outer parts of the region. Excellent aromatic power, round and fruity so mixable with fruit juice. No caramel, no burn, makes it an ideal mixer for cocktails.

* VSOP: Still the standard by which all others are measured. Up to 15 years old. Very spicy, bread, candied fruit, long.

1738 Accord Royal: (the year Rémy Martin got royal permission to plant more vines). Untypically for Rémy it is rich, smooth, concentrated, spicy, would be good with cigars and chocolate.

* XO Excellence: 85 degrees. GC, 10–35 years old, average 23 years. Again, rich *fruits confits*, apricot, orange, prune so concentrated that you don't even have to put your nose into the glass – so it's okay to put a little ice in the drink.

Extra 35: Mostly GC, rich *rancio*, spicy, and gingery.

Louis XIII: Quintessence of the Rémy style in a special Baccarat bottle which contributes to the – to me excessive – price.

Vintages: The only major firm to launch a series of specially selected vintages under the name The Centaur's Collection, selected from a mere couple of hundred casks out of a total of 200,000.

The 1965 has a little wood and *rancio* but it's still young and fresh, with a lovely long spiciness.

RÉMY TOURNY

Domaine de Montlambert, 16100 Louzac St André, Tel: 33 5 45 82 27 86, remytourny@wanadoo.fr

C&C

Family with 30-ha estate in the heart of the Borderies. Since M. Tourny himself died in 1996, his daughter and granddaughter decided to start selling some of his older brandies.

Fine Borderies 30: Deep almond/violetty nose, ends nice and nutty, though lacks concentration on the middle palate.

ROULLET

Le Goulet de Foussignac, 16200 Jarnac, Tel: 33 5 45 36 16 00

For nearly four centuries the Roullet family has been growing grapes – which still include a little Colombard and Folle Blanche – on a 22-ha estate the heart of the Premiers Fins Bois de Jarnac. This excellent grower now sells brandies from its extensive stocks of very old cognacs.

LOUIS ROYER

23 Rue Chail, BP 12, 16200 Jarnac, Tel: 33 5 45 81 02 72,

cognac@louis-royer.com

Founded in the nineteenth century, this firm used to specialize in bulk cognacs, including those treated (denatured) with salt and pepper. Since it was taken over by the Japanese drinks giant Suntory in 1989 after a family row it has been very enterprizing, introducing excellent cognacs from different sub-regions in a five-pack of 20cl bottles called Distilleries Collection, a clear and effective imitation of major whisky firms.

VSOP: GC. ISC Bronze 2000, Silver 2001, 2002 & 2003.

FC: ISC Bronze 2001.

Distilleries Collection

BBA: Floral warmth most unusual in a mere BB.

* FB: Light milk, fruit-and-nut chocolate nose and palate. ISC Gold 2001, Bronze 2002.

Borderies: Good nut chocolate on nose, but slightly burnt feel on the palate.

* PC: Richly floral, elegant, sippin' cognac. ISC Bronze 2001.

GC: Again, the rich chocolatey feel with some *rancio* and good concentration.

SALIGNAC

Place du Château, 16200 Jarnac, Tel: 33 5 45 35 55 55

Famous firm, now a subsidiary of Courvoisier, making only an unremarkable VS destined for the US market with brandies from the Bons Bois west of Cognac.

A TESSERON

16120 Châteauneuf-sur-Charente, Tel 33 5 45 62 52 61

Traditionally a wholesaler holding the region's largest stock of old cognacs. Now sells some to a few lucky buyers. It gets round the ban on dates by numbering its cognacs by the approximate date (e.g. 90 for the 1990).

Lot 90: Rich, earthy blend.

Lot 76 Tradition: GC, good nose and warmth, elegant, clearly mature but still some burn on the nose.

* Lot 53 Topaz: Up to 50 years old but comes over as younger. Delicious light *rancio* combined with all the firm's traditional elegance.

* Domaine St Seurin: A single-vineyard PC cognac from near Châteauneuf. Young – around 12 years old – with some Folle Blanche and Colombard; a most subtle, light, and floral cognac.

Lot 29 Tresor: This combines the delicacy and richness of the best cognacs from Delamain. Old but no *rancio*.

TIFFON
29 Quai de l'Ile Madame, 16200 Jarnac, Tel: 33 5 45 81 08 31

Founded by one Médéric Tiffon in 1875, it was bought in 1946 by the Braastad family – see Courvoisier and Delamain – and since then has naturally concentrated on selling to the Scandinavian drinks monopolies.

TRIJOL
17520 St-Martial-sur-Né, Tel: 33 5 46 49 53 31

Edevie

The Trijol family has been growing grapes and distilling wine since 1859 and is now a major distiller with eighteen stills, so only a proportion of its brandies come from its 30 ha of vines. Used to sell its brandies under the name of Duboigalant, the maiden name of Mme. Maxime Trijol.

VSOP: GC. ISC Trophy 2003.

XO: 30 years old. GC. A little *rancio*, well-balanced, rich florality on the nose and grapiness on palate.

Cigar blend: 35 years old. GC. Good fruit, some wood on the finish, more new oak than usual, strong structure, good to cope with cigars.

UNICOGNAC
Route de Cognac, 17500 Jonzac, Tel: 33 5 46 48 10 99

One of the major cooperatives in the Cognac region with 3,000 members, 250 of them growers owning 5,000 ha of vines in the PC and FB.

Ansac: special blend for the US market.

Prestige brand Roi des Rois: Various crystal or porcelain containers.

See also Jules Gautret

UNICOOP

49 Rue Lohmeyer, 16102 Cognac, Tel: 33 5 45 82 45 7

With Unicognac one of the two major cooperatives in the region, with 3,600 members who distil 250,000 hl between them in all the major regions, although forty-five per cent are in the Fins Bois and thirty-five per cent in the Bons Bois. Its business relies heavily on producing the ultra-premium Grey Goose vodka. In 1969 it bought the old firm of H. Mounier.

Prince Hubert de Polignac: GC. ISC Bronze 2001.

XO Royal: ISC Bronze 2001.

Dynastie: ISC Bronze 2002.

Glossary

For legal definitions of types of cognac see p. 209.

Acquit officiel. Certificate of origin of an alcoholic drink.

Acquit jaune d'or. Special type of *Acquit* required for cognac.

Alembic Charentais. (Originally called *cucurbit* and also known as *chaudière d'eau-de-vie*). Literally a spirit boiler. In reality the pot still, the vat used for distilling cognac.

Appellation d'Origine Contrôlée. Legal guarantee that a wine or spirit conforms to certain provisions as to its geographical origin, the methods used in its production, the varieties of grape from which it is made, the maximum yield of the vines, etc.

Arrondissement. Old name for a canton [q.v.]. Not to be confused with the Parisian variety.

Assignats. Rapidly depreciating monetary certificates issued by the early Revolutionary governments after 1789.

Ban de vendanges. Official starting date for the grape harvest. Before 1789 a feudal right which ensured that the landlord's grapes were picked before those of the peasantry.

barrique de Cognac. Before 1789 this held twenty-seven *veltes* [q.v.]. By 1900 it held 275 litres, now usually 350 litres.

bassiot. Basin, bucket or other receptacle to catch the newly distilled cognac as it emerges from the still.

BNIC. See Bureau National de Cognac.

bois. Formerly wooded sub-regions representing the majority of the Cognac region. Before they were formally defined they were known by a wide variety of names, including Premiers Fins Bois, Deuxième Bois, Bois Communs, etc.

Bois Ordinaires. Outer semi-circle of the Cognac region with only a few hectares of vines.

Bons Bois. The middle ring of vines in the Cognac appellation.

bonbonne. Glass jar holding approximately twenty-five litres used to store old cognacs.

bonne chauffe. Second distillation which produces cognac.

Borderies. Small rectangular sub-region north of Cognac which produces very special nutty brandies.

bouilleur. Distiller.

bouilleur de cru. Grower allowed to distil only his own wine.

bouilleur de profession. Professional distiller allowed to distil wines from other producers.

brandewijn, brandwin, brandywijn. Literally "burnt wine". Dutch term for brandy.

brouillis. Spirit of about thirty degrees produced by the first distillation.

brulerie. Literally "burning house". In fact, a distillery.

Bureau National de Cognac (BNIC). Cognac's ruling body set up in 1946 which supervizes the production and sale of Cognac.

buyer's own brand (BOB). Cognacs bottled under their own names by major buyers such as supermarkets or state liquor monopolies.

campagne. The Cognac year which runs from September 1 to August 31.

Campanian (Fr: Campanien). A type of chalky soil found only in the Grande Champagne.

canton. Administrative district, part of a *département* [q.v.] once called an *arrondissement*.

Champagnes. Regions which produce the finest brandies, named after the Roman Campania. See Grande & Petite Champagne.

chapelet. The white circular head formed by newly distilled cognac when poured into a glass.

chapiteau. Literally a circus tent, the "big top", a small, round container

which traps the alcoholic vapours from the alembic below.

chaudière d'eau de vie. Former name for an alembic [q.v.].

chauffe. Literally "heating". Term used for one of the two passes through the still required to produce cognac.

chauffe-vin. Cylinder in which wine is heated by the heat from the newly distilled brandy before it is distilled.

chlorosis (Fr: chlorose). Disease caused by an excess of chalk in the soil which chokes the vines.

coeur. The heart of the distillation, the only portion which should be extracted.

col. The neck of the still.

col de cygne. Literally "swan's neck". The modern shape of the *col*.

Colombard. Also called Colombat or French Colombard. Grape variety widely planted in Cognac in the eighteenth century. Still scattered plots.

comptes. Term describing the age of cognacs (see p. 211).

courtiers. Cognac brokers.

Cru. Term describing the subdivisions of the Cognac region.

cucurbite. See alembic.

Département. French administrative unit, similar to a British county.

early landed. Cognacs shipped in cask soon after distillation to Britain where they are aged until bottled (hence the term Early Landed Late Bottled).

eau-de-vie. Any brandy distilled from fruit.

esprit de vin. Term dating back to the eighteenth century for especially strong brandy.

fine. French term for any brandy.

Fine a l'eau. Brandy and water, formerly a favourite French apéritif.

Fine Champagne. A blend of brandies from the Grande and Petite Champagne, with at least half coming from the Grande Champagne.

Fins Bois. Large and very varied region; cf. Bons Bois, Fins Bois, Bois Ordinaires.

Folle Blanche. Grape variety much planted in Cognac before phylloxera, which produced floral brandies. Now rare because of tendency to rot. Also called Folle in Cognac and Gros Plant in the mouth of the Loire valley.

fureur de planter. Mania for planting vines that swept through France in the early eighteenth century.

gabare. Barge used for transporting brandy.

gabelle. Salt tax levied from the Middle Ages until 1789.

groies. Special clay soil found only in the Borderies.

lees. The detritus, leaves, skins and other solids left in the vat after fermentation.

Limousin. Open-grained oak, originally from the forests around Limoges (hence the name), major source of wood for brandy casks (see also Tronçais).

maître de chai. "Cellar master" responsible for the distillation, maturing and blending of cognacs.

malolactic fermentation (Fr: le malo). Secondary fermentation in which the harsh malic acids in the wine are transformed into the smoother lactic acid.

moût. Must, unfermented grape juice.

Napoléon. Name attached to a legally undefined quality of cognac, above VSOP [q.v.] and below XO [q.v.].

oidium. Fungal disease that afflicted the Cognac vineyards during the 1850s.

paradis. Chai holding older cognacs.

part des anges. Literally "the angels' share", local term for spirit lost through evaporation.

petites eaux. Mixture of brandy and water employed when reducing the strength of cognac before bottling.

Phylloxera vastatrix. "Wine louse" which devastated Cognac and France's, and indeed Europe's, other wine regions from the last quarter of the nineteenth century.

Pineau des Charentes. Local apéritif made by adding brandy to grape juice and thus preventing fermentation. Legally Pineau must be between sixteen and twenty-two degrees of alcohol and be aged in wood for at least a year.

pipe. (Now used only for port.) Barrel containing 600 litres.

preuve. Strength of brandy. In the eighteenth century *Preuve de Cognac* was about sixty degrees of alcohol, *Preuve d'Hollande* about forty-nine degrees, and *Preuve de Londres* about fifty-eight degrees.

quart de sel. Tax of twenty-five per cent paid in the Middle Ages whenever salt changed hands.

queues. French term for tails [q.v.].

rancio Charentais. Rich, complex flavours combining nuts and candied fruits developed by the best cognacs after twenty years or more in wood.

rimé. A cognac that has been

overheated in the still and has developed burnt flavours.

St-Emilion. Alternative name for Ugni Blanc [q.v.].

Saintonian (Fr Saintonien). Type of chalky soil found almost exclusively in the Petite Champagne.

secondes. Low-strength brandy from the later stages of distillation.

serpentin. The cooling coil attached to the still.

tails. The modern term for secondes.

terroir. French term covering the geological, physical, and chemical composition of a vineyard, including the weather and the aspect.

tête. The "head" or first brandy from a distillation.

tête de Maure. Old-fashioned type of col, supposedly the shape of a Moor's head. complete with turban.

tierçon. Pre-1789 measure holding two barriques. then about 404 litres.

tonneau. In Cognac this means any large cask (in Bordeaux a measure meaning 900 litres).

tonnelier. Cooper.

tonnelerie. Wood-working shop where casks are made; a cooperage.

Torula compniacensis richon. Fungus that lives off the fumes from cognac and blackens the roofs of chais.

Three-Star. Older name for the basic quality of cognac, now called VS.

Tronçais. With Limousin, the type of oak used in Cognac. Its grain is tighter. Its name comes from the forest of Tronçais in Central France.

Ugni Blanc. The basic grape variety used in Cognac where it makes neutral, low-strength, and acid wine.

velte. Dutch measure which represented eight *pintes de Paris* or six *pintes d'Angoulême* – what in Britain would be called an Imperial gallon.

vins vinés. Fortified wines.

VS. The basic quality of cognac. Legally the youngest cognac in the blend must be at least thirty months old (i.e. *Compte 2*).

VSOP. Originally called Very Special Old Pale. The quality above VS, in which the youngest cognac in the blend must be at least four-and-a-half years old (i.e. *Compte 4*).

XO. Stands for Extra Old. A superior type of cognac, generally but not universally comprising cognacs which are at least ten years old.

Appendix

Production of cognac
(Millions of bottles, annual average)

1879	107.6 – pre phylloxera peak
1889	16.4 – post-phylloxera low
1891–1900	22.2
1901–1910	32.2
1911–1920	31.1
1921–1930	39.9
1931–1940	38.4

Sales
(Millions of bottles, annual average)

1947–56	37.2
1957–66	60
1967–76	92.9
1977–84	141
1985–92	142
1993–2002	120

Campaign years run from 1 September to 31 August.
Includes sales of cognac in the form of fortified wines.

VINTAGES

Because so few single-vintage cognacs are available for tasting it is impossible to give the sort of yearly guide which is normal with wines. I can only provide some indications of quality – bearing in mind that even in mediocre vintages there may be a few brandies worthy of vintage status.

Classic older vintages

1953 Hine produced one of the great cognacs of all time.

1955 Hot but excellent year.

1959 Ripe grapes, round brandies.

1961 Rather too soft.

1962 Hot year with some fermentation difficulties but some fine cognacs.

1963 Only a few single-vintage cognacs were good, but these were superb.

1965 As with 1963.

1972 Excellent.

1973 Far too much wine, and not strong enough to make decent brandy.

1975 "All I love about cognac", according to Maurice Fillioux.

1976 A very hot year, too much rain at harvest time, flat cognacs.

1978 Variable, some good cognacs.

1980 Late, cold year resulting in thin and flat cognacs.

1981 Spring frosts produced more concentrated wines and cognacs.

1984 Poor.

1987 No real depth or intensity.

1988 Superb balance between fruit and acidity.

1989 Wine too strong, liable to accidents in vinification.

1991 Deadly spring frosts, little cognac but good concentrated stuff.

1992 Heavy rain at harvest time.

1993 A great deal of rot.

1994 A handful of good brandies from a generally poor year.

2002 Will be an excellent year with complex brandies.

Bibliography

Mac A Andrew *Cognac an Independent Guide*, Lusina, Deptford NJ 08096 USA, 1999.

Anon, *A Sad Picture of Rustic Folk*, 1786.

Baudoin, A, *Les eaux-de-vie et la fabrication du Cognac*, 1983.

Berry, Charles Walter, *In Search of Wine*, London, Constable, 1935.

Bertall, *La vigne*, 1878.

Boraud, Henri, *De l'Usage commercial du nom du Cognac*, Bordeaux, 1904.

Bures, Maurice, "Le type saintongeais", *La Science Sociale*, vol. 23, Paris, 1908.

Butel, Paul, *Histoire de la Société Hennessy*, Hennessy, PLACE, 1995.

Caumeil, Michel, *Pour la science*, December 1983.

Chardonne, Jacques, *Le bonheur de Barbezieux*, Stock Paris, 1938.

Chardonne, Jacques, *Chronique Privée de l'an 1940*, Stock, Paris 1941.

Coquand, H, Description Physique, Paris, 1858.

Coste, Michel, Cognac: les clés de la fortune, Librairie du Château, PLACE, 2001.

Corlieu, *Receuil en forme d'histoire*, Jeanne Laffitte, Marseille, 1976.

Coussie, Jean-Vincent, *Le Cognac et les aléas de l'histoire*, BNIC, 1996.

Cullen, Professor Louis, *The Brandy Trade under the Ancien Régime*, Cambridge, 1998.

Cullen, Professor Louis, *The Irish Brandy Houses of Eighteenth-Century France*, Lilliput, PLACE, 2000.

Daniou, Patrick, *Annales GREH*, 1983.

Delamain, Robert, *Histoire du Cognac*, Paris, Stock, 1935.

Demachy, JF, *L'Art du distillateur des eaux fortes,* Paris, 1773.

Diderot etc, *Encyclopedie ou dictionnaire des arts et metier*, Paris 1770.

Doléances de la Senechaussee d'Angoulême pour les Etats Generaux de 1789.

Enjalbert, Etudes locales 1939, no 192-1193.

Flanner, Janet, *Paris was Yesterday*, Angus & Robertson, London, 1973.

Forbes, RJ, *A Short History of the Art of Distillation*, Leiden, 1970.

Gervais, Jean, *Mémoire sur l'angoumois* (reprint), SAHC, 1964.

International Wine & Spirit Record, London.

Julien-Labruyère, François, *Paysans Charentais*, vol I, Rupella, La Rochelle, 1982.

Julien-Labruyère, Francois, *A la récherche de la Saintonge,* Maritime, Versailles, 1974.

Lafon, R, Lafon J, & Coquillaud, P, Le Cognac: sa distillation, JB Baillière et fils, Paris, 1964.

Landrau, Marguerite, *Le Cognac devant la loi*, Cognac, L'Isle d'Or, Cognac, 1981.

Leauté, Robert, "Distillation in Alembic", *American Journal of Enology and Viticulture*, Vol 4, No 1, 1990.

Long, James, *The Century Companion to Cognac and Other Brandies*, London, Century, 1983.

Lys, Jean, *Le Commerce de Cognac*, Université de Bordeaux, 1929.

Martin-Civat, Pierre, *La monopole des eaux-de-vie sous Henri IV,* IOOème Congrès Nationale des Sociétés Savantes, Paris, 1975.

Mejane, Professor, *Annales de technologie agricole*, 1975.

Monnet, Jean, *Memoires*, Paris, Fayard, 1976.

Munier, Etienne, *Essai sur l'Angoumois a la fin de l'Ancien Régime,* Bruno Sepulchre, Paris, 1977.

Munier, Etienne, *Sur la manière de bruler ou distiller les vins,* Bruno Sepulchre, Paris, 1981.

Néau, *De la crise viticole en Charente*, Paris, 1907.

Neon, Maurice, *De la Crise viticole en Charente*, Paris, 1907.

Norois, Paris.

Petit, Catherine, *Les Charentes: pays du Cognac*, ACE, Paris, 1984.

Plante, La société en Charente au XIX, CRDP, Poitiers, 1976.

Quenot, J-P, *Statistique du Département de la Charente*, 1818.

Ravaz, Louis, and Vivier, Albert, *Le pays du Cognac*, Angoulême, 1900.

Revue Periodique Mensuelle , Paris, 1892.

Savary, Abbé PL, *Dictionnaire universel du commerce*, Paris, 1823.

Sepulchre, Bruno, *Le Livre de Cognac*, Hubschmid & Bouret, Paris, 1983.

Taransaud, Jean, *Le Livre de la tonnellerie*, La Roue a Livres Diffusion, Paris, 1976.

Tovey, Charles, *British and Foreign Spirits*, Whittaker, London, 1864.

Verdon, JA, *Une commune rurale vue par son instituteur d'alors: Malaville en 1901*, Annales GREH, 1982.

Index